Lex Orandi Series

Sacramental Orders

Lex Orandi Series

John D. Laurance, S.J.
Editor

Sacramental Orders

Susan K. Wood, S.C.L.

A Liturgical Press Book

 THE LITURGICAL PRESS
Collegeville, Minnesota

www.litpress.org

Cover design by Greg Becker.

Cover illustration: Alberto Arnoldi (fl. 1351–64). Holy Orders. Museo dell'Opera del Duomo, Florence, Italy. Scala/Art Resource, New York. Used with permission.

Excerpts from the English translation of *Ordination of Deacons, Priests, and Bishops* © 1975, International Committee on English in the Liturgy, Inc. (ICEL); excerpts from the English translation of *Documents on the Liturgy, 1963–1979: Conciliar, Papal, and Curial Texts* © 1982, ICEL; excerpts from the English translation of *Ceremonial of Bishops* © 1989, ICEL; excerpts from the English translation of *Rites of Ordination of Bishops, Presbyters, and Deacons* © 1993, ICEL; excerpts from the English translation of *Rites of Ordination of a Bishop, of Priests and of Deacons* © 1999, ICEL. All rights reserved.

The Scripture quotations are from the New Revised Standard Version Bible, Catholic edition, © 1989 by the Division of Christian Education of the National Council of Churches of Christ in the U.S.A. Used by permission. All rights reserved.

1   2   3   4   5   6   7   8

Library of Congress Cataloging-in-Publication Data

Wood, Susan K.
    Sacramental orders / Susan K. Wood.
        p.   cm. — (Lex orandi series)
    Includes bibliographical references and index.
    ISBN 0-8146-2522-3 (alk. paper)
    1. Clergy—Office.   2. Catholic Church—Clergy.
3. Ordination—Catholic Church.   4. Catholic Church.
De ordinatione episcopi, presbyterorum et diaconorum.
5. Catholic Church—Doctrines.   I. Title.   II. Series.

BX2240.W66   2000
264'.02084—dc21   00-032132

Contents

Preface to the *Lex Orandi* Series

T he theology of the seven sacraments prevalent in the Catholic Church through most of the second millennium interpreted those rites more as sacred objects to be *passively* received than as *active* participations in Christ's paschal mystery. And their meaning was to be derived, not from the shape of their liturgical celebration, but from the Church's official teaching, teaching typically occasioned by historical challenges to her faith. Whereas in patristic times Church writers expounded the theology of the sacraments from the rites themselves, with the later expansion of Christianity into central Europe, confidence waned that the form and enactment of the liturgy in any way *manifested* the Mystery it contained. As the *Adoro Te Devote,* a medieval hymn on the Church's use of bread in the Eucharistic Liturgy, puts it, "Seeing, tasting, touching are in Thee deceived."

In recent times, however, there has been a kind of "Copernican revolution" in sacramental theology. Not only have sacraments come to be understood as actions of God *and* the Church, the truth of the ancient adage, *lex orandi, lex credendi* (how the Church prays expresses what she believes), has also been seen in a new light. Theologians have come to realize that if all Church dogma is rooted ultimately in her faith-experience of God, so too must her understanding of the sacraments derive from her experience of their liturgical celebration. Sacraments, too, must *manifest* the Mystery they contain. Consequently, in the tradition of ancient mystagogies, "liturgical theology"—that is, God's word ("first theology") to the Church through her worship—has come to be understood, along with official Church teaching, as an indispensable source for sacramental theology. And sacramental theology itself has returned to its proper place within a larger "theology of liturgy." The works of theologians such as Guardini, Casel, Rahner, Schmemann, Kilmartin, and Chauvet mark various stages in this historical development.

Although much has been written on the role of the celebrating Church, up until now no set of studies on all seven sacraments that we know of has attempted to exegete their meaning primarily from their typical celebrations. The aim of this present series, then, is precisely to investigate the sacraments as liturgical events in order to discover in them the faith understanding of Christian life of which they are both the source and the summit (SC 10).

However, since the theology of liturgy is but one part of the whole of systematic theology, liturgical events can be adequately interpreted as witnesses to the Church's faith only in light of the other ways she experiences God's word. Accordingly, individual volumes in this series analyze typical experiences of the rites they cover against the background of the rest of the Church's traditional life and teaching, and they do so guided by the unique synthesis of that tradition that each author, as theologian, brings to the work. To do anything less would be to fail in the task of theology. On occasion, then, authors will offer their own critique, whether of the rites themselves or of how they have experienced their celebration, doing so on the basis of other theological sources as well (including, for example, the official instructions introducing each rite).

Sacraments as liturgical *events* are not understood by most theologians today as they once were, that is, as so-called "moments of consecration" (the "This is my Body"; the pouring of water ". . . in the name of the Father . . .," etc.). Rather, similar to how Aristotle's *Poetics* envisions Greek tragedies, sacraments are seen as events extended through time, having beginnings, middles, and ends. True, as protracted events they include indispensable high points, but separated off from the whole liturgical celebration, those key moments, at least in the short run, lose much of their intelligibility and intensity and, therefore, their efficacy as well (cf. SC 14). Accordingly, volumes in this series attempt to study each sacrament as it unfolds through its total performance, discerning especially its basic structure and how various elements contribute to its overall faith meaning.

The motivating purpose of this new series on the sacraments is ultimately a pastoral one: to help foster the fuller liturgical participation called for by Vatican II, and not necessarily to "break new ground" in sacramental theology. The readership envisioned by the series, therefore, is a broad one, not confined just to liturgical experts. Individual volumes presuppose only a beginner's familiarity with Christian theology, such as that possessed by university upper-level undergraduate or master's level students.

Finally, the rites studied in this series are those of the Roman Rite of the Catholic Church in use today. As valuable as a comparison of various Christian liturgies would be, no one series can do everything. At the same time, it is hoped that efforts made here toward understanding the Roman Rite might help inspire other, more explicitly ecumenical studies of Christian liturgy.

John D. Laurance, S.J.
Marquette University

Introduction

L iturgical rites teach through gestures, symbols, prayer texts, and liturgical actions. Consequently, rites must be clear in their organization, and the gestures and words must communicate the theology of the sacrament. The Constitution on the Sacred Liturgy, *Sacrosanctum concilium,* promulgated on December 4, 1963, articulated the general principles—simplification, clarification, and return to ancient sources—that directed the reform of the liturgy: "In this restoration both texts and rites should be drawn up so as to express more clearly the holy things which they signify. The Christian people, as far as possible, should be able to understand them with ease and take part in them fully, actively, and as a community."[1]

The 1968 Revision of the Rites of Ordination

The revised rites of ordination, promulgated in 1968,[2] only five years after the Second Vatican Council had mandated revision, comprised the first of the reformed liturgical books of the Roman Rite of the sacramental rites. At the time of the Second Vatican Council the rites for ordination were in serious need of revision. Those in use up to 1968, promulgated by Pope Clement VIII in 1595, were a compilation of texts and ceremonies from several earlier sources, reflecting doctrinal and cultural influences from the fifth to the end of the thirteenth century.[3] Essential rites, such as the laying on of hands, were buried under secondary rites. Some formulas were not compatible with current theology. For example, theologians in the Middle Ages considered the handing over of the paten and chalice to be the essential rite of ordination. But Pius XII, in his apostolic constitution *Sacramentum ordinis,* reestablished the laying on of hands and the consecratory prayer as the essential rites. The Roman Pontifical of 1596 reflected the allegorizing mentality of the Middle Ages, which interpreted persons, events, and rites of the Old Testament in terms of the New Testament. For example, the bishop's miter was described as the horns of both Testaments and represented the horns of Moses as he came down from the mountain with tablets of the covenant.[4] The 1968 rite removed such allegorical interpretations of ritual actions. The miter was retained, but its conferral occurred in silence. Where previously elements of the rite of ordination were scattered throughout the Eucharistic Liturgy, they were consolidated to occur between the Liturgy of the Word and the Eucharistic Liturgy, the same moment used in the celebration of baptism, confirmation, and matrimony. In the former rite each gesture was accompanied by a formula, but the words did not always match the objective meaning of the gesture. For example, the formula "Receive the Holy Spirit" had accompanied the imposition of hands. This made it look like this prayer for the Holy Spirit was an essential part of the sacrament, when, in reality, the prayer that followed was really the consecratory prayer. Consequently, the 1968 rite suppressed the prayer, "Receive the Holy Spirit" and the imposition of hands occurs in silence.

From the 1968 Rite to the 1990 Rite

Pope Paul VI had foreseen that adjustments would have to be made in the rites after a number of years of experience with the revised rite. Since the 1968 text was one of the first of the liturgical books desired by the Second Vatican Council, it was not able to profit from the fruits of the pastoral experience acquired in the process of publishing and using other rites.

Two major deficiencies were experienced in the rites of ordination: the lack of a general introduction comparable to those in the liturgical books published later, and the need for a new ordination prayer for priests, one which focused more on the priesthood of Christ than on the Old Testament priesthood. On June 4, 1973, the Congregation for Divine Worship wrote a letter to the Vatican Secretary of State requesting permission to produce a more uniform edition of all the reformed rites which would bring the terminology and rubrics of the various books into harmony with each other. The letter stated the congregation's desire to prepare a "General Introduction" for the volume containing the ordination rites.[5]

The congregation never received a response to its letter. Nevertheless, a study group was formed[6] which worked on an Introduction. This study group also addressed the inclusion of the rite of acceptance of celibacy in the rite of diaconal ordination (required in 1972 by Pope Paul VI), a new redaction of the ordination prayers for priests and deacons, and a proposed change in the layout of the book according to which the rite of episcopal ordination would come first. The work of this group did not see the light of day.

On July 17, 1975, Pope Paul VI issued his apostolic constitution *Constans Nobis Studium,* establishing a new Vatican congregation, the Sacred Congregation for the Sacraments and Divine Worship. This took the place of the former Congregation for the Discipline of the Sacraments (created by Pius X in 1908) and the Congregation for Divine Worship (created by Paul VI in 1969). With the suppression of the Congregation for Divine Worship, the work of the study group ended up in the archives, and Pierre Jounel reports that the production of liturgical materials in Rome languished for a dozen years after that.[7] A committee, Concerning Holy Orders (Coetus De Ordinibus sacris) under the leadership of Reiner Kaczynski, completed the revision of the rites. The Congregation for the Sacraments and Divine Worship reviewed the work of the committee on May 20–24, 1985, and approved their schemas with some modifications.[8] On June 29, 1989, by the decree "Ritus Ordinationum," the Congregation for Divine Worship and the Discipline of the Sacraments promulgated the *editio typica altera* of the rites of ordination for a bishop, presbyters, and deacons in the Roman Rite.[9] The revision of the rite was published under a 1990 copyright date. Even though ten years later the English-speaking world still did not have a confirmed English translation of the rite and was still using the 1968 rite, the second "typical" edition, confirmed in its Latin form by the Vatican, constituted the current official and normative rite of the church from the date of its promulgation in Latin.

The major changes in the second typical edition of the Roman Pontifical are:

1. The insertion of the Praenotanda, a General Introduction[10] to all the rites of ordination, and the development of the introductions for the various particular rites of ordination.

2. Reorganization of the chapters within the pontifical in a descending rather than an ascending order: bishop, presbyter, deacon.

3. Changes in the prayer of ordination for presbyters and deacons.

4. Supplemental promises in the rite for presbyters.

5. Promise of celibacy in the rite for deacons. Even those who have made profession of perpetual chastity in a religious institute are bound to make this commitment to celibacy.

6. Promise of obedience and respect to the local bishop by religious candidates.

7. Insertion of the rite of admission to candidacy for Holy Orders in the appendix of the pontifical.

The Present Study

This volume of the *Lex Orandi* Series is a liturgical and theological study of ordained ministry grounded in the liturgy of the 1990 typical edition of the rites. It addresses the three orders within the one Sacrament of Order: bishop, presbyter, and deacon. By including each order with this study, the interrelationship between the three becomes more apparent, and the theology of one is allowed to inform the theology of the others. One of the challenges in theologies of ordained ministry today is to distinguish a bishop from a presbyter when both are ordinations to the priesthood and presbyters are assuming a greater ministry of oversight as they pastor more than one parish, and to distinguish deacons from presbyters at a time in Church history when deacons are assuming more presbyteral functions.

Ordained ministry cannot be understood by itself in isolation or only exclusively in its relationship with Christ. It must find its identity in relationship to the Church, for it exists to serve and build up the

Church. This study begins, therefore, by placing a theology of ordained ministry within its ecclesial foundations, identifying four conceptualizations of the Church within the Dogmatic Constitution on the Church, *Lumen gentium*. It identifies a monarchical and hierarchical conceptualization with clear separation between the ordained and the laity; a eucharistic, collegial model of ministry representing the communion of particular churches; a theology of the threefold paradigm of priest, prophet, and king, which structures the concept of the church as the people of God as well as the theologies of ordained ministry and the laity; and finally, a theology of the Church as a sacrament of Christ and ordained ministry as a sacrament of the Church. Each of these conceptualizations sheds light on different aspects of ordained ministry in its relationship to the Church. For the most part, it is not a question of choosing one conceptualization over the others but, rather, different ways of viewing the Church that illumine different aspects of ordained ministry in its ecclesial relationships.

There is a mutual reciprocity in the relationship between liturgical rite and the theology of the sacrament as explicated in ecclesial documents. The ordination rites reflect the theology articulated by the Second Vatican Council and yet also present a theology of the sacrament embedded in the liturgical texts and actions. This study explores that relationship by presenting two chapters on each order, bishop, presbyter, and deacon. The first consists of a theological commentary on the 1990 rite while the second examines a theology of that particular order from a more systematic perspective. These do not pretend to exhaust the theology of that particular order but, rather, address some aspect of each order that arises from a theology of the rite. Thus, what is most significant about the rite for the ordination of bishops is precisely the fact that it is a sacramental ordination, following the teaching of Vatican II on the sacramentality of the episcopacy. Chapter three consequently explores a theological understanding of that sacramentality. Chapter five examines the identity of the presbyterate in terms of four relationships: presbyter to Christ, presbyter to bishop, presbyter to presbyter within the presbyterium, and presbyter to the Church. Chapter seven addresses several questions concerning the diaconate: the normativity of the permanent diaconate for a theology of the diaconate, whether the Church should retain the transitional diaconate, the diaconate as a vocation, and the relationship between the diaconate and lay ministry.

ICEL, the International Commission on English in the Liturgy, was kind enough to provide me with the latest translations of the liturgical rite while they were still in the process of discussion and approval by the American bishops. Every attempt has been made to accurately present the latest translation. However, readers need to be aware that the process of approval by the episcopal conference and confirmation by the Vatican was still in process at the time that this book was sent to press.

In conclusion, I would like to acknowledge and thank those who have assisted me in this project. Saint John's University, Collegeville, Minnesota, granted me a sabbatical 1998–99 during which I was a scholar at the Institute of Ecumenical and Cultural Research in Collegeville. The time and resources provided by both enabled me to complete most of the manuscript during that year. I am also grateful to the Sisters of Charity of Leavenworth, Kansas, my religious community, who made it possible for me to accept a full year's sabbatical and who encourage me personally and professionally. I finish this project with renewed appreciation for conversation and critical comments from readers and colleagues. John Laurance, S.J., the series editor, Michael Downey, and Rene McGraw, O.S.B., read the entire manuscript in draft form. Others who read parts of the manuscript include Patrick Henry, Charles Bobertz, Joseph Feders, O.S.B., and Martha Reeves. Finally, I am grateful for my family who unfailingly cheers me on.

Notes, Introduction

[1] *Sacrosanctum concilium* 21.

[2] Pope Paul VI issued his apostolic constitution, "Approval of New Rite for the Ordination of Deacons, Presbyters, and Bishops," on June 18, 1968. On July 12, 1977, the Congregation for the Sacraments and Divine Worship received from the Cardinal Secretary of State the English translation of the sacramental form for the ordination of bishop, priest, deacon as definitively approved by Pope Paul VI. On August 12, the congregation approved the entire "White Book" (definitive version) for *The Ordination of Deacons, Priests, and Bishops* as prepared by ICEL in 1975 and approved by the NCCB in 1976. The commission charged with the revision of the pontifical of the ordination rites include Bernard Botte, president, Kleinheyer, secretary, Lengeling, M. Vogel, P. Jounel, Nabuco, and P. Lécuyer.

[3] The history of this ordination rite has been studied by Bruno Kleinheyer, in *Die Priesterweihe im Römischen Ritus* (Trier, 1962). See Bernard Botte, *From Silence to Participation* (Washington, D.C.: The Pastoral Press, 1988) 133–43; Anni-

bale Bugnini, *The Reform of the Liturgy 1948–1975*, trans. Matthew J. O'Connell (Collegeville: The Liturgical Press, 1990) 708–23; and Frederick R. McManus, "The New Rite for Ordination of Bishops," *American Ecclesiastical Review* 159 (1968) 410–16.

[4] Interestingly, the Latin Vulgate mistranslated the Hebrew text. The vulgate version of Exodus 34:29 is: Cumque descenderet Moyses de monte Sinai tenebat duos tabulas testimonii et ignorabat quod cornuta esset facies sua ex consortio sermonis Domini. See also Exodus 34:35: qui videbat faciem egredientis Mosi esse cornutam sed operiebat rursus ille faciem suam si quando loquebatur ad eos.

[5] The text of this letter and the history surrounding it appears in Annibale Bugnini, *The Reform of the Liturgy 1948–1975*, 721.

[6] The members were B. Kleinheyer, chair, R. Kacynski, secretary, P. M. Gy, P. Jounel, J. Lécuyer, E. Lengeling, M. Lessi, A. Nocent, and F. Bär. A. Duman and P. Coughlan were added later.

[7] Pierre Jounel, "La Nouvelle Édition Typique du Rituel des Ordinations," *La Maison-Dieu* 186 (1991) 10.

[8] F. Dell'Oro, "La 'Editio typica altera'del Pontificale Romano delle Ordinazione," *Revista Liturgica* 78 (1991) 287–92.

[9] Congregatio de cultu divino et disciplina sacramentorum, "Acta: De Ordinatione Episcopi, Presbyterorum et Diaconorum," *Notitiae* 26 (1991) 74–75. The rites themselves have been published as *Pontificale Romanum ex decreto Sacrosancti Oecumenici Concilii Vaticani II renovatum auctoritate Pauli Pp. VI editum Joannis Pauli Pp. II cura recognitum. De Ordinatione Episcopi, Presbyterorum et Diaconorum, Editio Typica Altera* (Vatican City: Typis Polyglottis Vaticanis, 1990).

[10] The Constitution on the Sacred Liturgy of Vatican II decreed that "the instructions prefixed to the individual rites in the Roman Ritual, whether they be pastoral and rubrical or whether they have a special social import, shall not be omitted" (63b).

Chapter One

The Ecclesiological Foundations of Ministry

Ordained ministry arises from within the Church and reflects the structure of the Church. How we conceive of the Church will largely determine how we see ministry functioning within it. Since the rites of ordination were revised to reflect the ecclesiology within the documents of Vatican II, a study of this sacrament must begin with the ecclesiology of the Second Vatican Council.

There is, however, no one ecclesiology in these documents. The council became the focus of various converging ecclesiologies received from various strata of the tradition. Two conflicting groups of bishops struggled to represent their view of the Church. Traditional bishops proposed an understanding of the Church according to Counter-Reformation theology and practices. More progressive bishops supported a more historical view of the Church, emphasis on the local church and episcopal collegiality, a more pastoral approach, and dialogue with the contemporary world. Even though the more progressive bishops prevailed, the final documents reflect the influence of both groups.

The First Vatican Council in 1870 had articulated a theology of the papacy, but ended before it could develop a theology of the episcopacy. A council responding to what it perceived to be the dangers of modernism and liberalism, it refuted error and defined doctrine, notably the doctrine of papal infallibility. By contrast, the Second Vatican Council was not convened to refute error, but to engage the contemporary world in dialogue. The spirit of the council is perhaps best expressed in the opening words of the Pastoral Constitution on the Church in the Modern World:

1

The joys and hopes and the sorrows and anxieties of people today, especially of those who are poor and afflicted, are also the joys and hopes, sorrows and anxieties of the disciples of Christ, and there is nothing truly human which does not also affect them. Their community is composed of people united in Christ who are directed by the holy Spirit in their pilgrimage towards the Father's kingdom and who have received the message of salvation to be communicated to everyone. For this reason it feels itself closely linked to the human race and its history.[1]

In comparison with Vatican I, the documents of Vatican II reveal the Church to be less defensive and more open; less self-promoting and triumphalistic as it looks less to itself and more to Christ; less self-assured as it describes the Church as a mystery, less static and more historical. The Church is more decentralized in the shift from Roman primacy to universal episcopacy, from hierarchical ministry to the People of God, from identifying itself as coextensive with the Church of Christ to recognition of the ecclesiality of other Christian churches, from Rome to the Church worldwide.[2]

The history of the council chronicles the struggle between bishops of the Curia who fashioned the preparatory document, *De ecclesia,* presented to the council fathers in November 1962 and the reform bishops who rejected it.[3] A comparison of the original schema of 1962 and the final schema of 1964 reveals the difference. The first emphasized the hierarchy and authority while the second situated the Church in the mystery of the Trinity, emphasized the Church as the People of God, and taught that all are called to holiness:

Original Schema of 1962

1. On the Nature of the Church Militant
2. Membership in Church and its Necessity for Salvation
3. Office of bishop, as Highest Degree of Ordination
4. On Residential Bishops
5. The States of Evangelical Perfection
6. Concerning the Laity
7. Magisterium
8. Authority and Obedience in the Church
9. Relations between Church and State

10. Necessity of Church to Evangelize All Nations

11. Ecumenism

Final Schema of Lumen gentium *(November 21, 1964)*

1. The Mystery of the Church

2. The People of God

3. The Hierarchical Constitution of the Church and in Particular the Episcopate

4. The Laity

5. The Universal Call to Holiness in the Church

6. Religious

7. The Eschatological Character of the Pilgrim Church and Its Union with the Heavenly Church

8. The Blessed Virgin Mary, Mother of God, in the Mystery of Christ and the Church

Much of the council's teaching on the sacrament of order sought a balance between a theology of the episcopacy with its emphasis on collegiality, the sacramentality of the episcopacy, and episcopal authority described as "proper, ordinary, and immediate," and a theology of the papacy as developed in Vatican I. Consequently, in the third chapter of *Lumen gentium* on the hierarchical Church, sentences describing episcopal authority are frequently followed by affirmations of papal authority. The two are maintained in balance and counterbalance. The theology of the hierarchy in chapter three is in turn contextualized by its position after chapter one, on the mystery of the Church, and chapter two, on the Church as the People of God. This placement shifts the emphasis from an institutional and structural view of the Church to one which envisions it as a community of believers characterized by communion, mystery, and grace.

The Dogmatic Constitution on the Church reflects all these forces. It is hardly surprising, then, that at least four different models or conceptualizations of the Church are discernible within the documents. The differing models reflect different relationships between the ordained and lay faithful. First, vestiges of an older monarchical ecclesiology remain. Second, the council is in continuity with the ecclesiology of the Mystical Body brought into prominence by Pius XII's encyclical, *Mystici corporis* (1943). This correlates with a eucharistic ecclesiology associated with a definition of a particular church as an altar community around a bishop. Third, the Church is described as the People of God in chapter 2 of *Lumen gentium,* emphasizing that the Church is a community of the baptized. The fourth model envisions the Church as a sacrament of the unity between God and his people, although the theological implications of this view of the Church are more explicitly developed in the theological literature than in the conciliar documents themselves. In 1985 the Extraordinary Synod of Bishops determined that communion was the dominant image of the Church at the council.[4] Communion, however, is not itself a separate model, but a characteristic of the Church when viewed from the perspective of baptism and the Eucharist, the foundational sacraments which bring us into communion with God and the Church.

If the Roman Catholic ecclesiology of the recent past is perceived as clerical and hierarchical, the ecclesiology of the present is heavily sacramental. It remains identified by objective criteria, especially the sacraments of baptism, Eucharist, and a sacrament of order believed to be in apostolic succession. Even though *Lumen gentium* identifies preaching as the primary responsibility of the bishop, Roman Catholicism has not been primarily identified as a community of faith gathered by the word. Even though the People of God are those "who in faith look towards Jesus, the author of salvation and the principle of unity and peace,"[5] the priestly community that this people forms is "brought into operation through the sacraments and the exercise of virtues."[6] Baptism is the sacrament of faith and the objective means by which a person participates in the new People of God: "Believers in Christ have been born again not from a perishable but from an imperishable seed through the word of the living God (see 1 Pet 1, 23), not of flesh but of water and the holy Spirit (see John 3, 55-6); and they have been finally set up as 'a chosen race, a royal priesthood, a holy nation, God's own people . . . once no people but now God's people'" (1 Pet 2, 9-10).[7]

The Church of the present has not ceased to be clerical even while it attempts to distance itself from clericalism. Clericalism is the attitude that the ordained comprise the active elite corps in the Church, having sole responsibility for the Church's mission. Within clericalism clerics absorb all power, ecclesiastical privilege, and churchly identity to themselves while the laity remain passive, mere participators in the apostolate of the hierarchy. After the council many applauded, claiming that the Church had moved from a hierarchical Church to a Church of the laity. Although it would be conceptually simpler to turn from a hierarchically conceived Church to a democratic Church of the laity, the reality is much more complex. The ecclesiology of Vatican II, while identifying the Church as the People of God and grounding ecclesial identity in baptism, nevertheless notes that "Christ the Lord instituted a variety of ministries which are directed towards the good of the whole body. Ministers who are endowed with sacred power are at the service of their brothers and sisters, so that all who belong to the People of God, and therefore enjoy real Christian dignity, by cooperating with each other freely and in an orderly manner in pursuit of the same goal, may attain salvation."[8] The People of God is an ordered people with a variety of orders within the Church. Chapter 3 of *Lumen gentium* still speaks of a "hierarchically constituted society."[9] This complex reality includes a people endowed with baptismal dignity who have a responsibility towards the Church by reason of their baptism, who share in the priestly, prophetic and kingly office of Christ, and who are appointed directly to the apostolate by the Lord through baptism and confirmation, on the one hand, and the ordained ministers of the Church invested with "sacred power"[10] on the other hand. The People of God is comprised of both laity and the ordained rather than either one or the other exclusively.

The four conceptual models, although distinctive, are not absolutely mutually exclusive. The temptation exists to make things tidy and neat so there is no overlap between them, or to force a choice among models, or to rank them evaluatively. Different models elucidate different aspects of the Church. No model is complete in itself. One can, however, offer critical assessments of those aspects of the Church not accounted for in a particular model. There can also exist tensions between them that may even border on contradictions. These four models are presented here as descriptive accounts of four discernible patterns of Church structure within the documents of Vatican II.

Because various models exist simultaneously within the Church, they tend to balance, correct, and limit each other. For example, the collegiality inherent in the eucharistic model qualifies the theology of those aspects of the papacy best described within the monarchical model. The baptismal theology represented by the concept of the People of God complements the eucharistic theology of the Church seen as the Mystical Body of Christ at the same time as it corrects a monarchical model.

The concept of Church as sacrament prevents too close an association of the Church with Christ in the eucharistic model.

The construction of new models for viewing ecclesial relationships is often accomplished within a dialogue, if not a polemic, with an older conceptualization of authority and structure in the Church. The dominant model on the eve of Vatican II was a monarchical or pyramidal model of the Church. According to this view, the secular sphere is separate and distinct from a clerical world. The laity are passive receptors, and there is no participation of the faithful in ecclesial decisions. An example of such an ecclesiology is found in Bellarmine's Counter-Reformational view of the Church as a perfect society. Bellarmine institutionally defines the Church: "The one true Church is the society of men bound together by profession of the same Christian faith, and by communion of the same sacraments, under the rule of legitimate pastors and in particular under the one vicar of Christ on earth, the Roman Pontiff. . . . And it is as visible as the Kingdom of France or the Republic of Venice."[11] Such a model can be depicted thus:[12]

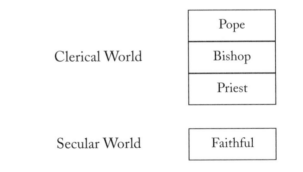

Schillebeeckx notes that this monarchical model of the Church is theologically founded in (1) the predominance of a christology which omitted the influence of the Spirit on the lowermost levels of the Church and (2) the social significance of papal infallibility where the Pope is seen as the representative of Christ in this world in an analogous fashion to how the governors were the representatives of the Roman emperor in distant places.[13] He further observes that this view robs all the other institutional authorities in the Church, including the bishops and the community of faith, of their original Christian authority and authenticity.[14] As important and essential as the Petrine ministry is for the unity and communion of the Church, it is one ministerial service among others in the Church.

Vestiges of this model are apparent in the documents of Vatican II in the clear distinction between the secular and sacred orders, with the secular order of temporal affairs the responsibility of the laity and sacred ministry the principal and express purpose of ordained ministry.[15] When the pope is described in the Preliminary Explanatory Note as the Vicar of Christ and the pastor of the universal Church, the subject of supreme and entire power of the whole Church,[16] this is a monarchical description even though, strictly speaking, the Preliminary Explanatory Note is not part of the conciliar document since it was not passed by a vote of the bishops. It is an explanation supplied by the doctrinal commission, announced by the Secretary General of the council, and published as an appendix to the official Latin version of *Lumen gentium*. Its intent was to clarify the pope's relationship to the episcopal college. The description of the papacy is stated more monarchically in the Preliminary Explanatory Note than in *Lumen gentium* 18.

Two developments in the ecclesiology of Vatican II seriously challenged the monarchical or pyramidal model: (1) the development of the principle of collegiality and the affirmation of the sacramentality of episcopal consecration, and (2) the image of the Church as the People of God. The first affirmed that the bishops possess powers by virtue of their episcopal consecration that are not juridically delegated to them by the pope even though they exercise these powers in communion with him. The second affirmed that the Church is not exclusively identified with the hierarchy or its juridical organization, but is the communion of its members. This understanding led to a renewed theology of the laity.

The Mystical Body and a Eucharistic Ecclesiology

The view of the Church as the Mystical Body of Christ became prominent with the publication of Pius XII's encyclical in 1943, *Mystici corporis*. *Lumen gentium* develops it at length in article 7. The Church considered as the body of Christ has the advantage of being a strongly biblical image that resonates with the Church's worship and its experience of communion around the Lord's table. Two distinct and slightly different scriptural foundations for this image appear in the New Testament. In the epistles to the Ephesians and Colossians the relationship between Christ and the community is a covenanted one, in a relationship of head and body, for only in these epistles is Christ mentioned as the head of the body. By contrast, in 1 Corinthians 12 and Romans 12:4-8, Christ is equated with the entire body or community, membership in the body of Christ being conferred by baptism. The texts from Colossians and Ephesians, by emphasizing the distinction between the head and the body, distinguishes the Church from Christ more than those texts from First Corinthians and Romans. This distinction between Christ and the Church makes it impossible to identify the Church as a prolongation of the incarnation in such a way that the uniqueness and particularity of the historical Jesus Christ is lost. This distinction also assures that the Church always remains subordinate to its head, Christ, and does not claim for itself what is uniquely Christ's.

Within the sacramental life of the Church, the Eucharist is not only the visible sign of communion in and with Christ, but is also constitutive of ecclesial communion, for in partaking of one bread we become one body (1 Cor 10:16-17). There is a density of ontological realism here that extends not only to the sacramental realism of the presence of Christ under the species of bread and wine, but also the sacramental realism of the Church, for where the Eucharist is, there is the Church. There exists an intrinsic relationship between the historical Christ, the sacramental Christ of the Eucharist, and the ecclesial Christ. Church, sacrament, and historical person are different modes of existence of the same person seen through a theology of a real symbol or efficacious sacramentality. The Eucharist is not exactly the same thing as the Church although it is a sacrament of it; the Church is not Christ, although it is a sacrament of the "whole Christ." Furthermore, while safeguarding a doctrine of the Real Presence, the Eucharist is not identical with the historical Christ; it is more properly termed a sacrament of Christ. The Eucharist is the sacramental Real Presence of Christ, and the Church, in sacramental union with its head, constitutes the "whole Christ." Within this communion ecclesiology there is an ontological density to the Eucharist by which real communion of the members of the Church with each other and with and in Christ is effected. This does not deny the sacramental incorporation in Christ in baptism, but as the unity of the rites of initiation indicates, the Eucharist is the culmination of baptism. What is begun in baptism, namely, incorporation in Christ and the Church, finds repeated visible expression in the Eucharist. Sacramental realism exists on several levels: the body of Christ is truly present in the Eucharist and so is the ecclesial body, the Church.

One can find this close association between the eucharistic body and the Church in both Scripture and in the theology of Augustine. In First Corinthians, Jerome Murphy-O'Connor finds it habitual in Paul's vocabulary to attribute the name "Christ" to the community.[17] This is not an identification between the community and the historical Christ, but indicates that the community performs the same function as Christ.[18] A similar association of the ecclesial with the eucharistic body occurs in Augustine of Hippo's Easter sermons, addressed to the newly baptized, and his sermons on the Gospel of John. The neophytes are included in the eucharistic symbolism of the bread and wine so that he can say: "There you are on the altar, there you are in the chalice."[19]

The unity of the bread is a type or sacramental symbol of the unity of the ecclesial body. The bread is a sacrament of the Church not just because it belongs to the Church, but because it signifies the Church. This leads to the assertion that where the Eucharist is, there is the Church. This statement means not only that the Church is present where the Eucharist is celebrated, but also that the Church is sacramentalized, that is, signified and present, in the Eucharist. The sacramental realism of the historical Christ leads to the sacramental realism of the ecclesial Christ. Affirmation of the christological reality leads to the affirmation of the ecclesial reality. The presence of the latter is as real as the presence of the first. When we commune with the sacramental Body of Christ, we commune with the resurrected Christ and the Church, which is also the Body of Christ.

The Roman Catholic Church identifies the basic unit of the Church as the altar community around the bishop.[20] Thus the local church is defined as a eucharistic community even though the only time the people usually experience themselves as gathered around the eucharistic table of the local bishop, unless they happen to reside in the cathedral parish, is for special occasions like confirmation in their local parish. The local church as a eucharistic community cannot exist alone as church all by itself, but must be united to its bishop and through the bishop to all the other eucharistic communities within the Church. The local church, although wholly church, is not the whole Church.

The universal Church is the communion of these altar communities. The universal Church is one, although it subsists in each particular church in an analogous way to how the Eucharist or Body of Christ is present on many altars though there is just one Body. A primary function of pastoral leadership is to maintain the community in unity and communion, both within the local church and with the other local churches. Governance and liturgical presidency coincide since the presider at the Eucharist, the sacrament of ecclesial unity, and the person responsible for maintaining the community in unity is the bishop. Liturgical presidency is the sacramentalization of that person's role in the community.

We might represent this conceptualization of the Church thus:

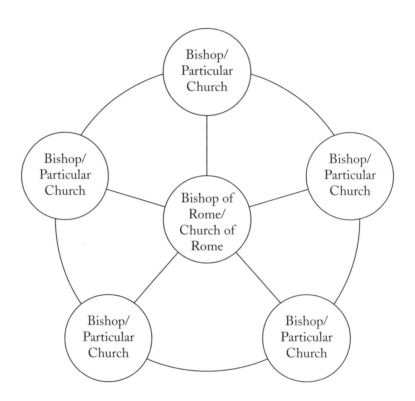

In this model each particular church is in communion with every other particular church and the Bishop of Rome who exercises the ministry of safeguarding the unity and communion of the particular churches. This communion is personalized and objectively sacramentalized in the college of bishops to which each bishop is admitted upon consecration. The bishops in their persons represent their churches.

This model represents a eucharistic ecclesiology since the paradigm of this relationship and the basis of communion is the Eucharist. This model of Church communion remains largely a clerical model since the interrelationship of the particular churches it illustrates is objectified and sacramentalized by the interrelationship of bishops. It also appears to be predominantly Christomonistic[21] to the exclusion of a viable pneumatology since it emphasizes the Church as the body of Christ. However, if ecclesiology is brought into a closer conversation with a liturgical theology of the Eucharist, which stresses the epicletic action of the Spirit and pays attention to the fact that the Eucharistic Prayer is addressed to the Father, it becomes evident that the Eucharist is ultimately trinitarian rather than exclusively christological. This model includes all the People of God as subject of the liturgical action and is intimately related to baptism as a sacrament of initiation since both sacraments incorporate us into the Church.

Elements of a eucharistic, Mystical Body of Christ model of the Church within the documents of Vatican II include: the definition of the local church as an altar community, the episcopal collegiality described in chapter three of *Lumen gentium,* and the relationship between the one universal Church and the many local churches. The statement in *Sacrosanctum concilium* that the Church is most manifestly itself when it celebrates the Eucharist could not be clearer: "The church is displayed with special clarity when the holy People of God, all of them, are actively and fully sharing in the same liturgical celebrations—especially when it is the same Eucharist—sharing one prayer at one altar, at which the bishop is presiding, surrounded by his presbyterate and his ministers."[22]

The People of God

The third model, the description of the Church as the People of God, is the subject of the second chapter of *Lumen gentium.* A product of the research activities of German theologians in the 1930s,[23] this description emphasizes the Church's historical character, the unity of the history of God with his people, and the eschatological goal of the Church. Since within this model there are various ways of being joined or related to the Church which are possible and real beyond the confines of its visible boundaries, it is ecumenical.[24] In addition to avoiding a view of Church membership that is too rigid and exclusive, it avoids identifying the Church as a prolongation of the incarnation. At the time of the council it was seen as a more flexible concept than "Mystical Body." One of the great advantages of the Church seen as the People of God is that the Church is not exclusively identified with its institutional structures or the hierarchy, but is seen as being first a community, a people, inclusive of clerical leaders and laity. This gives all the people of the Church a renewed sense of responsibility for the Church according to their place in it. This image of the Church has done more than anything else to promote the role of the laity in the Church.

The "People of God" is not a synonym for the laity, but includes everyone—lay, ordained, and religious. The chapter's position in *Lumen gentium,* immediately following the chapter on the mystery of the Church and before the chapters on the hierarchy and the laity, signals the prior unity of all the faithful within the one People of God on the basis of their baptism before they are identified in their diversity. The importance of its position cannot be overestimated. The Church cannot be identified with the hierarchy, but is the community of people consecrated by baptism and the anointing of the Holy Spirit.

The Threefold Office in Vatican II

A major principle of organization of *Lumen gentium*'s discussion of the People of God is the threefold motif of priest, prophet, and king.[25] The people as a whole is priestly, prophetic, and kingly as is each constitutive group within it. This model of the Church can be diagramed like this:

People of God

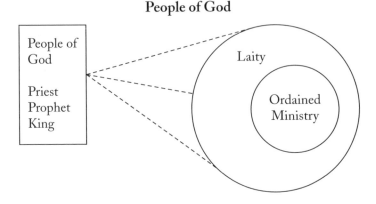

The new People of God become a priestly people through baptism. Their baptismal character gives the priestly people a place in Christian worship, particularly in the Eucharist. The practice of dismissing catechumens after the Liturgy of the Word reflects this theology since they are not deputed to participate in the Liturgy of the Eucharist until after their baptism.

The two images of the Church, the Mystical Body of Christ and the People of God, are not in competition, but actually complement one another. The new people is a holy priesthood because of its relationship to the priesthood of Christ. In other words, it is a holy priesthood because it is the Mystical Body of Christ. It does not constitute a priesthood apart from Christ who is the one priest. The images are two aspects of the same relationship, but aspects that emphasize different characteristics of the Church. The image of the Mystical Body emphasizes its sacramental nature and eucharistic origins, but can be somewhat ahistorical and static, while the image of the People of God is historical, dynamic, and rooted in baptism.

Vatican II carefully points out that the common priesthood of the faithful and the ministerial or hierarchical priesthood, although ordered to one another, differ essentially and not only in degree.[26] The ministerial priest "forms and governs the priestly people, effects the eucharistic sacrifice, and offers it to God in the name of all the people." Unfortunately, this difference is described in terms of the sacred powers and functions of a ministerial priest rather than in terms of a more developed theology of a ministerial priest's relationship to Christ or the ecclesial community. Chapter five will argue that in the universal or common priesthood, the members represent Christ in his body as members of that body, while in the ordained priesthood, priests represent Christ in his headship of the body and officially represent the body in its totality.

The holy People of God shares in Christ's prophetic office through their anointing in baptism and confirmation. They exercise this office particularly by witnessing to Christ through their lives of faith and love. However, Vatican II also teaches that by virtue of this prophetic office and the indwelling of the Spirit, the whole People of God cannot err in matters of belief.[27] This *sensus fidei*, the sense of the faith, of the whole people is exercised when all the people, inclusive of the bishops to the last of the faithful, "manifest a universal consent in matters of faith and morals."[28] This does not mean that only where there is 100 percent agreement on the part of all the Catholics in the world does a true *sensus fidei* obtain in regard to any Christian doctrine, or that the majority opinion represents the action of the Holy Spirit. In fact, there has never been a truly universal consensus in any significant case. It does mean that infallibility does not belong solely to the hierarchy or solely to the believing people, but that there is a mutual interdependence between the teaching of pastors and the belief of the people since both are assisted by the Holy Spirit.[29] Also associated with the prophetic office are the charisms, gifts of the Spirit, given in great variety and diversity to the People of God for the renewal and building up of the Church.[30]

All the People of God belong to Christ's kingdom, "whose nature is not earthly but heavenly."[31] The kingly office of the People of God is to seek "for the return of all humanity and all its goods under Christ the Head in the unity of his Spirit."[32] *Lumen gentium* associates this kingdom with a catholic unity prefiguring and promoting universal peace. The kingdom is all-inclusive since everyone is called by God's grace to salvation. Everyone belongs to it, including the Catholic faithful, others who believe in Christ, and all humankind.

Bishops, with priests and deacons as helpers, exercise this threefold office in their service of the community, "presiding in the place of God over the flock, whose shepherds they are, as teachers of doctrine, priests of sacred worship and ministers of government."[33] The use of the three offices in *Lumen gentium* indicates that the power to sanctify, teach, and govern are conferred by ordination to the episcopacy. This power comes not from the Church or from the pope, but from Christ.[34] According to the older division between office *(munus)* and power *(postestas)*, the power of sanctifying was conferred by episcopal consecration and the office of governing by a canonical mission of jurisdiction. With the threefold office, all episcopal powers are seen as having a sacramental origin.[35] For this reason, not only diocesan bishops, but also all bishops, including titular and auxiliary bishops, have the right to attend a council. All belong to the episcopal college by virtue of their episcopal ordination and not by virtue of a jurisdictional appointment to a diocese.

Here the kingly role is interpreted as governance and pastoral leadership, the prophetic role as preaching and teaching, and the priestly role as leadership in sacred worship. The exercise of these roles is specific to the episcopal office. For example, governance is collegial within the college of bishops and in union with the Bishop of Rome. Preaching is the preeminent responsibility of the bishop who is the authentic teacher endowed with the authority of Christ.[36] The bishop, invested with the fullness of the sacrament of order, is the "high priest of his flock."[37] The principal manifestation of the Church occurs with the full, active participation of all God's people at the Eucharist at which the bishop presides surrounded by his priests and the other ministers.[38]

Presbyters, as helpers to the bishop, also exercise these same roles. They are consecrated "in order to preach the Gospel and shepherd the faithful as well as to celebrate divine worship as true priests of the New Testament."[39] The exercise of their power is dependent upon the bishop, but they share ministerial priesthood with the bishop. They form a college with other presbyters and exercise a limited authority over a portion of the flock assigned to them. They are really understood as extensions of the bishop since they are his "cooperators, support and mouthpiece."[40]

Lumen gentium does not explicitly develop a theology of the diaconate with respect to the threefold office. Deacons are ordained "for the service of the liturgy, of the Gospel and of works of charity."[41] Since they are not ordained to the ministerial priesthood, as are bishops and presbyters, their liturgical ministry must be interpreted as an exercise of the common or universal priesthood shared by all the People of God. They are authorized, however, to exercise official liturgical leadership not generally permitted to other baptized Christians such as presiding at solemn baptism, witnessing Christian marriage, and officiating at funeral and burial services. This raises questions beyond the scope of the present study regarding why these sacraments are appropriately administered or witnessed by an official representative of the Church, which a deacon is, but do not require an ordained priest. Today deacons exercise their prophetic function by proclaiming the gospel, preaching, and teaching. Their governing role is simply referred to as "functions of administration." Their service of charity traditionally involves the administration of the temporal goods of the community.

This same triad structures sections 34, 35, and 36 of the chapter on the laity in *Lumen gentium*. The laity exercise their priestly office by offering spiritual worship both in the Eucharist and everywhere by their holy actions.[42] They exercise their prophetic office through evangelization by word and testimony of life, especially through the structure of their secular lives and through married and family life.[43] The lay faithful spread the kingdom by ordering the whole of creation to the praise of God and by helping one another "achieve greater holiness of life, so that the world may be filled with the spirit of Christ and may the more effectively attain its destiny in justice, in love and in peace."[44] The laity accomplish this through their competence in secular disciplines, human labor, technical skill, and civil culture.

The extensiveness of the threefold schema in *Lumen gentium* ties together the description of the Church as the People of God and the image of the Church as the Body of Christ, since the paradigm of the Church is Christ who was Priest, Prophet, and King. It links the rest of *Lumen gentium* with the first chapter, which describes how we are formed in the likeness of Christ through baptism.[45] Finally, it emphasizes the unity of all the members of the Church who exercise the same threefold office according to their place in the Church.

The Historical Origins
of the Priest, Prophet, and King Paradigm

The use of the tripartite division to describe Christ and all the faithful dates from the early Church.[46] Its use to describe ministry, however, is rather recent despite its extensive occurrence in *Lumen gentium*. The term *Christus* means the "anointed one." Eusebius, the fourth-century bishop of Caesarea and chronicler of the early Church, recalls that among the Jews high priests, kings, and prophets were anointed, thus making them *christs*.[47] The evidence for the anointing of prophets, however, is rather thin. The only Old Testament references are Psalm 105:15, "Do not touch my anointed ones; do my prophets no harm," cited in 1 Chronicles 16:22, and 1 Kings 19:16, where the Lord tells Elijah to anoint Elisha son of Shaphat of Abel-meholah as prophet in his place, and Sirach 48:8, a reference to 1 Kings 19:16. There are other texts, especially Deuteronomy 18:18, which speak of God raising up a prophet, but these are not associated with anointing. Later tradition usually refers to the anointing of Elisha for evidence of prophetic anointing.

Jesus Christ is clearly and directly identified as High Priest (Heb 3:1) and King (John 18:33-37, 19:14-22). Once again, the evidence for identification as a prophet is more oblique. Disciples, although none of the Twelve, identify Jesus as a prophet in John 4:19, 6:14, and 9:17. In Acts 3:22-26 the implication is that Jesus is a prophet like Moses. Jesus seems to refer to himself as a prophet in Luke 4:24 by the words, "No prophet is accepted in his native place." The author of the Gospel of John seems to agree with this designation for Jesus, but Jesus never directly calls himself a prophet, and the evidence is less direct than for his identity as priest and king. Christ's messianic anointing, however, is closely associated with his prophetic function (Isa 61:1, Luke 4:18-19, Acts 10:38). He does receive the titles "Rabbi" and "Teacher" and so functions like a prophet.[48] Later Church tradition, including the Council of Trent, attributes the three titles to Christ on the basis of his anointing.[49]

John Chrysostom applies the roles of priest, prophet, and king to all the faithful in his commentary on 2 Corinthians 1:21-22.[50] This passage from Paul, however, does not make this application, but only speaks of our anointing. The early fifth-century bishop, Fastidius, also applies the threefold pattern to the Christian faithful on the basis of their having been anointed in baptism like Christ the anointed one.[51] The priestly, prophetic, and royal triad is attributed to the Christian people by virtue of their baptismal incorporation into Christ.

However, Peter J. Drilling's study of the triad concludes that "none of the texts cited from the first twelve hundred years of the Church's history applies the three, as three that are inseparable, as titles or as characteristics of the ministry of the ordained."[52] John Calvin's *Institutes* (1545) was the first work to show how the threefold offices of Christ continue to function in the Church.[53] At the Council of Trent, the threefold office appears in the preparation of the decree on the sacrament of order, referring there to priests.[54] In fact, it is not until the First Vatican Council in the nineteenth century that it is used to describe the role of bishops and the pope. It was included in the schema for the dogmatic constitution on the Church, *Tametsi Deus Ecclesiam.* Pope Pius XII continued to apply the threefold pattern to bishops in *Mystici corporis,* June 29, 1943, and it appears in the revised Baltimore Catechism in 1948.[55] The influence of threefold office on the text of *Lumen gentium* was most likely due to the work of Sebastian Tromp, a member of the Doctrinal Commission which drafted *Lumen gentium,* who had developed this theme in a book republished on the eve of the council, and Yves Congar, who developed the theme in reference to the laity.[56] Vatican II replaced royal terminology with pastoral terminology, shifting the imagery from Christ the King to Christ the Good Shepherd. Pastoral leadership and governance become two aspects of the same office, thus joining Christ's identity as Good Shepherd and King.[57]

This is done for pastoral reasons, but it also illustrates that office and function are essential within the Church rather than their explicit connection with anointing. The biblical association of the priest, prophet,

and king triad with Old Testament anointings seems to be less important than the link between the Christian community and Christ. A
shepherd, the image which tends to replace the notion of king, is not
anointed. Baptism effects our incorporation in Christ and does entail
anointing in its solemn form, but our likeness to Christ does not exclusively lie in the anointing.

Historically, the triad was first applied to Christ, then to Christians,
next to hierarchical ministry within the Church, and, finally, in the
twentieth century, to the tasks of the Church itself. The Church itself is
prophetic, priestly, and royal. This trajectory is not surprising, given that
ecclesiology did not develop as a formal theological discipline until the
nineteenth century. The triad expresses the activities essential for the
Christian community: ministry to sacrament, word, and pastoral service.[58] They are activities essential for the Church to be Church, enabling
the Church to perpetuate itself and to engage in mission to the world.

The triad also speaks to the inner coherence of christology, ecclesiology, and the Christian activity of the baptized and the ordained. The
triad appears in different forms for the faithful and the ordained. When
Vatican II speaks of the faithful, the triad appears as "priest, prophet,
king" while in reference to the ordained it becomes "teacher, priest,
shepherd/king." Although the application of the threefold office to both
the nonordained faithful and the ordained emphasizes their unity in
Christ, the offices are not exercised in the same manner by the ordained
and the nonordained. The People of God become a priestly community
through baptism, which incorporates them into the ecclesial body of
Christ and orients them to participation in Christ's eucharistic Body.
They share in Christ's priesthood as members of his churchly body. Ordination identifies a person with Christ, the head of the body. This difference points to the difference in essence and not only in degree that
distinguishes the ordained from the nonordained baptized.[59] The prophetic office of the faithful is associated with their testimony of life
while the prophetic office of the ordained, particularly bishops, is identified with their authoritative teaching. The kingly role of the baptized
is to work to spread the kingdom, particularly in the secular world,
while the shepherding/governing office of the ordained is to provide
pastoral leadership within the Church. Although these offices are characteristics of the Church as a whole and ministry in its totality, the triad
in and of itself does not necessitate that every ministry in the Church
subsume all three offices to itself in its public ministerial form. As we
have seen, Vatican II did not explicitly apply the triad to the diaconate.

The identification of both the People of God and the ordained with Christ through the threefold office would seem to contribute to a Christomonistic view of the Church to the exclusion of an adequate pneumatology. The original association of the threefold office with anointing, however, offers an important corrective to this, since the anointing is always by the Spirit. A person is conformed to Christ only by the power of the Spirit. Baptism and ordination are primarily sacraments of the Spirit that have a christological effect.

The Church as Sacrament

A fourth model of the Church in the documents of Vatican II is that of sacrament. Three different articles in *Lumen gentium* identify the Church as a sacrament, each with a slightly different nuance:

> And since the church is in Christ as a sacrament or instrumental sign of intimate union with God and of the unity of all humanity, the council, continuing the teaching of previous councils, intends to declare with greater clarity to the faithful and the entire human race the nature of the church and its universal mission (Article 1).

> Christ, when he was lifted up from the earth, drew all people to himself; rising from the dead, he sent his life-giving Spirit down on his disciples and through him he constituted his body which is the church as the universal sacrament of salvation. . . . (Article 48).

> God has called together the assembly of those who look to Jesus in faith as the author of salvation and the principle of unity and peace, and he has constituted the church that it may be for one and all the visible sacrament of this saving unity (Article 9).

These three passages from *Lumen gentium* give three slightly different identifications of what the Church signifies as sacrament: intimate union with God and the unity of humanity, salvation, and saving unity. This suggests that the salvation consisting in union with God does not exist apart from unity within humanity.

Yves Congar notes three occurrences of an identification of the Church as sign in the Constitution on the Sacred Liturgy.[60] In Article 2 the Church is "an ensign raised for the nations, under which the scattered children of God can be brought together into one until there is one fold and one shepherd." Article 5 speaks of the sacrament of the whole Church arising from the side of Christ as he slept on the cross. Article 26 cautions against a privatization of the liturgy, noting that "liturgical events are not private actions but celebrations of the Church which is 'the sacrament of unity,' the holy people drawn into an ordered whole under the bishops." The first and third of these passages stress the Church as a sacrament or sign of unity while the second passage associates the Church with the blood and water issuing from the side of Jesus, symbols of baptism and Eucharist.

The identification of the Church as a sacrament occurs within a chain of sacramentality in the theological writing of Edward Schillebeeckx and Karl Rahner.[61] Christ is a sacrament of the Father. The Church is a sacrament of Christ, and the seven sacraments are sacraments of the Church. The sign or sacrament is the actualization in the world of that which is signified, namely, God, Christ, and the Church, respectively. This model can be diagramed thus:

$$\textbf{God} \longrightarrow \textbf{Christ} \longrightarrow \textbf{Church} \longrightarrow \textbf{Sacraments}$$

The idea of the Church as sacrament is closely related to the image of the body of Christ. From a biblical perspective, the body is that which makes a person present and active. The Church as the body of Christ is the sacramental presence of Christ in the world in an analogous way to how Christ is the sacrament of the Father. In the concept of sacrament, there is both unity and difference, unity between the sign of the sacrament and what is signified, difference, because what is signified is not absolutely identical with the sign which makes it present. Historical presence and sacramental presence are two different modalities.

Two examples may clarify this relationship. The resurrected Christ is really present in the sacrament of the Eucharist, but does not bleed or suffer pain when consumed. Christ is the image of and self-expression of the Father. The one who sees the Son sees the Father (John 14:9). In Karl Rahner's theology the Son is a real symbol, which means Real Presence under sign, of the Father. He shares the same divine nature as the Father (unity) and yet is distinct from the Father as the Father's object of self-knowledge. The identity between Father and Son lies in the identity of their divine nature, and their difference lies in their relationship. The Father generates the Son and the Son is begotten of the Father. The Son does not generate and the Father is not begotten.

They are so close, however, that in Edward Schillebeeckx's theology, we encounter God when we encounter Christ.

A sacrament is "a symbol of a sacred reality, a visible form of invisible grace."[62] In the case of the Church, the visible sign includes the institutional and social aspect of the Church, that is, all that is manifest in history and located in space and time. The referent of the sign is the resurrected Christ. As with the incarnation, in the Church there is the union of the divine and the human, the human being the manifestation and revelation of the divine. Henri de Lubac draws this analogy: "The Church is here below the sacrament of Jesus Christ, as Jesus Christ himself is for us, in his humanity, the sacrament of God."[63] The human element becomes the manifestation and revelation of the divine. *Lumen gentium* expresses this relationship thus:

> This society, however, equipped with hierarchical structures, and the mystical body of Christ, a visible assembly and a spiritual community, an earthly church and a church enriched with heavenly gifts, must not be considered as two things, but as forming one complex reality comprising a human and a divine element. It is therefore by no mean analogy that it is likened to the mystery of the incarnate Word. For just as the assumed nature serves the divine Word as a living instrument of salvation inseparably joined with him, in a similar way the social structure of the church serves the Spirit who vivifies the church towards the growth of the body (see Eph 4, 16).[64]

Even though the concept of the Church as the sacrament of Christ is closely related to the image of the Church as the Mystical Body of Christ, it avoids a major weakness of this image of being too close an identification between Christ and the Church. The concept of sacrament is able to express the unity between the sign and the referent of that sign at the same time that it maintains the distinction between sign and referent. For example, equating the relationship of Christ to his Father with that of the Church to Christ ignores the fact that the Church has not fully arrived at the eschaton. The Church is in a state of becoming and its expression as sign is not fully complete. Yet, as we have seen, the modality of a sacrament maintains a distinction between sign and referent at the same time that it expresses their unity. This unity and distinction is analogous to the relationship between the divine and human natures in Christ: "as with Christ the distinction between his Godhead and his humanity remains without confusion though they are inseparable signs and reality, manifest historical form and Holy Spirit are not the same in the Church, but as in Christ, are not separable any more either."[65]

The Church is most visibly a sign of grace and union with Christ in the Eucharist since the Eucharist is "indivisibly Christological and ecclesiological."[66] The Eucharist is both the sign and the instrument of the union of the People of God with God and with one another. However, not only the Eucharist, but also all the sacraments have the Church as their referent, which is to say that sacraments are signs of the Church. The sacraments relate to the Church as the self-expression of the Church. They are "the essential functions that bring into activity the very essence of the Church."[67] The moments of the seven sacraments are, then, the moments of self-actualization of the Church.

The nature of the Church is evident through each of the sacraments. In the Eucharist we know the Church to be the body of Christ. We are incorporated into that body, both the Church and the body of Christ, in baptism. We are reconciled to both Christ and the Church in the sacrament of penance. Marriage, the covenant between two human beings, is a sign of the relationship between Christ and the Church. So, too, what is "ordered" in the sacrament of order is the Church. In this sacrament the ordained person is ordered to both Christ and the Church in such a way that the ordained is representative of both. As will become evident in the course of this study, the sacrament of order reveals the nature of the Church: a communion of communions represented by the college of bishops, a priestly community, and a community of charity.

Traditional theologies of ordination frequently locate the essence of the sacrament in the configuration of the ordained person to Christ. A direct line of authority extends from Christ to the apostles to the bishops who are the successors of the apostles. Bishops take the place of Christ himself and act as his representatives. This theology, developed by St. Ignatius of Antioch and St. Irenaeus to assert episcopal authority against the Gnostic heresies of the time,[68] is still strongly present in chapter three of *Lumen gentium*.[69] This theology of ordination supports the teaching authority of the bishops and pope. Within sacramental theology it also enables the Church to assert that Christ, rather than the minister, is the principal actor when the sacraments are administered.

This is accurate, but incomplete, for in this view ordination occurs without any reference to the Church. Other strands within the tradition balance this one-sided christological view of ordination with attention to the ecclesiological and pneumatological location of ordination. These include the prohibition against absolute ordination apart from ordination to a particular ecclesial community and the rites of election and acclamation within the ordination rites. A theological view of the chain of sacramentality wherein sacraments are sacraments of the Church and the Church is a sacrament of Christ also contributes to this balance, for the Church mediates the presence of Christ in the sacraments. Ordination is a sign of the Church, and by way of the Church, of Christ. This does not democratize the theology of ordination or minimize christological representation insofar as the Church is seen as the body of Christ, and ordination is seen as accomplished by the laying on of hands by ministers in apostolic succession and invocation of the Spirit.

Other possible models exist which are not present in these documents. For example, Leonardo Boff develops a model of the Church based on his experience of base Christian communities in Brazil. He begins with the assertion that the community as the People of God exists antecedently to the Church as organization.[70] According to this view, the risen Christ and the Spirit are immanently present in the community. Ministries arise from the community and exist for service to the community. According to Boff, these communities are characterized "by the absence of alienating structures, by direct relationship, by reciprocity, by a deep communion, by mutual assistance, by communality of gospel ideals, by equality among members."[71] Institutional characteristics such as "rigid rules, hierarchies, prescribed relationships in a framework of a distinction of functions, qualities, and titles" are absent. Here the basis for communion is the faith of the Church and the sharing in the gospel. This model of the Church functions along a Word/laity axis rather than the Eucharist/clerical axis characteristic of institutional and eucharistic ecclesiologies. Models such as this, however, do not inform the ordination rites which were revised to reflect the ecclesiology of Vatican II.

Elements of the four conceptualizations of the Church presented here—monarchical, Mystical Body of Christ, People of God, and sacrament—are evident in the conciliar documents and influence the theology and practice of ordained ministry today. The monarchical model still dualistically divides the world between the sacred and the profane, allocating the sacred to the ordained ministers and the profane to the laity. Perhaps the lines are not as clearly drawn as they once were, but such recent documents as "Some Questions Regarding Collaboration of Nonordained Faithful in Priests' Sacred Ministry" witness to its continued presence.[72] The interest in lay ministry today finds theological foundations in the baptismal theology of the People of God. This raises new questions about priestly identity and the distinction between the common or universal priesthood and the ordained priesthood. This chapter has shown the close connections between the view of the Church as the Mystical Body of Christ and the Church as sacrament of Christ. The view of the Church as sacrament and the seven sacraments as sacraments of the Church has given us a renewed understanding of sacraments as not only the acts of Christ, but as acts of the Church that reveal the nature of the Church. This understanding of the Church has the important effect of broadening an understanding of ordained ministry from a private relationship between the ordained person and Christ to an emphasis on the ordained person's relationship to the Church. Christ acts through the sacraments by means of his body, the Church, acting. The ordained minister is authorized by the Church,[73] an authorization inseparable from the gift of the Holy Spirit invoked in the epiclesis of ordination, to minister in the name of the Church and Christ, the first being the sacrament and body of the second.

Notes, Chapter One

[1] *Gaudium et spes* 1, in *Decrees of the Ecumenical Councils,* Vol. Two: *Trent to Vatican II,* ed. Norman P. Tanner (Washington, D.C.: Georgetown University Press, 1990).

[2] See Edward Schillibeeckx, *L'Eglise du Christ de l'homme d'aujourd'hui selon Vatican II* (Paris: Mappus, 1965).

[3] The final vote approving *Lumen gentium* on November 21, 1964, was 2151 *placet,* 5 *non-placet.*

[4] The Final Report, "The Church, in the World of God, Celebrates the Mysteries of Christ for the Salvation of the World" (National Catholic News Service), II, C, 1.

[5] *Lumen gentium* 9.

[6] *Lumen gentium* 11.

[7] *Lumen gentium* 9.

[8] *Lumen gentium* 18.

[9] *Lumen gentium* 20.

[10] *Lumen gentium* 18.

[11] Robert Bellarmine, *Of Controversies of Christian Faith Against Heretics of Today* (1586).

[12] Leonardo Boff, *Ecclesiogenesis*, 26.

[13] Edward Schillebeeckx, *Church: The Human Story of God* (New York: Crossroad, 1990) 198.

[14] Edward Schillebeeckx, *Church: The Human Story of God*, 199.

[15] *Lumen gentium* 31.

[16] *Lumen gentium*, Preliminary Explanatory Note 3.

[17] Jerome Murphy-O'Connor, O.P. *1 Corinthians* (Wilmington, Del.: Michael Glazier, 1972) 115.

[18] Ibid.

[19] Sermon 6.

[20] *Lumen gentium* 26.

[21] A Christomonistic model of the Church is one that identifies the Church exclusively with Christ without accounting for the presence and action of the Holy Spirit.

[22] *Sacrosanctum concilium* 41.

[23] Cardinal Ratzinger, "The Ecclesiology of Vatican II," *Origins* 15 (22) (November 14, 1985) 374.

[24] Ibid., 372.

[25] For a history of the development of *Lumen gentium* according to this tripartite paradigm, see Peter. J. Drilling, "The Priest, Prophet and King Trilogy: Elements of its Meaning in *Lumen gentium* and for Today," *Église et Théologie* 19 (1988) 179–206.

[26] *Lumen gentium* 10.

[27] *Lumen gentium* 12.

[28] Ibid.

[29] See Avery Dulles, *"Sensus Fidelium,"America* 155 (Nov. 1, 1986) 240–42, 263.

[30] *Lumen gentium* 12

[31] *Lumen gentium* 13.

[32] *Lumen gentium* 13.

[33] *Lumen gentium* 20.

[34] Bonaventure Kloppenburg, *The Ecclesiology of Vatican II*, trans. Matthew J. O'Connell (Chicago: Franciscan Herald Press, 1974) 222–23.

[35] K. Rahner, "The Dogmatic Constitution on the Church," *Commentary on the Documents of Vatican II*, vol. I, H. Vorgrimler, ed. (New York: Herder and Herder, 1967) 188–95.

[36] *Lumen gentium* 25.

[37] *Sacrosanctum concilium* 41.

[38] Ibid.

[39] *Lumen gentium* 28.

[40] Ibid.

[41] *Lumen gentium* 29.

[42] *Lumen gentium* 34.

[43] *Lumen gentium* 35.

[44] *Lumen gentium* 36.

[45] This, of course, constitutes a very Christocentric notion of the Church. Vatican II has been frequently criticized for its comparatively weak pneumatology.

[46] For histories of this trilogy see Yves Congar, "Sur la triologie: Prophète-Roi-Prêtre," *Revue des Sciences Philosophiques et Religieuses* 67 (1983) 97–115; L. Schick, *Das Dreifache Amt Christi und der Kirche.* Zur Entstehung und Entwicklung der Trilogien (Europäische Hochschulschriften, Reihe XXIII Theologie Bd. 171). (Frankfurt/M.—Bern, Peter Lang, 1982).

[47] Eusebius, *Historica Ecclesiastica,* I, 3, in *Patrologia Graeca,* vol. 20, cc. 68–73, and in Hugh Jackson Lawlor and John Ernest Leonard Oulton, eds. and trans., *The Ecclesiastical History and the Martyrs of Palestine* (London: SPCK, 1954), 12; *Demonstratio Evangelica,* Lib. IV, 15, in PG 22, 290–91 and in William John Ferrar, ed. and trans. *The Proof of the Gospel* (Grand Rapids, Mich.: Baker Book House, n.d.), 191 ff. Cited by Peter J. Drilling, "The Priest, Prophet and King Trilogy," 188.

[48] See Ch. H. Dodd, "Jesus als Lehrer u. Prophet," in *Mysterium Christi* (Berlin, 1931) 69–86; J. Daniélou, "Le Christ prophète" in *La Vie spirituelle* (February 1948) 154–70; F. Gils, *Jésus Prophète d'après les Evangiles synoptiques* (Louvain, 1957); F. Normann, *Christos diadaskalos.* Die Vorstellung von Christus als Lehrer in der christlichen Literatur des ersten u. zweiten Jahrhunderts (Munster, 1967). Cited by Congar, "Sur la triologie: Prophète-Roi-Prêtre," 103, n. 36.

[49] *Catechimus Tridentinus,* I, cap. 3, q. 7 (Typis Seminarii Patavini, 1930).

[50] John Chrysostom, in *2 Cor homilia 3,5* in PG 61, 411 and in *A Library of the Fathers, The Homilies of St. John Chrysostom on the Second Epistle of St. Paul the Apostle to the Corinthians* (Oxford: John Henry Parker, 1948) 43. Cited by Peter J. Drilling, "The Priest, Prophet and King Trilogy," 188.

[51] Fastidius, *De Vita Christiana,* 1, in *Patrologia Latina,* vol. 50, c. 394. Ludwig Schick notes two patristic references not included in the 1963 draft of *Lumen gentium:* Peter Chrysologus's sermons LIX and CXXVI, and a homily by the Persian Asphraates. Chrysologus uses the trilogy as a christological formula, and Aphraates to describe the effects of the baptismal anointing upon the Christian people. See Ludwig Schick, *Das Dreifache Amt Christi und der Kirche* (Frankfurt am Main: Peter Lang, 1982) 60–62, 65, 65–57. Cited by Peter J. Drilling, "The Priest, Prophet, and King Trilogy," 188–89.

[52] Peter J. Drilling, "The Priest, Prophet, and King Trilogy," 189.

[53] See Josef Fuchs, "Origines d'une Trilogie ecclésiologique à l'époque rationaliste de la théologie," *Revue des Sciences Philosophiques et Théologiques* 53 (1969) 185–211.

[54] "Aptissime enim [ritus unctionis] unctionem eam spiritalem repraesentat, quam sacerdotes per ordinationem a Christo Domino trahentes, participes quodammodo fiunt regni, prophetiae, et sacerdotii eius, quatenus ad regnodos et docendos populos atque ad offerenda pro eis sacrificia idonei redduntur." *Concilum Tridentinum* Ed. Goerresgesellschaft, Vol. VIII, 486, 3–6. Cited by Yves Congar, "Sur la triologie: Prophète-Roi-Prêtre," 104.

[55] *A Catechism of Christian Doctrine, No. 3: A Text for Secondary Schools and Colleges,* revised edition (Paterson, N. J.: St. Anthony Guild Press, 1948), nos. 143–46.

⁵⁶ Sebastian Tromp, *Corpus Christi Quod Est Ecclesia,* vol. II, *De Christo Capite Mystici Corporis* (Rome: Gregorian University, 1946). This was republished in 1960 with minor revision. For the threefold office see pp. 318–38. Yves Congar, *Lay People in the Church* (Westminster, Maryland: The Newman Press, 1965). This was first published in 1956. Joseph H. Crehan, "Priesthood, Kingship, and Prophecy," *Theological Studies* 42 (1981) 216–31, claims that Vatican II derived its teaching on the threefold office of Christ from Newman. Peter Drilling refutes this in "The Priest, Prophet and King Trilogy," 199.

⁵⁷ This point is made by Peter Drilling in "The Priest, Prophet and King Trilogy," 205. See *Lumen gentium,* 20, 21, 27, 28.

⁵⁸ See Bernard Cooke, *Ministry to Word and Sacrament* (Philadelphia: Fortress Press, 1976), Edward Farley, *Ecclesial Reflection: An Anatomy of Theological Method* (Philadelphia: Fortress Press, 1982) 253.

⁵⁹ *Lumen gentium* 10.

⁶⁰ Yves Congar, *Un peuple messianique: L'Eglise: sacrement du salut, salut et libération* (Paris: Edition du Cerf, 1975) 31.

⁶¹ Karl Rahner, *The Church and the Sacraments* (New York: Herder and Herder, 1963); Edward Schillebeeckx, *Christ, the Sacrament of the Encounter with God* (Kansas City, Mo.: Sheed Andrews and McMeel, 1963). See also Avery Dulles, *Models of the Church* (New York: Doubleday & Co., 1974); Gustave Martelet, "De la sacramentalité propre à l'Eglise," *Nouvelle revue théologique* 95 (1973) 25–42; P. Smulders, "L'Eglise sacrement du salut," in G. Barauna (ed.), *L'Eglise de Vatican II,* vol. 2 (Paris: Cerf, 1967) 313–38; Jan Groot, "The Church as Sacrament of the World," *Concilium,* vol. 1, no. 4 (London: Burns & Oates Ltd., January 1968).

⁶² DS 1639.

⁶³ Cited by G. Martelet, "De la sacramentalité propre à l'Eglise," 26.

⁶⁴ *Lumen gentium* 8.

⁶⁵ Karl Rahner, *Studies in Modern Theology* (London: Burns & Oates, 1964) 201.

⁶⁶ Dulles, 74.

⁶⁷ Rahner, *Church and Sacraments,* 22.

⁶⁸ See St. Irenaeus, *Adv Haer.* III, 3,1; PG 7, 848; III, 2, 2; PG 847; St. Ignatius, Martyr, *Philad.* Praef, 1, 1. Cited in *Lumen gentium* 20.

⁶⁹ So *Lumen gentium* 21.

⁷⁰ Leonardo Boff, *Ecclesiogenesis: The Base Communities Reinvent the Church* (Maryknoll, New York: Orbis Books, 1986) 26.

⁷¹ Ibid., 4.

⁷² "Some Questions Regarding Collaboration of Nonordained Faithful in Priests' Sacred Ministry," *Origins* 27 (24) (November 27, 1997) 397, 399–409.

⁷³ See Thomas P. Rausch, "Priestly Identity: Priority of Representation and the Iconic Argument," *Worship* 73 (March 1999) 169–79.

Chapter Two

The Liturgical Rite
of the Ordination of a Bishop

The greatest impetus to the liturgical revision of the rite of the ordination of a bishop was the theology of the episcopacy articulated by the Second Vatican Council. In developing a doctrine of episcopal collegiality with the bishop as the recipient of the fullness of the sacrament of orders,[1] the council resolved a disputed theological question: is episcopal consecration a sacramental ordination or a juridical, nonsacramental consecration?[2] This *Lex Orandi* series looks to the liturgical rite for a theology of the sacrament. However, the rite itself also reflects the theology of the Church. The interrelationship between the theology of episcopacy embedded in the ordination rite and the conciliar teaching is a striking example of the mutual and reciprocal relationship of the rule of prayer and the rule of faith, the *lex orandi* and the *lex credendi* of the Church.

The differences between the 1990 and the 1968 rites of ordination of a bishop, though few, are significant. The revised rite reflects the emphasis on episcopal consecration as sacramental, speaking of the *ordination* of a bishop, thus departing from the traditional employment of "consecration" to designate what happens to a bishop. The new rites likewise speak interchangeably about the "consecratory" prayer of deacons, priests, and bishops. The 1990 rite was corrected to use the language of ordination with respect to bishops more consistently than the 1968 did.[3] All three rites now speak of both "ordinations" and "conse-

28

crations." Finally, the rite now includes a General Introduction in keeping with the structure of the rites of the other sacraments.

The revised *Pontificale Romanum* (1990), the liturgical book containing the rites of ordination, begins with the ordination of the bishop in accordance with the ancient tradition of listing the bishop first.[4] Within a study of the sacrament of order, this gives priority to the order of bishop and his threefold office of governing, sanctifying, and teaching in imitation of Jesus Christ who was Shepherd, Priest, and Teacher. This contrasts with the practice prior to Vatican II, which tended to view the priesthood, with reference to the order of the presbyterate, as the principal manifestation of the sacrament of order. The new sequence reflects both the dependence of the other two orders on the bishop and the theology of the episcopacy as the fullness of orders. It also corrects an emphasis on the personal powers received within an ascending sequence of ordinations.

The episcopate, the presbyterate, and the diaconate are the three orders that now comprise the ranks of the clergy. The rite of ordination for each order has a common parallel structure. Paul VI suppressed first tonsure, minor orders, and the subdiaconate in his *motu proprio, Ministeria quaedam,* August 15, 1972. At the same time he established the ministries of reader and acolyte. "Candidates for ordination as deacons or priests are to receive these ministries and exercise them for a suitable time in order to be better disposed for the future service of the word and of the altar."[5] These formal and canonical institutions to ministry by the bishop are also open to lay men. Reader and acolyte are now ministries rather than minor orders and can be entrusted to lay people who do not aspire to the presbyterate. These formal ministries have not entered the life of the church in a significant way because they are limited to lay men, while women, who can be and are commissioned to serve as extraordinary ministers of Communion and lectors, cannot be admitted to these formal canonical ministries.[6]

The outline of the 1990 rite is as follows:[7]

Introduction to the Rite of Ordination of a Bishop
(Praenotanda)

Importance of the Ordination

Duties and Ministries

Celebration of the Ordination

Requisites for the Celebration

Outline of the Rite of Ordination of a Bishop

INTRODUCTORY RITES

LITURGY OF THE WORD

LITURGY OF ORDINATION

    Preparatory Rites

        Hymn

        Presentation of the Bishop-elect

        Apostolic Letter

        Assent of the People

        Homily

        Promises of the Elect

        Litany of Supplication

            Invitation to Prayer

            Litany of the Saints

            Concluding Prayer

    Laying on of Hands and Prayer of Ordination

        Laying on of Hands

        Book of the Gospels

        Prayer of Ordination

        Explanatory Rites

            Anointing of the Bishop's Head

            Presentation of the Book of the Gospels

            Investiture with Ring, Pallium (if appropriate), Miter and Pastoral Staff

            Seating of the Bishop

            Kiss of Peace

LITURGY OF THE EUCHARIST

CONCLUDING RITE

    Hymn of Thanksgiving and Blessing

    Solemn Blessing

The Rite of Ordination of a Bishop

Introduction

The Constitution on the Sacred Liturgy, no. 63b, foresaw that revisions of the rites would contain introductions. It prescribed that collections of rites adapted to the needs of the different regions should include the instructions prefixed to the individual rites in the Roman Ritual, "whether they be pastoral and rubrical or whether they have special social import." Before the council, the introductions in the Roman Pontifical had been limited to rubrical and juridical instructions.[8] The sacrament of order, the first sacrament to be revised after Vatican II, did not have a General Introduction in the 1968 revision. The second typical edition (1990) now includes a three-part General Introduction that discusses a theology of ordination, the structure of the celebration, and adaptations for different regions and circumstances. Each rite of ordination also begins with its own four-part introduction giving information on the importance of the ordination, the duties and ministries of participants in the ordination, instructions on the celebration of the ordination, and requisites for the celebration.

In the rite for bishops, the first section briefly summarizes the importance of the ordination by quoting key sentences on a theology of the episcopacy from the Dogmatic Constitution on the Church (LG 11, 22–26, 28, 29), the Constitution on the Liturgy (SC 41), the Decree on the Pastoral Office of the Bishops in the Church (CD 2), and the Decree on the Ministry and Life of Priests (PO 2). Additional sources include the apostolic constitutions of Pius XII, *Sacramentum Ordinis* (November 30, 1947), and Paul VI, *Pontificalis Romani recognitio* (June 18, 1968), which stipulate the essential matter and form[9] of the sacrament of ordination for the three rites. Although the introduction to the rite of the ordination of a bishop draws heavily on these documents, it does so sketchily, with the result that significant aspects of a theology of the episcopacy are not mentioned.

The introduction begins not with the individual powers or responsibilities of a bishop, but with his collegial relationships. The first effect of episcopal ordination is to make a person a member of the episcopal college: "A person is constituted a member of the episcopal college in virtue of episcopal ordination and hierarchic communion with the head and members of that college."[10] Bishops are successors to the apostles,[11] and the order of bishops is a collegial body, a permanent assembly, that is the successor of the college of the apostles. Here the emphasis is on bishops and apostles, not as individuals, but as members of a larger body that exercises its ministry corporately. The mission of the bishops is that of the apostles: to preach the gospel so that all people may attain salvation by faith, baptism, and obedience to the commandments. The episcopal college united under the pope, who is the successor of Peter, expresses the unity, diversity, and universality of the flock of Christ.[12]

The bishop is ordained for a particular church, exercises his pastoral government over the portion of the People of God entrusted to him, and is the visible principle and foundation of unity in his particular church.[13] Individual bishops exercise their pastoral office over the people in their own particular church, not over another particular church or the universal Church. These particular churches are fashioned in the image of the universal Church. It is in and from these particular churches that the Catholic Church has its existence. A point made in *Lumen gentium,* that although each bishop represents his own church, the bishops as a collegial body together with the pope represent the whole Church, is not explicitly cited in the introduction. Also not mentioned in the introduction is the fact that the bishop's office, precisely because of its collegial character, is also the link between that local church and the larger communion of local churches. This relationship is the foundation for one of a bishop's fundamental tasks, namely, the oversight of the catholicity of the Church.[14]

The introduction emphasizes the preeminent obligation of the bishop to preach the gospel in the service of evangelization. Specifically mentioned in connection with the office of sanctifying are the bishops' control of the conferral of baptism, their role as the original ministers of confirmation, their conferral of sacred orders, and their regulation of the penitential disciplines. Their stewardship of the supreme priesthood is especially exercised in the Eucharist, which they regulate and offer or cause to be offered.

The bishop presiding over the Eucharist in his church is normative for both our understanding of the Eucharist and our understanding of the Church. As no. 41 of the Constitution on the Liturgy from Vatican II puts it:

> The bishop is to be considered as the High Priest of his flock from whom the life in Christ of his faithful is in some way derived and upon whom it in some way depends.

Therefore all should hold in the greatest esteem the liturgical life of the diocese centered around the bishop, especially in his cathedral church. They must be convinced that the principal manifestation of the Church consists in the full, active participation of all God's holy people in the same liturgical celebrations, especially in the same Eucharist, in one prayer, at one altar, at which the bishop presides, surrounded by his college of priests and by his ministers.

It is here that we have the symbol and reality of unity and collegiality that is indicative of what the Church is as the body of Christ. The bishop is the minister of unity in his church and becomes the symbolic focal point of it in his presidency at the Eucharist. However, he is not there alone. It is not the private Eucharist of the bishop that manifests the Church, but it is in the full, active participation of the people in the Eucharist that the Church is manifested. Ideally, it is also a Eucharistic Liturgy in which the various ministers assume their proper roles, thus witnessing to the diversity of roles and charisms within the Church. This is why, in Roman Catholicism, the particular church, which we most often experience as the diocese, is the cell unit of the Church. The universal Church exists in and from the particular church.[15] That is to say, the particular church is wholly church even though it is not the whole Church in isolation. The whole Church only exists as a communion of particular churches, although the elements necessary for the Church exist concretely in a particular church. This is where the Roman Catholic Church differs from some Protestant churches in which the parish or local worshiping assembly, rather than a diocese, convention, or synod, is the basic unit of the Church.

The Constitution on the Liturgy, no. 42, clearly states that the establishment of parishes and of priests as pastors who take the place of the bishop is a concession to the impossibility of the bishop's always and everywhere presiding over the whole of his church. Consequently, every effort must be made to foster an understanding of the relation of the liturgical life of the parish to the bishop.[16]

The offices of teaching and governing can be exercised only in hierarchical communion with the head and members of the episcopal college.[17] If a bishop breaks communion with the college of bishops, he loses his ability to teach and rule in the name of the Church. However, since the Donatist controversy in the time of Augustine, an ordained minister out of communion with the Church does retain the ability to confer the sacraments validly even though these are considered to be illicit, that is, unlawful. Augustine's teaching, adopted by the Church, is that it is Christ who primarily acts in the administration of the sacraments, not the minister.

An application of this teaching in our own time can be found in the case of Archbishop Marcel Lefevre of Econe, Switzerland. In ordaining three bishops against the explicit directive of Pope John Paul II, he incurred automatic excommunication. The three bishops were validly ordained bishops, but from that moment they and Archbishop Lefevre were in formal schism with the Roman Catholic Church and could not teach or govern in the name of the Church.

Frederick McManus has drawn attention to a number of omissions in the list of episcopal duties in no. 14: the absence of explicit reference to pastoral government, even though already mentioned in nn. 12 and 13, the lack of emphasis on the sacramentality of episcopal orders despite its significance in the teaching of the Second Vatican Council, and the omission of the responsibility of the individual bishop, as a member of the college, for all the other particular churches.[18] These omissions reveal the extremely brief and summary character of the introduction.

Part II of the introduction outlines the duties and ministries within the ordination rite as these specify the liturgical ministry of the various persons participating in the rite. It begins with the role of the faithful and then discusses the role of bishops, presbyters, and deacons. Part III refers to the various ritual acts.

Theological meaning is embedded in these directives, specifically the collegial nature of the order of the episcopate and a theology of the local church. In conformity with ancient custom, the principal ordaining bishop associates at least two other bishops with himself in celebrating the ordination. Canon 4 of the Council of Nicaea ruled that all the bishops of the province should be involved, but if that were not possible, then there should be a minimum of three. These bear witness to the apostolic faith and ministry of the Church, transmit the apostolic ministry to the bishop-elect, receive the new bishop as the representative of his church to other churches, receive him into the episcopal college, and minister the gift of the Spirit to him.[19] The purpose of requiring a minimum of three bishops is not to assure validity, but to represent episcopal collegiality into which the new bishop is received. For this same reason it is also appropriate that all the bishops present participate in the ordination by laying on of hands, the recitation of the designated part of the prayer of ordination, and the greeting with the kiss of peace.[20] The 1968/1990 rites consider the active participation of all the bishops as normal, not only for the ordination, but also for the concelebration of the eucharistic Liturgy.

Frederick McManus observes that "nothing is more clearly insisted upon in the new rite than the bishop's relation to his church."[21] Ordination is only conferred in the context of community and in the context of the Eucharist. Since the bishop is ordained for the sake of the entire local church, it is appropriate that great numbers of clergy and faithful attend the ordination.[22] To make this possible, the ordination takes place within a Mass on Sunday. The feast day of an apostle has traditionally been an appropriate day for the ordination of a bishop, but it is preferable to schedule the ordination to facilitate as large a gathering of the faithful as possible. The bishop should be ordained in the Christian community he is going to serve, not at home among his fellow priests and friends.

The Eucharist is the appropriate setting for the celebration of ordinations since that is where the Church is most fully manifest. The Eucharist is an exercise of the priestly office of Jesus Christ and of his body, the Church.[23] It expresses the eschatological meaning of ordained ministry for it is here that the dispersed people of God gather around the bishop in the diversity of the charisms of the people of God as the body of Christ and the temple of the Spirit.[24] In this convoked eucharistic assembly the unity of the eschaton is sacramentally represented.

The importance of the local church is further emphasized by the fact that two presbyters of the diocese for which the bishop-elect is being ordained assist him in the celebration of his ordination. One of them, in the name of the local church, requests the ordaining bishop to confer ordination on the bishop-elect.[25] After his ordination the new bishop takes his place in the bishop's chair of his church and presides at the Eucharist following his ordination. He presides over the Eucharist because he presides over the communion of this local church. Presbyters from the local diocese concelebrate the Liturgy of the Eucharist with the new bishop. All of this is the natural assumption of his role as pastor of this church that he is to serve. Throughout the entire rite, the norm is clearly the ordination of a residential bishop who will be pastor of a particular church defined as an altar community under the sacred ministry of the bishop.[26] The directive that the ordination is to be celebrated within the context of a stational Mass[27] liturgy further emphasizes this relationship between the bishop and his altar community. Given this emphasis on the particular church, it is curious that Part III does not mention the silent prayer of the people during the laying on of hands and the consecratory prayer or their assent.[28]

Preparatory Rites

The rite of ordination begins with the hymn *Veni Creator Spiritus* that occurs only in the rite for the ordination of a bishop, although the rubrics state that another hymn similar to it may be sung.[29] The bishop-elect is presented for ordination by the presbyters assisting him. If he is to be ordained a residential bishop, they say, "Most Reverend Father, the Church of N. asks you to ordain this priest N. to the office of the episcopate." In this instance the request for ordination is made in the name of the local church. If he is not to be ordained as a residential bishop, they say, "Most Reverend Father, our holy mother the Catholic Church asks you to ordain this priest N. to the office of the episcopate."[30] This ritual variation underscores the theological tension in the theology of the episcopacy and its relation to the local and universal Church. The first instance reflects a communion ecclesiology where the universal Church is a communion of churches. A bishop is ordained for a specific church. In the second instance, the bishop is not rooted in a particular church, and simply the Catholic Church in a nongeographic sense requests his ordination. Titular bishops, that is, auxiliary bishops or bishops in diplomatic or administrative posts, are given the title of an extinct see as a reminder that the office of bishop has its primary purpose in caring for the people of a Christian community.

The papal letter of appointment is then read and the entire assembly gives its consent to it by saying "Thanks be to God" or by giving their assent to the choice in some other way. In the United States this assent is often accompanied by applause. The presbyters have presented the bishop-elect in the name of the clergy and the local church. Here the people give their assent and accept him publicly.[31]

Two different Latin words are used in the 1990 text to indicate the action of the people. In no. 33, if the bishop is ordained in his own cathedral church, the people listen to the apostolic letter and respond with the acclamation "Thanks be to God" or some other response. Here the Latin word is *acclamo* which means "to cry out with approval." In no. 38 the verb is *assentor* which meant "to assent to" or "to confirm." The latter term has a stronger connotation of ratification and reception.

In the *Apostolic Constitution* the election of a bishop by the entire people preceded his ordination. Historical evidence shows that this was still the rule in the fourth century.[32] Election by a church, however, was never sufficient, for one was only consecrated bishop through the imposition of hands by other bishops. In other words, a local church cannot survive in and of itself and is incapable of perpetuating itself apart from other churches. It can only present a candidate for ordination. It is the task of other bishops who minister the gift of the Spirit bestowed by the imposition of their hands to accept him into their college through ordination.[33] The bishops are witnesses of the apostolic faith and receive the new bishop into his role of guarantor of apostolic faith. This election of a bishop by the people should not be understood as pointing to some notion of the ideal of democracy in early Christianity or to a principle, at least at first, that a congregation had the right to choose its own ministers. However, the election of a candidate for ordination "was understood as the means by which God's choice of a person for a particular ecclesiastical office was discerned and made manifest."[34] The consecratory prayer makes it very clear that it is God who chooses and ordains the ministers through the action of the Church.

We do not now have this tradition of election in the Church since the papal nuncio[35] typically has more influence over the selection of bishops than the conference of bishops. The people have a minimal role, if any at all. Nevertheless, the rite has retained the acclamation of approval by the people. Even without an election, this is appropriate, for ordination is entrance into a pastoral relationship. The acclamation affirms that the people are willing to enter into this relationship with their minister. Without the community's consent a minister simply cannot minister.[36]

The assent of the people is also theologically significant because it is one of two places within the rite of ordination, the other being the litany of supplication, where they have a vocal role. Without the rite of assent, ordination becomes a completely clericalized affair, and it would be easy to forget that ordination occurs for and within the Church. Its purpose is not to accumulate powers for an individual, or even to create a certain relationship between the minister and Christ. Ministry is always a relationship with the People of God. The people are a communion, and ordained ministry is in service of that communion. It is therefore appropriate that the people take an active role in the rite.

The 1992 *Newsletter* of the United States Bishops' Committee on the Liturgy suggests a possible territorial adaptation to give greater attention to the legitimate and active presence of and participation of the laity at ordinations. They suggest the inclusion of a formula more clearly eliciting the assent of the people before the election of presbyters and deacons and after the reading of the apostolic mandate at the ordination of a bishop. Another possibility is the inclusion of a question in the promises of the elect regarding his willingness to consult or work with the laity.[37]

The Homily

After the assent of the people, the ordaining bishop addresses first the congregation and then the bishop-elect. This address was an innovation in the 1968 rite as the previous pontifical had included no address for the ordination of a bishop. The suggested homily is a model which may be adapted by the ordaining bishop. Adaptation is particularly necessary if the one being ordained will not be a residential bishop.

The homily first addresses the Church, stressing the continuity between Christ, the apostles, and the bishops through the apostolic succession effected through the laying on of hands and the gift of the Spirit. It emphasizes the bishop as the presence of Christ in our time who continues Christ's ministry by preaching the gospel, by conferring the mysteries of the faith on those who believe, and by guiding the people. It teaches that the bishop possesses the fullness of the sacrament of orders.

The homily then asks the Church to receive the bishop-elect who is about to be received into the college of bishops, repeating some of the themes of the first paragraph. The ritual assent of the people has actually preceded the homily, but the more important reception occurs within the life of the Church where the relationship between bishop and people is lived out in concrete, historical circumstances.

Then the homily addresses the bishop-elect, reminding him that he is appointed to act for men and women in relation to God and that his title is one of service rather than honor. It recalls his pastoral tasks of preaching, ensuring sound teaching, praying, and offering sacrifice, and his responsibility to govern and protect the Church. It then gives pastoral advice: to love those in his care, his co-ministers, the priests and deacons, as well as the poor and infirm, strangers and the homeless. It encourages collaboration with the faithful, reminds him that he is incorporated into the college of bishops, and urges him to have concern for all the churches and to come to the support of those churches in need. It ends with an exhortation to attend to the flock in the name of the Father, whose image the bishop represents in the Church; the Son, whose office of Teacher, Priest, and Shepherd the bishop undertakes; and in the name of the Holy Spirit who gives life to the Church and supports weakness.

Promises of the Elect

An examination and responses in the form of promises of the bishop-elect immediately follow the homily. In the 1596 rite this examination had been an interrogation into the orthodoxy of the elect in light of heresies. The purpose of the scrutiny was to ascertain that the bishop-elect held the apostolic faith. However, in the 1968/1990 rite, the examination and promises of the bishop-elect repeat the essential points made in the final section of the homily and pertain to the commitment of the bishop to the Church and to the people. The bishop-elect makes the following promises:

1. Promise to discharge until death the office received from the apostles and transmitted to the ordinand by the laying on of hands.

2. Promise to preach the gospel with constancy and fidelity.

3. Promise to guard the deposit of faith, entire and incorrupt, as handed down by the Apostles and kept by the Church everywhere and at all times.

4. Promise to build up the body of Christ, the Church, and to remain united to it within the order of bishops under the authority of the successor of Saint Peter the Apostle.

5. Promise of obedience to the successor of the apostle Peter.

6. Promise to guide and sustain the people of God in the way of salvation as a devoted father with the help of the priests and deacons.

7. Promise to be welcoming and merciful to the poor, strangers, and all those who are in need.

8. Promise to seek out the sheep who stray and to gather them into the fold of the Lord.

9. Promise to pray for the People of God without ceasing and to carry out the office of high priest without reproach.

Litany of Supplication

The bishop-elect prostrates himself and the cantors sing the litany with everyone responding. At this moment the prayer of the assembly unites with the prayer of the communion of saints on behalf of the bishop-elect. The litany used for the ordination of a bishop names all twelve apostles, the reason why an invocation to "Saint James" occurs twice. The revised litany moves the three prayers for the elect from the conclusion of the third part of the litany and inserts them into the text after the prayer for the pope and before the prayer for all peoples.

Laying on of Hands and Prayer of Ordination

The essence of the sacramental rite consists of the laying on of hands and the prayer of ordination.[38] The biblical gesture of laying on of hands may be of Jewish origin, although this is disputed.[39] It constitutes the oldest Roman ritual of ordination whether for deacon, presbyter, or bishop. The principal elements of episcopal ordination in Acts 13:2-3 include a preliminary fast, imposition of hands, and prayer. This simple gesture was gradually enriched with a large number of symbols, rites and prayers in accordance with the different historical periods during which they were added. The result verged on a sacred drama.[40] This was in stark contrast to the sobriety of the ordination rite in the *Apostolic Tradition*[41] in which the substantial elements are: imposition of hands by bishops and priests in silence, silent prayer, possibly a second imposition of hands on the head of the elect by all of the bishops present,[42] and a prayer of consecration made only by the ordaining bishop, and the kiss of peace. Scholars identify the first imposition of hands as a designation of the candidate, reserving the consecratory value to the second.[43]

The gesture of the laying on of hands has multiple meanings.[44] It can mean invocation of the Holy Spirit who gives the bishop the spiritual gift to be leader and high priest of the People of God, conferral of powers, confirmation of the selection of the ordinand, and reception into the episcopal college. It recalls the enthronement of Joshua and the consecration of kings and high priests in the Old Testament. It evokes the descent of the Spirit on Christ in the Jordan and on the apostles at Pentecost in the New Testament. This gesture, common to all ordinations, "symbolizes the Church's conviction that it does not derive its life from itself but from Christ and his Spirit and that the ministries which communicate, sustain, develop, and express its life derive their power, not from the community and not from the individuals selected, but from God."[45] Symbols, by their nature, are polyvalent, so it is not necessary to choose one meaning to the exclusion of the others. However, a sacramental theology, an ecclesiology, and a theology of the episcopacy in relation to a pneumatology emerge in the interplay of these meanings.

In both the *Apostolic Tradition* and the 1990 rite, all the bishops present impose hands to represent their reception of their fellow bishop into the college of bishops. An individualistic idea of episcopal consecration according to which one individual communicates the powers he possess to another individual is simply incompatible with the collegial character of the episcopacy. Episcopal ordination is a collective act of the episcopal body incorporating the newly elect into the order of bishops.[46] A bishop becomes a member of the episcopal body by sacramental consecration and hierarchical communion with the head and members of the college.[47]

The laying on of hands is traditionally understood as a conferring of the Holy Spirit and so is an epicletic[48] gesture. The consecratory prayer is also epicletic in its petition for the effusion of the "governing Spirit" for the bishop-elect. The ordaining bishops are the visible sign within the community of the Spirit's presence. In laying on their hands, they communicate the power of the Spirit to the new bishop. Since the Spirit conferred is the "governing Spirit," this is seen as a conferring of ministerial power.

The laying on of hands is the essential gesture for ordaining or establishing a person in the sacred ministry. This can result in a channel theory of transmission by which the bishops transmit the power they possess to another. One consequence of this view is a certain view of apostolic succession as a linear transmission of authority in an unbroken chain of succession. J. Kevin Coyle refers to this traditional understanding of what happens in the laying on of hands as the "conferral model."[49] The conferral model has several weaknesses. It lacks the ecclesial context within which the action of laying on of hands occurs. This includes an understanding that the ordaining bishops do not act just on behalf of the college of bishops, but on behalf of the churches. It corresponds to what Zizioulas calls the historical model, which only considers one aspect of the mission of the Church to the exclusion of the pneumatological and eschatological dimensions of the Church.[50] Finally, it emphasizes the transmission of personal power to consecrate and absolve rather than the ministerial office of presiding at the building up of the Church.[51]

This restriction of the act of ordination to the ordaining bishops without taking into account their ecclesial role and context raises several theological questions. Is it the bishops who ordain, or is it the

Church that ordains through the ministry of the bishops? Is the Spirit of governance given in the act of ordination, or does the presence of the Spirit precede the ordination? Is the act of laying on of hands a recognition of the preexistent Spirit of governance in the bishop-elect instead of or as well as the conferral of that Spirit? That the laying on of hands be both a recognition of the preexistent Spirit of governance as well as a conferral of the Spirit does not seem so unlikely when we remember that the sacrament we call confirmation bestows the Spirit even though we acknowledge that the Spirit is already present in the confirmand. In sacramental theology we affirm that sacraments confer grace, which is to say that they confer the presence of the Spirit. However neither the presence of grace nor the Spirit is restricted to the sacramental act. Just because the Spirit is present, we do not cease asking for the Spirit to be present or ritualize that request and presence through liturgical actions. However this is interpreted, something new does occur, namely, the official designation of this individual within a context of prayer and invocation of the Spirit to govern this particular church and represent Christ to it.

Edward Schillebeeckx has suggested another interpretation of the laying on of hands. He suggests that this gesture is a ratification of the choice of ministers on the part of the community. He concludes that the recognition and sending by the Church is the decisive event. Even though the laying on of hands is a clear fact of the tradition, it is not primary or decisive.[52] This choice is concretized in a liturgical laying on of hands. This represents a theology of ordination "from below" which contrasts with what he claims became a clerical mandate "from above." The weakness of Schillebeeckx's understanding of the laying on of hands as a liturgical ratification of the community's choice is that election appears to be more the act of the community than of God. If we look for inner coherence within the rite, this theory is inconsistent with the theology embedded in the consecratory prayer that stresses God's election. It is also inconsistent with the belief that it is the Spirit who bestows the grace and charism of governance.

J. Kevin Coyle proposes what he calls a "recognition model" of the laying on of hands. According to this model, the laying on of hands is the community's recognition that the Spirit has chosen this person for the ministry at hand. This theory has the advantage of emphasizing that the choice of a bishop, however that occurs, is a process of discernment of the presence of the Spirit of governance rather than merely a discernment of natural qualities of leadership. It does not intend that this historic gesture be reduced to something merely symbolic without any deeper substance.

Historians have long demonstrated that an unbroken linear succession of ministers appointed by the laying on of hands is untenable in the earliest period of the Church. This poses a problem to the conferral model. Yet the Church also considers a succession in apostolic communities apart from their ministers to be insufficient. It is possible to locate a third possibility in the relationship between ministers and communities which involves an interpretation of the laying on of hands as being both a designation for ministry by the community and an epicletic invocation of the Spirit.

The ordaining bishops minister in the name of the Church through an epicletic gesture and prayer for the Spirit. Ordination is both epiclesis and human choice.[53] It is not necessary to choose between them. The Spirit is present in both the ordaining bishops and the community. The laying on of hands by the ordaining bishops and the assent by the people represent a recognition prompted by the presence of the Spirit within the bishops and within the community to recognize the Spirit within the one who is ordained. At the same time it is a prayer for that Spirit to dwell within this person that he may govern in the Spirit. Hervé-Marie Legrand reminds us that modern writers have a tendency to restrict the action of the Spirit solely to the laying on of hands by the bishop, while, in reality, the Spirit is active at every moment in the election-ordination.[54] This supports a theology of apostolic succession as both a succession of ministers who have received the laying on of hands and a succession of apostolic communities which have retained the apostolic faith. The key lies in the relationship between the minister and the community. These are not two separate and unrelated successions, but one succession in which the minister is in communion with the community, articulating, personifying and representing the apostolic faith of that community, and the community recognizing itself in its minister. There is a mutual inclusion between the community and the bishop, expressed in St. Cyprian's well-known formula: "The Bishop is in the Church and the Church is in the Bishop."

Just prior to the prayer of consecration the principal ordaining bishop places the open Book of the Gospels upon the head of the bishop-elect. Two assisting deacons hold the Book of the Gospels above his head until the prayer of consecration is completed. The origins of this gesture remain a mystery. One possibility is that it originated when a separate episcopal office first emerged from a corporate presbyterate and it was thought inappropriate for a lower rank to lay hands on a higher rank. Another possibility is that the imposition of the Book of the Gospels solved the problem of who should impose hands on the ordinand when neighboring bishops began to attend episcopal ordinations and challenge the right of the local presbyterate to conduct the ordination. This solution symbolized the action of Christ himself ordaining the bishop.[55]

Tradition gives us various interpretations of this gesture. Severian of Gabala (b. fourth cent.; d. after 408) interpreted it as being a symbol of the descent of the Spirit on the ordinand. He believed that the appearance of the Holy Spirit in the form of tongues of fire on the apostles at Pentecost was the sign of their ordination. Since the descent of the Holy Spirit is invisible, the gospel is placed on the head of the one being ordained high priest. The Book of the Gospels represents a tongue of fire. The tongue signifies the preaching of the bishop, and the fire refers to the saying "I have come to cast fire on the earth."[56] This gesture suggests that the new bishop is subject to the gospel.

In the Syrian-Jacobite rite the gospel book is open to Luke 4:18 (i.e., Isa 61:1): "The Spirit of the Lord is upon me." In this context the gesture emphasizes the epicletic nature of the laying on of hands. The interpretation is also applicable to the context in the pontifical of G. Durandus where it is accompanied by a brief formula *"Accipe Spiritum Sanctum."*[57]

Another interpretation comes to us from John Chrysostom (ca. 349–407), or possibly a Pseudo-Chrysostom,[58] who interprets the gesture as a symbol of the submission of the bishop to the law of God and the equivalent in the New Covenant of the high-priestly crown of Aaron:

> In the ordinations of priests [i.e., bishops] the gospel of Christ is placed on the head so that the ordinand may learn that he receives the true crown of the gospel, and so that he may learn that even if he is the head of all, yet he acts under these laws, ruling over all and ruled by law, judging all and being judged by the Word. . . . The fact that the high-priest has the gospel is a sign that he is under authority.[59]

A third interpretation, from Pseudo-Dionysius, is that the Book of the Gospels represents the word of the gospel and work of proclaiming it given to the bishop. Bernard Botte suggests that it refers to the power of the gospel which comes to fill the ordinand when the Holy Spirit is invoked upon him.[60] Paul Bradshaw suggests that these various interpretations may indicate that "they are attempts to find a meaning for a ceremony the earlier sense of which had been forgotten."[61]

The language of the gesture itself inherently contains many of the meanings just cited, although Severian of Gabala's interpretation may be a bit too allegorical for contemporary sensibilities. These interpretations give us insight into the responsibilities and duties of the bishop. The bishop is subject to a higher authority, the law of the gospel. The faithful preaching of the word of God is the foremost office of the bishop.[62] Bishops are heralds of the faith, authentic teachers who are endowed with the authority of Christ and given the duty to preach the faith to the people assigned to them.

The consecratory prayer is the verbal specification of the laying on of hands.[63] As we have seen, both are epicletic in that they call for the descent of the Spirit on the new bishop.[64] One of the most significant changes in the 1968 rite, retained in the 1990 rite, was to replace the consecratory prayer of the bishop with the prayer from the *Apostolic Tradition* of Hippolytus. This prayer is biblically based, noted for its Christocentrism, its sobriety, clarity, and its rich doctrinal content. It introduces the concepts of apostolic succession and collegiality into the consecratory prayer which were not present in previous texts.

In the *Apostolic Tradition,* during the imposition of hands, all present are to keep silence, praying in their heart for the descent of the Spirit. Then one of the bishops imposes his hands again while he prays the consecratory prayer. The prayer of the faithful for the descent of the Spirit in the *Apostolic Tradition* indicates that the epiclesis is effected by all the community present.[65] James Puglisi, for example, compares ordination to the Eucharist. Both are the work of all in that all celebrate while only one presides. He interprets this epiclesis of the liturgical assembly as a sign that the bishops are the ministers of the Spirit in the communion of the Church.

Unfortunately, the directive in no. 7 of the General Introduction to the 1990 rites of ordination of bishop, priest, and deacon for the silent prayer of the people during the laying on of hands and the prayer of ordination is not repeated as a rubric within the text of the ordination rites. This directive was not present at all in the 1968 rite, which did not have a General Introduction. The directive states: "While the laying on of hands is taking place the faithful should pray in silence. They take part in the prayer of ordination by listening to it and by affirming and concluding it through their final acclamation." It would be very helpful to include this directive within the worship aids for the ordinations of bishops, presbyters and deacons, so the faithful may be informed of their participation. Otherwise it would appear that their role is primarily limited to their assent and to the litany of supplication. The directives in the 1990 rite do not specify that this prayer is for "the descent of the Spirit" as do the directives in the *Apostolic Tradition,* in which the epicletic nature of this prayer is evident.

The retrieval of a communion ecclesiology in the post-Vatican II Church emphasizes the reciprocal nature of the relationship between a bishop and his church and the fact that ministry arises from and is exercised on behalf of the Church. The silent prayer of the people accompanying the prayer of the ordaining bishops witnesses to this relationship. As was the case with their assent, this moment of prayerful, silent participation renders them active participants, not merely passive spectators. It also emphasizes that the whole Church and not only the ordaining bishops participate in the invocation of the Holy Spirit. This in no way detracts from the necessary role of the ordaining bishops, but indicates his communion with the Church and the Church with him.

The consecratory prayer for the bishop was completely revised in the 1968 rite. Instead of the lengthy medieval prayer in the form of a preface we now have a prayer from the *Apostolic Tradition* of Hippolytus of Rome, the oldest extant text of episcopal consecration.[66] This text is simpler and clearer and has the added ecumenical advantage of being used in the Coptic Rite and, in a fuller version, among the West Syrians.

The following chart shows the normative Latin text of the consecratory prayer for a bishop, the 1999 translation, biblical references, and alternative translations:[67]

Prayer of Ordination for a Bishop

Editio Typica Altera, 1990[68]	English Translation, March 2000, ICEL[69]	Commentary
Deus et Pater Domini nostri Jesu Christi	God and Father of our Lord Jesus Christ,	Eph 1:3; 2 Cor 1:2
Pater misericordiarum et Deus totius consolationis	Father of mercies and God of all consolation	2 Cor 1:3
qui in excelsis habitas, et humilia respicis,	you dwell on high and look on the lowly;	Ps 112:5-6; 137:6
qui cognoscis omnia antequam nascantur,	You know all things before they come to be;	Dan 13:42

tu qui dedisti in Ecclesia tua normas[70] per verbum gratiae tuae,	through the word of your grace you established order in your Church.	Literally: you gave the rules of your Church by the word of your grace. Acts 14:3; 20:32
qui praedestinasti ex principio genus justorum ab Abraham	From the beginning, you predestined a righteous nation, born of Abraham.	Literally: the race of the just (descendants) of Abraham
qui constituisti principes et sacerdotes,	You appointed rulers and priests	
et sanctuarium tuum sine ministerio non dereliquisti,	And did not leave your sanctuary without ministers.	
cui ab initio mundi placuit in his quos eligisti glorificari:	From the foundation of the world it has pleased you to be glorified in those you have chosen.	Matt 25:34 Doxological conclusion to the first section.

The following part of the prayer is prayed by all the ordaining bishops with hands joined, in a low voice, in order that the voice of the principal ordaining bishop may be clearly heard.	**The following words of the prayer constitute the form of the sacrament[71] and are required for validity.**	
Et nunc effunde super hunc electum	So now pour out upon this chosen one	
eam virtutem, quae a te est, Spiritum principalem,	that power which is from you, the governing Spirit,	Literally: the Spirit of authority[72] Ps 51:14
quem dedisti dilecto Filio tuo Jesu Christo,	Whom you gave to your beloved Son, Jesus Christ,	
quem ipse donavit sanctis Apostolis,	the Spirit whom he gave to the holy Apostles,	
qui constituerunt Ecclesiam per singula loca ut sanctuarium tuum,	who founded the Church in every place to be your temple	
in gloriam et laudem indeficientem nominis tui.	for the unceasing praise and glory of your name.	1 Thess 2:13; 1 Thess 5:17 Doxological conclusion to the second section.

The principal ordaining bishop continues alone:

Da, cordium cognitor Pater,	Father, you know all hearts,	Acts 1:24; 15:8
huic servo tuo, quem elegisti ad Episcopatum,	Grant that this, your servant, whom you have chosen for the office of Bishop	Acts 1:15-26
ut pascat gregem sanctum tuum,	may shepherd your holy flock,	Acts 20:28; 1 Pet 5:2 John 21:16
et summum sacerdotium tibi exhibeat sine reprehensione, serviens tibi nocte et die	and, serving you night and day, fulfill before you without reproach the ministry of high priest;	
ut incessanter vultum tuum propitium reddat	so may he intercede always with you to look kindly upon us	
et offerat dona sanctae Ecclesiae tuae;	and may he offer the gifts of your holy Church.	Reference to the Eucharist: Clement 44, 4
da ut virtute Spiritus summi sacerdotii	Grant that by the power of the Spirit, who bestows the office of high priest,	
habeat potestatem di-mittendi peccata secun-dum mandatum tuum;	he may have the power to forgive sins according to your command,	John 20:20-23
ut distribuat munera se-cundum praeceptum tuum	assign ministries according to your decree,	1 Pet 5:3
et solvat omne vinculum secundum potestatem quam dedisti Apostolis;	and loose every bond in accord with the authority you gave the Apostles.	Matt 18:18
placeat tibi in mansue-tudine et mundo corde,	May he please you by his gentleness and purity of heart,	Matt 3:5, 8 2 Tim 2:25
offerentes tibi odorem suavitatis,	Presenting a fragrant offering to you,	Eph 5:2
per Filium tuum Jesum Christum, per quem tibi gloria et potentia et honor, cum Spiritu Sancto in sancta Ecclesia et nunc et in saecula saeculorum. Amen.	through Jesus Christ, your Son, through whom glory and power and honor are yours with the Holy Spirit in the holy Church, now and for ever. (All answer) Amen.	Doxological conclusion

The ordination prayer has three parts, the end of each signaled by a reference to the glorification of God. It begins with the initial benediction of the second letter to the Corinthians, stressing the omniscience of God, God's plan for the Church, and the carrying out of this plan through the election of rulers and priests who continue the line of Abraham. The emphasis is clearly on election by God. J. Lécuyer points out the remarkable similarity between the Prayer of Hippolytus and the text in *Lumen gentium* 2: "The eternal Father, in accordance with the utterly gratuitous and mysterious design of his wisdom and goodness, created the whole universe. . . . All the elect, before time began, the Father 'foreknew and also predestined to become conformed to the image of his Son . . .'" The common elements are God's mysterious design, his prescience, and the predestination of those who are elected. Thus, God's pleasure in Jesus (Matt 3:17; Mark 1:11; Matt 17:5; 2 Pet 1:17), his election of Jesus (Matt 12:8 citing Isa 42:1), and his glorification in Jesus (John 13:31) are now applied to God's relationship to the bishop-elect.[73] The relationship that God has with Jesus is now attributed to God's relationship with the bishop through the association between the text of the consecratory prayer and the biblical allusions. However, the same thing could be said of all Christians, for Christ's relationship to his Father is ours through adoption. We are destined and chosen for adoption in Christ through the good pleasure of his will (Eph 1:5, Rom 8:29). The mystery of God's will is that we, along with all things in heaven and on earth, be gathered up in Christ (Eph 1:10). We live for the praise of God's glory (Eph 1:12). Nevertheless, the themes of election and glorification are more specific in the ordination prayer since the bishop is elected for a specific office in the Church. It is imperative that the bishop not arrogate this office to himself, but that he be chosen for it by God.

Paul VI referred to the entirety of the consecratory prayer as the "form" of the sacrament in the Latin Church, but only identified the second section of the prayer as the essence of the form and therefore necessary for sacramental validity.[74] The consecratory prayer asks the Father to pour out on the bishop-elect the power of the Spirit of authority, which will enable the bishops to govern the particular church. The power of the Spirit guided Jesus at the beginning of his Galilean ministry and descended upon the apostles at Pentecost to empower them to be witnesses to Christ to the ends of the earth.[75] This power now guides the bishop in his ministry.

This Spirit was first given to Christ, then to the apostles, and now to the bishop-elect. This traces a clear line of authority from Christ to the apostles and then to the bishop. The bishop is a prolongation of the visible presence of Christ and the apostles since he has received their powers and essential functions. Notably absent in this prayer is a theology of the community that is enspirited. Nor is the bishop chosen from among the people. The prayer in and of itself is not contextualized ecclesially. Any ecclesial context for this will have to come from other elements within the larger rite.

The expression *spiritus principalis* raises certain difficulties and has been variously translated into modern languages. Bernard Botte notes that there are two problems which must not be confused. The first is the meaning of the phrase in Psalm 51:4. The second is its meaning in the ordination prayer. In his opinion the second has nothing in common with the first. He explains the meaning in the prayer as follows:

> The three orders constitute one gift of the Spirit, but it is not the same for all. For the bishop, it is the *spiritus principalis;* for the priests, who are the council of the bishop, it is the *spiritus consilii* [spirit of counsel]; for the deacon, who is the right arm of the bishop, it is the *spiritus zeli et sollicitudinis* [spirit of zeal and care]. It is evident that these distinctions are made according to the functions of each minister. It is therefore clear that *principalis* must be put into relation with the specific functions of the bishop. . . .

> The point of departure for the author is the typology of the Old Testament. God never left his people without a leader, nor his sanctuary without a minister; it is the same for the new Israel, the Church. The bishop is simultaneously the leader who must govern the new people and the high priest of the new sanctuary, which is established in every place. The bishop is the leader of the Church. . . . [The *spiritus principalis*] is the gift of the spirit appropriate for a leader. The best translation would perhaps be "Spirit of authority."[76]

The third section of the ordination prayer cites the duties of the bishop.[77] He is to shepherd the flock as Christ did and exercise the supreme priesthood in imitation of Christ, the high priest. He offers the holy gifts of the Church, a reference to his function in the Eucharist. In its original context within the *Apostolic Tradition,* the eucharistic anaphora immediately followed this prayer. By the authority of the apostles he forgives sins in response to the commandment in John 20:23 and the example of Christ. He distributes the ministries of the Church. Here the reference is to the bishop's responsibility to distribute shares in his ministry by establishing presbyters and deacons who will help him in his ministry.[78] The sixth function is to exercise the power to loose bonds. This is analogous to the power to forgive sins, but refers further to the power to impose an interdict[79] or to raise it. Finally, the bishop must live a life pleasing to God in gentleness and purity of heart. In other words, the bishop must be conformed to the model of Christ.

In the *Apostolic Tradition* the bishop was seen as succeeding to a dual office, one of governance and priesthood. The first section mentions rulers and priests. References to the office of priesthood include the mention of not leaving God's sanctuary without a minister, the duties of the high priesthood of offering gifts and forgiving sin, and the exercise of the high priestly office, blamelessly ministering night and day. Duties of governance include assigning ministries and loosening bonds. The Spirit designated in the epiclesis is a "governing Spirit," which specifies the particular task for which the bishop receives the Spirit.

The ordination prayer does not refer to the bishop's teaching/prophetic or preaching responsibilities. Paul Bradshaw suggests that this may be evidence that such a ministry was not seen as fundamental to the episcopal office in the tradition in which the prayer arose.[80] This interpretation, however, is difficult to reconcile with the bishop's role with regard to the gospel. Nevertheless, the dual office evident in the prayer contrasts with the threefold office which is so predominant in the teaching on the episcopacy in Vatican II and which is mentioned in the apostolic constitution of Paul VI, "Approving New Rites for the Ordination of Deacons, Presbyters, and Bishops." The threefold office is either explicit or implicit in other aspects of the rite. It is mentioned in the homily, and the third function of teaching is implicit in the promise to proclaim the gospel.

Even though the prayer speaks of a dual ministry, the emphasis is ultimately on governance. Structurally, the prayer of ordination is an *inclusio*, that is, it has an A–B–A structure. Within this structure, the most important element thematically is the middle one, which is framed by the outside sections. There are three sections in the prayer, each clearly delineated by a reference to the glorification of God. Rulers and priests are mentioned in the first section. Ruling and priestly activities are spelled out in the third sections. However, in the middle section, the shortest section, the essence of the prayer is "pour out upon this chosen one the governing Spirit." Thematically, even though the bishop is a priest, he is a high priest, a leader among priests. This qualification of his priesthood subsumes it under governance. Finally, it should be noted that a feature of governance prominent in the rite, but not present in the prayer of ordination, is the collegiality the bishop is to share with fellow bishops.

These points of asymmetry with the rest of the rite of ordination point to the development in the office and theology of the episcopacy since the time of the *Apostolic Tradition*. The prayer of consecration is a great improvement over what existed before 1968 because it represents an ancient tradition in the Church, is noble in its simplicity, and relates the Old and New Testaments. Nevertheless, it does not perfectly coincide with the theology within the rite as a whole. This underscores the fact that the theology of ordination is embedded in the entire liturgical rite, inclusive of symbol, gestures, participants, rubrics, and not only in the prayer texts.

Explanatory Rites

The explanatory rites are different for the various orders and represent the offices that have been conferred through the laying on of hands and the invocation of the Holy Spirit.[81] These rites were not present in the early liturgy of Hippolytus, but developed over the course of time when the language of the ordination became inaccessible to the faithful. The visual symbolism of the explanatory rites communicated the meaning of the ordination to the people.

Anointing of the Bishop's Head

This anointing recalls the royal and prophetic anointing of David. According to the theological and liturgical tradition it makes the bishop a vicar of Christ (Amalarius), a high priest (Ambrosian Pontifical), and participant in the high priesthood of Christ (*Pontificale Romanum* 1968).[82] The anointing of the bishop's head recalls Psalm 133: "How very good and pleasant it is when kindred live together in unity! It is like the precious oil on the head, running down upon the beard, on the beard of Aaron, running down over the collar of his robes. It is like the dew of Hermon, which falls on the mountains of Zion. For there the Lord ordained his blessing, life forevermore." Aaron was a priest of the Old Testament, and the anointing with oil symbolizes the new bishop's participation in the high priesthood of Christ. Oil is also a symbol of anointing by the Holy Spirit. In the Old Testament the high priest was consecrated by anointing with oil and clothing with vestments. In the New Testament this was transposed to anointing with the Holy Spirit and the ornament of virtues.[83] The bishop's hands are not anointed since they have already been anointed in his presbyteral ordination.

Presentation of the Book of the Gospels

The principal ordaining bishop presents the Book of the Gospels to the newly ordained bishop, saying: "Receive the gospel and preach the word of God with all patience and sound teaching."[84] *Lumen gentium* teaches that "among the more important duties of bishops that of preaching the Gospel has pride of place."[85] The bishop builds up the people of God with the word of God.

Investiture with Ring,
Pallium (if appropriate), Miter and Pastoral Staff

Traditionally, the episcopal ring signified authority and jurisdiction.[86] This meaning originated during the period of lay investiture when within the feudal system the awarding of a bishopric was a benefice linked to feudal subjection. The prince gave the staff and ring as symbols of the bishop's authority and office.

The symbolism of nuptial fidelity, also present within the 1990 liturgy, supplanted these interpretations toward the tenth century.[87] The ring now symbolizes the bishop's fidelity to and nuptial bond with the Church, his spouse, and he is supposed to wear it always.[88] Up until the ninth century it was not licit for a bishop to change diocese lest he commit the sin of "adultery."[89] The practice of transferring a bishop from one diocese to another mitigates the nuptial symbolism, although most people would agree today that the practice of being able to transfer bishops from one diocese to another serves the good of the Church. This is another instance where we see a tension between a theology of the local church and a theology of the universal Church. A residential bishop is presented for ordination by presbyters of his church, and he is only ordained a bishop for a particular church. There are no absolute ordinations, that is, ordinations that are not ordinations for a particular church. The nuptial symbolism, therefore, pertains primarily to the particular church and secondarily to the universal Church.

This nuptial interpretation when applied to the bishop represents a significant migration from the earliest interpretation where the Church is the primary spouse of Christ. The ring was given to the pope so that he would guard the purity of heart of the mystical spouse, the holy and universal Church of God.[90] The bishop became the keeper of the bride of Christ, the Church, in which he himself became a participant.[91] This nuptial meaning as applied to the Church remains evident in the prayer which says: "Receive this ring, the seal of your fidelity: adorned with undefiled faith, preserve unblemished the bride of God, the holy Church." Although historically, in some mystical fashion, the bishop, too, became a spouse of his Church, there is a great difference between the two nuptial symbolisms from an ecclesiological and ministerial point of view. In the first, the ordained bishop or pope bears an ecclesial responsibility on behalf of and within the Church who is the bride. In the second, he himself becomes the bridegroom of the Church.

The pallium is a circular band of white woolen cloth worn around the shoulders over the chasuble. It has two strips hanging down, one in front and the other in back, and is marked by six purple crosses. The pallium is a symbol of the metropolitan bishop's authority in communion with the Church of Rome. A metropolitan bishop is the archbishop of an archdiocese and presides over an ecclesiastical province. It is both a sign of his authority to rule and of his authority to delegate by sending others in his name, namely, suffragan bishops. Canon law stipulates that the metropolitan must request the pallium of the Roman pontiff within three months from the reception of episcopal consecration or, if already consecrated a bishop, from the time of canonical provision.[92] The metropolitan can use the pallium within his own particular Church according to the norm of liturgical law, but never outside it. He must request a new pallium if he is transferred to another metropolitan see.

The 1914 code viewed the role of the metropolitan as a participation in papal power and restricted the exercise of certain archiepiscopal functions until the pallium had been obtained unless a special indult[93] permitted otherwise.[94] The 1983 code dropped these restrictions and no longer sees the role of the metropolitan as a participation in papal authority, but still requires that the metropolitan request the pallium and retains it as a symbol of authority.[95]

The miter is the headdress worn in liturgical functions by bishops and other ecclesiastical prelates such as mitered abbots. In earlier ordination rites it symbolized the horns of Moses when he descended from Sinai with the two tablets of the covenant. However, this was based on a mistranslation of Hebrew text in the Vulgate, the Latin translation of the Bible. The 1968 rite, in wishing to avoid the allegorizing of the medieval rites, decreed that the miter was to be placed on the bishop's head in silence and omitted any formula accompanying that action.

The 1990 rite subsequently added a formula signifying the bishop's re-solve to pursue holiness.[96] The *Ceremonial of Bishops* stipulates that the bishop uses the miter "when he is seated; when he gives the homily; when he greets the people, addresses them, or gives the invitation to prayer, except when he would have to lay it aside immediately after-ward; when he gives a solemn blessing to the people; when he confers a sacrament; when he is walking in procession."[97] He does not wear the miter when he leads the congregation in recited or sung prayer. The changing symbolism of the miter seems to indicate that it is one of the symbols of episcopal ordination in search of a theology.

The episcopal staff, sometimes called a crozier, symbolizes a shep-herd's crook and the bishop's role as shepherd of the church entrusted to him. One of the oldest and most prestigious of the auxiliary rites of episcopal ordination, it appears as a liturgical symbol in the seventh century, probably in Spain, when it signified the governance of a par-ticular church and the pastoral ministry entrusted to the bishop.[98] However it was originally a civil and/or military sign of honor which became associated with bishops once they were numbered among the important citizens. Its civil meaning was associated with investiture be-cause, along with the ring, it was part of the act with which the right of rule over a new fief or a city with its attendant territory was conferred on a vassal.[99] The sovereign intended to confer civil authority with the bestowal of these symbols of authority. The bishop carries a pastoral staff in his own territory as a sign of his pastoral responsibility. He may use it in another diocese when he celebrates with the consent of the diocesan bishop.

Seating of the Bishop

There is no "enthronement" of the new bishop. If he is in his own church, he is led to the cathedra, the bishop's seat, of his cathedral church, the place from which he presides over the Eucharist. If he is not in his own church, he is invited to take first place among the con-celebrating bishops.[100]

Kiss of Peace

The kiss of peace within the ordination rite does not replace the kiss of peace which takes place in the Communion Rite of the Eucharistic Liturgy and which is exchanged by all the faithful present with its usual significance. In the context of the ordination rite, the newly ordained bishop receives the kiss of peace from the principal ordaining bishop and all the other bishops. This signifies the newly ordained bishop's reception into the episcopal college and the collegiality of bishops.[101]

During this action Psalm 95 (96) may be sung with the antiphon, "Go into the world, alleluia. And teach all people, alleluia." Another appropriate song of the same kind with suitable antiphons may be used, especially when Psalm 95 (96) is used as the responsorial psalm in the Liturgy of the Word. The first suggestion emphasizes the teaching role of the bishop.

Conclusion

This examination of the liturgy of ordination has revealed how much theology is embedded in the liturgical rite. However, the rite itself is a hybrid product. The consecratory prayer is borrowed from the *Apostolic Tradition*. The introduction and homily reflect heavy indebtedness to *Lumen gentium*. The explanatory rites reflect accretions acquired between these two periods. The ritual assent of the people is important theologically, but originated with a practice of election by the people that no longer exists in the Church. In the case of the promises made by the bishop-elect, the particular structure of the rite has remained the same, that is examination and promise, but the content has changed. In sum, the history of the rite of ordination is one of continuity and discontinuity, stability and change.

If we identify the office of bishop as threefold—teaching, sanctifying, and governing—we see that these roles are not represented equally in the various ritual elements. The bishop's exercise of high priesthood in the Eucharist is most evident in his role of presiding at the ordination liturgy surrounded by the diversity of ministries represented by bishops, presbyters, deacons, acolytes, and readers in concert with the active participation of the faithful. The high priesthood of the bishop is mentioned in the ordination prayer, but is not represented in the explanatory rites. One reason for this is may be that the bishop is taken from the ranks of priests. Although ordination to the episcopacy is also an ordination to the priesthood, specifically the high priesthood, the rite shows a tendency to presume a priesthood already present within the ordinand rather than to celebrate in detail an ordination to high priesthood.

The bishop's responsibility for teaching is not mentioned in the ordination prayer, but is included in his promise to guard the deposit of faith and in the presentation of the Book of the Gospels with the accompanying injunction to "preach the word of God with all patience and sound teaching."[102]

The bishop's role in governance is especially prominent in the ordination rite in the references to shepherd with the accompanying symbolism of the pastoral staff, responsibilities to build up the Church, and in the ordination prayer for a governing Spirit. In addition, high priesthood, with the emphasis on the qualifier "high," is also related to governance. This suggests that the key to understanding the episcopacy is governance. The next chapter will explore this further by addressing the implications of the sacramentality of episcopal consecration for the collegiality of bishops and their relationship to the local and universal Church.

Notes, Chapter Two

[1] *Lumen gentium* 21, 22.

[2] See the discussion of this point in the next chapter.

[3] For example, no. 31 speaks of the "ordaining bishops" and "principal ordaining bishop" rather than "consecrating bishops" and "principal consecrating bishop" as in the introduction to the 1968 rite.

[4] The descending order (beginning with the bishop, then the presbyter, and last the deacon) is the older order. It is found in the *Apostolic Tradition,* in the Gregorian Sacramentary, and in the Barberini Euchologion. The ascending order appears in the *Missale Francorum* and becomes customary from the time of the Romano-Germanic Pontifical. Pierre-Marie Gy, O.P., "Ancient Ordination Prayers," *Studia Liturgica* 13 (1980) 76.

[5] Paul VI, *moto proprio, Ministeria quaedam,* August 15, 1972, XI.

[6] Botte's proposal that minor orders be retained if they can be conferred on those who habitually carry out their functions in the church was met in part. He had proposed the suppression of all minor orders except the subdiaconate. He would have preferred the title of subdeacon rather than acolyte, but conceded that in the end that is a question of semantics. See Bernard Botte, *From Silence to Participation,* trans. John Sullivan, O.C.D. (Washington, D.C.: The Pastoral Press, 1988) 139–43.

[7] From *Rites of Ordination of Bishops, Presbyters, and Deacons,* For Study and Comment by the Bishops of the Member and Associate-Member Conferences of the International Commission on English in the Liturgy. Prepared by the International

Commission on English in the Liturgy, A Joint Commission of Catholic Bishops' Conferences (Washington, D.C., October 1993) 28. This outline does not occur in the June 1999 ICEL translation because it does not occur in the Latin text. It is included here not as part of the text of the rite, but as a study aid.

[8] Bruno Kleinheyer, "Ordinationsfeiern," *Liturgisches Jahrbuch* 41 (2) (1991) 88–118.

[9] The "matter" of a sacrament is the material element and/or gesture necessary for the validity of a sacrament. For holy order, the matter of the sacrament is the imposition of hands on the head of the ordinand. The "form" of a sacrament is the verbal formula that so "shapes" the material element and ritual action prescribed by the rite that the sacrament is truly celebrated. The "form" of holy orders is that portion of the ordination prayers that Paul VI stipulated in this document.

[10] *Lumen gentium* 22.

[11] *Lumen gentium* 18. However, there is both similarity and difference between the role of the bishops and that of the apostles. The apostles are unique and unrepeatable insofar as they are eye witnesses of the resurrection. Bishops share with the apostles their commission from Jesus Christ to proclaim the gospel authoritatively.

[12] *De Ordinatione Episcopi, Presbyterorum et Diaconorum,* 12.

[13] *De Ordinatione Episcopi, Presbyterorum et Diaconorum,* 13.

[14] See *Lumen gentium* 23.

[15] *Lumen gentium* 23.

[16] Of theological interest for a theology of confirmation is the reference to bishops as the "primary" ministers of confirmation. In Canon 882, the bishop is called the "ordinary" minister of confirmation, while the Rite of Confirmation promulgated in 1971 speaks of the bishop as the "original" minister of confirmation. It then says, "Ordinarily the sacrament is administered by the bishop." The reason for the shift from "ordinary" is to account for the fact that when confirmation is administered during the Rite of Christian Initiation for Adults, it is the pastor who ordinarily confers the sacrament. If the bishop is present, however, he would confer it as he also does when confirmation is conferred outside of the Easter Vigil. The emphasis on "primary" emphasizes the fact that the sacraments are under the direction of the bishop. Presbyters participate in the priesthood of the bishop and act in his name in the exercise of their priesthood.

[17] *Lumen gentium* 21.

[18] Frederick R. McManus, "*Praenotanda* of Ordination: The Doctrinal Context of the Liturgical Law," 513–14.

[19] Hervé Legrand, "Theology and the Election of Bishops in the Early Church," *Concilium: Election and Consensus in the Church* (New York: Herder and Herder, 1972) 36–37.

[20] *De Ordinatione Episcopi, Presbyterorum et Diaconorum,* 16.

[21] Frederick R. McManus, "The New Rite for Ordination of Bishops," 413.

[22] *De Ordinatione Episcopi, Presbyterorum et Diaconorum,* 15, 22.

[23] *Sacrosanctum concilium* 7.

[24] See H. M. Legrand, "Inverser Babel, mission de l'Eglise," *Spiritus* 43 (1970) 323–46; John D. Zizioulas, *Being as Communion: Studies in Personhood and the*

Church (Crestwood, N.Y.: St. Vladimir's Seminary Press, 1985), "Ordination and Communion," *Istina* 16 (1) (1971) 5–12, "The Bishop in the Theological Doctrine of the Orthodox Church," *Kanon* 7 (1985) 23–35.

[25] *De Ordinatione Episcopi, Presbyterorum et Diaconorum*, 17, 24.

[26] *Lumen gentium* 26.

[27] The "stational Mass" is the new terminology for the pontifical Mass or pontifical high Mass. See the *Ceremonial of Bishops*, n. 119. Frederick McManus interprets the name change as emphasizing the gathered people rather than the presiding bishop in "pontificals." It emphasizes the church's preeminent manifestation in the "full, active participation of all God's holy people . . . at one altar at which the bishop presides." "*Praenotanda* of Ordination: The Doctrinal Context of the Liturgical Law," 523.

[28] Frederick R. McManus points out the absence of reference to the assent in, "*Praenotanda* of Ordination: The Doctrinal Context of the Liturgical Law," 515.

[29] *De Ordinatione Episcopi, Presbyterorum et Diaconorum*, 35. Before 1968 the hymn had been sung immediately after the laying on of hands. This mistakenly led to the belief that the Spirit had not yet come and that the essential rite was beginning. However, the essential rite, the laying on of hands, had just been completed. The commission revising the rite originally suggested first suggested that the hymn be suppressed. However, one consultor disapproved and contacted Paul VI who asked that the hymn be retained. It was then moved to the beginning of the ordination rite. See Bernard Botte, *From Silence to Participation*, 138.

[30] *De Ordinatione Episcopi, Presbyterorum et Diaconorum*, 38.

[31] Frederick McManus, "The New Rite for Ordination of Bishops," 413.

[32] Bernard Botte, "Collegiate Character of the Presbyterate," in *The Sacrament of Orders* (London: Aquin Press, 1962) 85. See also Hervé-Marie Legrand, "Theology and the Election of Bishops in the Early Church," *Concilium: Election and Consensus in the Church*, eds. Giuseppe Alberigo and Anton Weiler (New York: Herder and Herder, 1972) 31–42.

[33] Bernard Botte, "Introduction," in *Hippolyte de Rome, La Tradition Apostolique*, Sources chrétiennes, no. 11 (Paris: Cerf, 1984) 26.

[34] Paul Bradshaw, *Ordination Rites of the Ancient Churches of East and West* (Collegeville: The Liturgical Press, 1990) 22. So also Hervé-Marie Legrand, "Theology and the Election of Bishops in the Early Church," 40–41.

[35] The papal nuncio is the papal legate who represents the Apostolic See to a state or civil government and also represents the pope to particular churches in that state or nation. He has the rank of ambassador and acts as dean of the diplomatic corps.

[36] J. Kevin Coyle makes this point in "The Laying on of Hands as Conferral of the Spirit: Some Problems and a Possible Solution," *Studia Patristica* 18 (2) (1989) 349.

[37] *Newsletter* (September 1992) 34.

[38] See J. Behm, *die Handauflegung im Urchristentum nach Verwendung, Herkunft und Bedeutung in religionsgeschichtlichen Zusammenhang untersuch* (Leipzig, 1911; repr. Darmstadt, 1969); J. Coppens, *L'imposition des mains et les rites connexes dans le Nouveau Testament et dans l'Eglise ancienne* (Paris, 1925); J. Kevin Coyle, "The Laying on of Hands" *Studia Patristica*, Papers of the 1983 Oxford Patristics

Conference, ed. Elizabeth A. Livingstone, Vol. 18 (2) (Kalamazoo, Mich.: Cistercian Publications, 1989) 339–53; G. Diekmann, "The Laying on of Hands: The Basic Sacramental Rite," *Proceedings of the Catholic Theological Society of America* 29 (1974) 339–51; J.-T. Maertens, "Un rite de pouvoir: l'imposition des mains," *Studies in Religion/Sciences Religieuse* 7 (1978) 25–39; C. Vogel, "L'imposition des mains dans les rites d'ordination en Orient et en Occident," *La Maison-Dieu* 102 (1970) 57–72; C. Vogel, "Chirotonie et Chirothesie: Importance et relativité du geste de l'imposition des mains dans la collation des ordres" *Irénikon* 45 (1972) 7–21, 207–38; Everett Ferguson, "Laying On of Hands: Its Significance in Ordination," *Journal of Theological Studies* 26 (1975) 1–12.

[39] E. J. Kilmartin, "Ministère et ordination dans l'Eglise chrétienne primitive. Leur arrière-plan juif," *La Maison-Dieu* 138 (1979) 49–52, 91. However, Paul Bradshaw claims this is very uncertain in *Ordination Rites of the Ancient Churches of East and West* (Collegeville: The Liturgical Press, 1990) 33. See also E. Ferguson, "Jewish and Christian Ordinations: Some Observations," *Harvard Theological Review* 56 (1963) 13–19; L. A. Hoffman, "Jewish Ordination on the Eve of Christianity," *Studia Liturgica* 13 (1979) 11–41.

[40] Luca Brandolini, C. M., "L'Evoluzione Storica di Riti Delle Ordinazioni," in *De Ordinatione Diaconi, Presbyteri et Episcopi: Commento Al Nuovo Rite Delle Ordinazioni* (Rome: Edizioni Liturgiche, 1969) 68. Translation supplied by David Cotter, O.S.B.

[41] The *Apostolic Tradition*, attributed to Hippolytus and commonly dated ca. 215, contains the earliest ordination rites we have for bishops, presbyters, and deacons.

[42] The text of the *Apostolic Tradition* shows evidence of accretions which reflect the differing historical circumstances in which the text developed. The second imposition of hands may be one of these. See Paul Bradshaw, "Ordination" in *Essays on Hippolytus*, ed. Geoffrey J. Cuming (Grove Books, 1978) 34–35.

[43] M. Righetti, *Storia liturgica*, vol. IV, Milano, 1953, 319, cited by Brandolini, 70.

[44] Multiple meanings are present in the writings of the Fathers. See Joseph Lécuyer, "Le sens des rites d'ordination d'après les Pères," *L'Orient Syrien* 5 (1960) 463–75.

[45] Joseph A. Komonchak, "The Permanent Diaconate and the Variety of Ministries in the Church," *Diaconal Quarterly* 4 (1978) 19.

[46] Bernard Botte, "Holy Orders in the Ordination Prayers," in *The Sacrament of Orders* (London: Aquin Press, 1962) 20.

[47] *Lumen gentium* 22.

[48] An *epiclesis* is a prayer calling for the descent of the Holy Spirit. "Epicletic" is the adjective. An "epicletic gesture," usually the imposition of hands over someone, is a gesture signifying a prayer that the Holy Spirit come upon the person.

[49] J. Kevin Coyle, "The Laying on of Hands as Conferral of the Spirit: Some Problems and a Possible Solution," *Studia Patristica* 18 (2) (1989) 339–53.

[50] John Zizioulas, *Being as Communion*, 173.

[51] Puglisi, 205.

[52] E. Schillebeeckx, *Ministry: Leadership in the Community of Jesus Christ* (New York: Crossroad, 1981) 47–48.

[53] So Pierre-Marie Gy, "La théologie des prières anciennes pour l'ordination des évêques et des prêtres," *Revue des Sciences Philosophiques et Théologiques* 58 (1974) 607.

[54] Hervé-Marie Legrand, "Theology and the Election of Bishops in the Early Church," 38.

[55] Paul Bradshaw gives the history of this gesture and the various interpretations of it in *Ordination Rites of the Ancient Churches of East and West* (Collegeville: The Liturgical Press, 1990) 39–44.

[56] Severian of Gabala, PG 125–533. Cited by Bradshaw, *Ordination Rites of the Ancient Churches of East and West,* 40. See Joseph Lécuyer, "Note sur la liturgie du sacre des évêques," *Ephemerides Liturgicae* 66 (1952) 369–72.

[57] Antonio Santantoni, "Ordination and Ministry in the West," trans. David Cotter, O.S.B., in *Handbook for Liturgical Studies,* vol. 4 (Collegeville: The Liturgical Press, 2000).

[58] For a discussion of authorship see Paul Bradshaw, *Ordination Rites of the Ancient Churches of East and West,* 40.

[59] *De legislatore* (PG 56. 404). Cited by Bradshaw, *Ordination Rites of the Ancient Churches of East and West,* 40.

[60] Bernard Botte, "Holy Orders in the Ordination Prayers," in *The Sacrament of Orders* (London: Aquin Press, 1962) 14, 24.

[61] Bradshaw, *Ordination Rites of the Ancient Churches of East and West,* 42.

[62] *Lumen gentium* 25; *De Ordinatione Episcopi, Presbyterorum et Diaconorum,* 26.

[63] Godfrey Diekmann, O.S.B., "The Laying on of Hands: The Basic Sacramental Rite," *Proceedings of the Twenty-Ninth Annual Convention of the Catholic Theological Society of America* 29 (1974) 343.

[64] Pierre-Marie Gy, "La théologie des prières anciennes pour l'ordination des évêques et des prêtres," *Revue des sciences philosophiques et théologiques* 58 (1974) 607.

[65] James F. Puglisi, *The Process of Admission to Ordained Ministry: A Comparative Study,* vol. I: *Epistemological Principles and Roman Catholic Rites,* trans. Michael S. Driscoll and Misrahi (Collegeville: The Liturgical Press, 1996) 31.

[66] Joseph Lécuyer, "La prière d'ordination de l'évêque," *Nouvelle revue théologique* 89 (1967) 603.

[67] For a textual analysis of the prayer of consecration see Jean Magne, *Tradition Apostolique sur les charismes et Diataxeis des Saints Apôtres,* Origines Chrétienne I (Paris, 1975) 107–37.

[68] *Pontificale Romanun, De Ordinatione Episcopi, Presbyterorum et Diaconorum,* Editio Typica Altera (Rome: Typus Polyglottis Vaticanis, 1990) 24–25.

[69] English Translation from *Rites of Ordination of a Bishop, of Priests, and of Deacons,* Second Typical Edition, March 2000, prepared by International Commission on English in the Liturgy, A Joint Commission of Catholic Bishops' Conferences, no. 47, 28–29.

[70] This is from the *Apostolic Tradition* of Hippolytus. The original Greek, ὅρος, signifies a limit or a decree, used for the canons of church councils. Bernard Botte interprets it in this context to refer to the rule given "by the word of your grace," that is, by Holy Scripture. He notes that the Church is the new Israel and what was done in the Old Testament is the image of what must be done in the Church.

The word in the Latin text of the *Apostolic Tradition* is *terminos*. Bernard Botte, *La Tradition Apostolique d'après les anciennes versions,* 2nd rev. ed., Sources chrétiennes, vol. 11 (Paris: Editions du Cerf, 1984) 43.

[71] The "form of the sacrament" are the words required for the validity of the sacrament. Paul VI specified these in the apostolic constitution *Pontificalis Romani recognitio,* 18 June 1968.

[72] Bernard Botte, "'Spiritus Principalis' (Formule de l'Ordination Épiscopale)" *Notitiae* 10 (1974) 411.

[73] André Rose, "La prière consécration pour l'ordination épiscopale," *La Maison-Dieu* 98 (1969) 131.

[74] Paul VI, apostolic constitution *Pontificalis Romani recognitio,* 18 June 1968.

[75] André Rose, "La prière consécration pour l'ordination épiscopale," *La Maison-Dieu* 98 (1969) 133.

[76] Bernard Botte, "'Spiritus Principalis' (Formule de l'Ordination Épiscopale)" 410–11. See also Joseph Lécuyer, "Épiscopat et Presbytérat dans les Écrits d'Hippolyte de Rome," *Recherches de science religieuse* 41 (1953) 30–50.

[77] André Rose, "La prière consécration pour l'ordination épiscopale," 126–42.

[78] Ibid., 139.

[79] An interdict is an ecclesiastical penalty that prohibits a person from ministerial participation in public worship and from the reception of the sacraments and sacramentals.

[80] Paul Bradshaw, *Ordination Rites of the Ancient Churches of East and West,* 47.

[81] *De Ordinatione Episcopi, Presbyterorum et Diaconorum,* 8.

[82] Antonio Santantoni, "Ordination and Ministry in the West," trans. David Cotter, O.S.B., in *Handbook for Liturgical Studies,* vol. 4 (Collegeville: The Liturgical Press, 2000).

[83] Bernard Botte, *From Silence to Participation: An Insider's View of Liturgical Renewal,* 134.

[84] *De Ordinatione Episcopi, Presbyterorum et Diaconorum,* no. 50.

[85] *Lumen gentium* 25.

[86] Puglisi, 161.

[87] Ibid., 162.

[88] *Ceremonial of Bishops,* Revised by Decree of the Second Vatican Council and published by authority of Pope John Paul II, prepared by the International Commission on English in the Liturgy (Collegeville: The Liturgical Press, 1989) no. 58.

[89] Antonio Santantoni, "Ordination and Ministry in the West," (manuscript, 19).

[90] Antonio Santantoni, "Ordination and Ministry in the West," (manuscript, 26).

[91] Antonio Santantoni, "Ordination and Ministry in the West," (manuscript, 19).

[92] Canon 437.

[93] An indult is a permission given by the Holy See for nonobservance of a requirement of canon law.

[94] Canon 276.

[95] James A. Coriden and others, eds., *The Code of Canon Law: A Text and Commentary.* (Mahwah, New Jersey: Paulist Press, 1985) 355.

[96] *Pontificale Romanum, De Ordinatione Episcopi, Presbyterorum et Diaconorum,* Editio Typica Altera (Rome: Typis Polyglottis Vaticanis, 1990) no. 26. Pierre Jounel comments such an interpretation is closer to Amalarius and to Durandus of Mende (13th cent.) than it is to *Lumen gentium* in "La Nouvelle Édition Typique du Rituel des Ordinations" *La Maison-Dieu* 186 (1991) 11.

[97] *Ceremonial of Bishops,* 60.

[98] Isidore of Seville (d. 636) offered the earliest symbolic interpretation.

[99] Antonio Santantoni, "Ordination and Ministry in the West," (manuscript, 17).

[100] *De Ordinatione Episcopi, Presbyterorum et Diaconorum,* no. 55.

[101] *De Ordinatione Episcopi, Presbyterorum et Diaconorum,* no. 26.

[102] *De Ordinatione Episcopi, Presbyterorum et Diaconorum,* no. 50.

Chapter Three

The Sacramentality
of Episcopal Consecration

T he underlying thesis of this study is that the sacrament of
order signifies and reveals the nature of the Church. This insight directly follows from the teaching of *Lumen gentium* that
episcopal consecration constitutes the fullness of sacramental ordination
to office. To understand the sacrament of order and the relationship between the Church and an ordained person we must begin with the
bishop.[1] The teaching on the sacramentality of episcopal consecration
has far-reaching effects on the theology of both the episcopacy and the
presbyterate. When the episcopacy was viewed as an additional power
of jurisdiction, the episcopacy had a tendency to develop in an isolated
direction and become vulnerable to the pressure of secular models of
government and leadership at the same time that the presbyter was frequently reduced to a man empowered for cult.[2] Both orders were consequently impoverished, for jurisdiction and governance were cut from
their sacramental moorings,[3] while leadership of worship became divorced from leadership within the Christian community.

Before Vatican II the status of the episcopacy as an order remained a
disputed question in the Western Church, with the result that the point
of reference for discussions on ordained ministry was most frequently
the priesthood.[4] Now, in the light of contemporary sacramental theology, we must ask how and in what the episcopacy represents a fullness
above and beyond that of the presbyterate.[5] More importantly, how is
this sacrament a sacrament of the Church, that is, how is the nature of
the Church sacramentalized or manifested within episcopal ordination?

An examination of the ecclesial signification of the episcopacy is necessary in order to understand the function of the episcopacy within a "communion of communions" model of Church unity. In Roman Catholicism the theology of the particular church, the fundamental ecclesial unit, rests heavily upon the episcopacy, wherein the bishop functions as the representative of the local church and focus of ecclesial unity. He also embodies the link between a local church and other local churches. The communion among particular churches is objectified—one might also say sacramentalized—in the college of bishops.

Inadequate Distinguishing Criteria

Two criteria sometimes used to distinguish the episcopacy from the presbyterate, configuration to Christ and sacramental power, remain ultimately inadequate in and of themselves to determine either the essence or the uniqueness of the episcopacy. According to these views, the sacramental effect of ordination is commonly identified with the ordinand's configuration to Christ, which empowers the ordinand to teach, to govern, and to act in Christ's name in the administration of the sacraments. The episcopacy is then distinguished from the presbyterate in the powers proper to each "degree" of ordination. This equates fullness of orders with fullness of powers. Not the least problem associated with this view has been the difficulty in distinguishing the priesthood of the faithful and their configuration to Christ in baptism from that of the ordained minister.

According to the first view, both priest and bishop signify "Christ." The ordained person is *vicarius Christi*, a vicar of Christ, who acts *in persona Christi*, in the place of the person of Christ.[6] This view remains prominent in Vatican II's teaching that "through that sacrament priests by the anointing of the Holy Spirit are signed with a special character and so are configured to Christ the priest in such a way that they are able to act in the person of Christ the head."[7] In this view of the sacrament, the ordained person is "ordered" to Christ. This view has important ramifications for the other sacraments, since it is Christ who acts in the sacraments, as in the forgiveness of sin and in the consecration of the Eucharist.

Within this interpretation the sacrament of order is a sacrament essentially *for* the Church rather than a sacrament *of* the Church. In other words, it itself is not a sign manifesting the Church. This lack of appreciation for the ecclesial dimension of the sacrament of order was the precise reason why St. Thomas did not consider episcopal consecration to be a sacrament: he did not see how episcopal consecration empowered the bishop to consecrate more intensively the Body and Blood of Christ.[8] Even though the fullness of the sacrament of order conferred by episcopal consecration is called the "high priesthood," configuration to Christ does not distinguish the episcopacy from the presbyterate. We therefore have to look elsewhere to discover in what sense episcopal consecration is sacramental and contains a fullness beyond that of the presbyterate.

A second response locates the distinction between the order of the episcopacy and the priesthood in sacramental powers proper to each. To say that a bishop can ordain and confirm while a priest cannot does not take into account an evolving sacramental theology. In the revised rite of confirmation, it is now common practice for the bishop to delegate the administration of this sacrament to a parish pastor in certain circumstances, especially during the Easter Vigil. Karl Rahner has stated that "no truly definable borderline can be clearly and convincingly drawn between priest and bishop which is *absolute* as regards the power of order."[9] Documentation suggests that the valid ordination of a priest by another simple priest under certain conditions does not appear to be impossible.[10] The most theologically certain distinction in power is that a priest cannot ordain a bishop. We conclude, therefore, that the sign of episcopal consecration does not lie exclusively in the power it confers, even if by virtue of office the bishop is the primary minister of confirmation and orders.

Ecclesial Dimension of Sacrament

Contemporary sacramental theology identifies Christ as the fundamental sacrament, the Church as the sacrament of Christ, and seven sacraments as sacraments or signs of the Church.[11] That which is signified by a sacrament is made present in the "real symbol," which contains what it signifies.[12] Consequently the *res et sacramentum*, the sacramental reality, contains an ecclesial dimension in addition to the christological dimension as part of that which is signified by the sign of the sacrament, the *res sacramentum*.

The sacraments signify and effect a relationship with the Church as well as to Christ. For example, in baptism, in addition to participating in the death and resurrection of Christ, we are incorporated into the Church, not simply as an institution but as the body of Christ. In penance we are reconciled to the Church as well as to Christ. The bond of marriage is a sign of Christ's union with the Church.

This relationship, however, is most evident in the Eucharist. In the case of the Eucharist, the bread and wine are the *sacramentum tantum*. That which is signified, that is, the *res et sacramentum*, refers both to the Real Presence of the Body and Blood of Christ in the Eucharist and to the Church as the Mystical Body of Christ. There is a unity between the christological and the ecclesial effect of the sacrament because of the relationship between Christ and his body, the Church. This is what is meant when we say that the Church is constituted by the Eucharist.

This relationship is most vividly presented by Augustine's post-baptismal Easter sermons and his sermons on the Gospel of John. The Easter sermons were addressed to the newly baptized, represented their initiation into the mysteries of the Christian life, and were instructions on the sacraments of the altar.[13] He affirms that the bread that they see on the altar, consecrated by the word of God, is the Body of Christ and that the chalice holds the Blood of Christ. Then he asserts, "If you have received worthily, you are what you have received." He repeats 1 Corinthians 10:17 to support his assertion. In Sermon 6 he compares the neophytes, the newly initiated Christians, to the grain which has germinated, ripened, been winnowed, stored, threshed, treaded, milled and at last baked so as to emerge as bread. He also compares them to grapes that have been crushed and so formed into one sweet liquid in the chalice. He concludes: "There you are on the altar, there you are in the chalice."[14] In yet another sermon he exhorts: "Take, then, and eat the body of Christ, for in the body of Christ you are already made the members of Christ."[15]

At one level it would seem that Augustine is simply comparing the unity of the bread with the unity of the ecclesial body and that what we have is simply a literary device, a simile, or a metaphor. However, the unity of the body received at the altar is a sign and measure of the unity of the ecclesial body. The eucharistic sacrament is a sacrament of unity. This means that it signs, signifies, and creates the unity of the Church. Thus the bread is a sacrament of the Church, not just because it belongs to the Church, but because it signifies the Church. The sacramental realism of the historical Christ leads to the sacramental realism of the ecclesial Christ so that Augustine could say, "There you are on the altar, there you are in the chalice." Affirmation of the christological reality leads to the affirmation of the ecclesial reality. The presence of the latter is as real as the presence of the former. When we commune with the sacramental Body of Christ, we commune with the resurrected Christ and with the Church, which is also the Body of Christ. The referent of the sacrament is ecclesial as well as christological.

The sacrament of order also proclaims, realizes, celebrates, and signifies a reality beyond itself, and this reality includes the Church.[16] The ordained person officially and sacramentally represents the Church. In particular, a bishop represents his particular church within the communion of churches by his membership in the communion of bishops, the episcopal college. This representation of a particular church within the communion of churches ultimately distinguishes the episcopacy from the presbyterate. While it is true that the bishop also represents Christ, the theology of his Christic representation has frequently overshadowed his ecclesial representation with the result that we have forgotten that the sacrament of order signifies something about the Church.

An examination of several possibilities of what the sacrament of order might signify in the Church reveals that it must signify something about the structure rather than just the activity of the Church. If, for example, we were to say that the sacrament reveals that the Church nourishes, forgives, strengthens—those actions performed through ministry—one could respond that those aspects of the Church are revealed respectively in the sacraments of Eucharist, penance, and confirmation, and we still would not have discovered what is unique and specific to the sacrament of order. To answer that the sacrament of order reveals the teaching and governing authority of the Church does not in and of itself indicate the ecclesial basis of that authority.

Earlier writers have seen the connection between ordination and the nature of the Church. Although Rahner comments that the nature of the directive functions of the Church at the social level is determined by the nature of the Church herself, he does not develop what this nature is.[17] Edward Kilmartin identifies the ecclesial signification of apostolic office with the faith of the ecclesial community.[18] He traces the traditional view of apostolic office, according to which church leaders are empowered to act in the place of Christ, and criticizes the view that one can explain the representative role of the priest in relation to Christ in isolation from his representative role with respect to the Church as

Body of Christ. Basing his position on the necessity of faith for a sacramental event, he argues that office directly represents the faith of the Church and only to this extent can represent Christ. However, to say that the apostolic office represents the faith of the Church still does not identify in what respect it represents the nature of the Church. To argue from the necessity of faith to its signification in the episcopal college does not explain how a collegial structure is intrinsic to faith. Nor does it explain how the fullness of the episcopacy exceeds that of the priesthood.

Liturgical Evidence

Following the tradition of *lex orandi, lex credendi,* the principle that the Church believes as it prays, an important source for determining the distinguishing characteristic of episcopal consecration as well as its ecclesial signification is the rite of ordination of a bishop. The rite points to the close relationship between ordination and the ecclesial community, because ordinations always take place in the context of a eucharistic celebration and a bishop is ordained for a concrete eucharistic community, even if in our own time this is not absolutely true in the case of titular bishops.[19]

The ordination rite emphasizes the collegial character of the episcopacy. For example, in the examination of the candidate the principal ordaining bishop asks whether the bishop-elect is "resolved to build up the body of Christ, his Church, and to remain united to it within the order of bishops under the authority of the successor of Saint Peter the Apostle." Both the prayer inserted in Eucharistic Prayer I and the solemn blessing mention the "order of bishops" to which the newly consecrated bishop is raised by virtue of his consecration. The suggested homily asked the assembly to "gladly and gratefully, therefore, receive our brother whom we are about to accept into the college of bishops by the laying on of hands." Within this homily the bishop-elect is also admonished to "never forget that in the Catholic Church, made one by the bond of Christian love, you are incorporated into the college of bishops. You should therefore have a constant concern for all the churches and gladly come to the aid and support of churches in need." Furthermore, the rite itself includes a collegial act, the laying on of hands by the consecrating bishops. The rite of ordination thus clearly indicates the collegial character of episcopal consecration, since the bishop-elect is not merely consecrated a bishop but enters into the order of bishops,[20] and thereby is a member of the college of bishops.

This emphasis on episcopal collegiality is not the result of revised rites or the Second Vatican Council. Ten years before the council, Bernard Botte studied the prayers of ordination and concluded that the priesthood and the episcopate were essentially collegial.[21] He found that ordination seemed to be less the transmission of sacred or juridical powers from person to person than the conferring of a gift of the Spirit with a view to the growth of the Church as the body of Christ. He concluded that the local church could not be self-sufficient and that the Church is not composed of local communities existing alongside each other. It is the college of bishops which orders the Church, since the bishops constitute an "order."

Sacramental Episcopal Consecration in Vatican II

In *Lumen gentium* the effect of the sacrament is twofold: the gift of the Holy Spirit and the sacramental character which enables the bishop to represent Christ according to the threefold office of sanctifying, teaching, and governing. This last represents a significant advancement in the theology of orders by the council, whereby the three offices are conferred by sacramental consecration itself rather than being the result of a canonical mission from the pope. The limitation mentioned in the document is that the offices of teaching and governing "of their very nature can only be exercised in hierarchical communion with the head and members of the college."[22] Thus it is of the very nature of the episcopacy that a bishop exercises his office, even within his own particular church, only in relationship to the permanent body of bishops into which he is "incorporated" by his sacramental ordination.

Membership in and union with the college of bishops is consequently an essential element within episcopal consecration, and arguably represents the "fullness of orders" which sets the episcopacy apart from the other orders. What is sacramentally signified in episcopal consecration is the collegial nature of the Church as a "communion of communions." Thus I agree with Bernard Cooke that "the word 'fullness' can be truly used to describe the sacramental power of the episcopate, because it is the collegial dimension of the bishops' witness," although I disagree that it is primarily the faith of the entire Church that is the particular object of this witness.[23] What the college of bishops symbolizes is rather the unity that exists among the altar communities that each bishop represents in his office. Thus the "order" of the episcopacy truly reflects the ordering among eucharistic communities. The theological foundation for this position lies in a theology of the Eucharist and its interconnection with an ecclesiology of the Church as the Body of Christ.

Episcopacy and Eucharist

As David Power notes, "Safeguarding the unity of the Church in the one apostolic tradition, presiding over its essential unity, and presiding over its Eucharist all go together."[24] The episcopate witnesses to the unity of particular churches within the episcopal college, as well as the task of being the "visible source and foundation of unity."[25] The liturgical role of the bishop is the sacramentalization of his governing role, the "liturgical dimension of a pastoral charge."[26] The presidency of the bishop over the Body of Christ in the Eucharist parallels his governance of the ecclesial body of Christ. Thus the task of witnessing to unity in the Church is inseparable from the Eucharist, the sacrament of unity.

This is not surprising, given the identification between the Eucharist and the Church in the epistles of St. Paul. Paul's identification of the Church as the Body of Christ is well known (Rom 12:4ff.; 1 Cor 12:12ff.; Eph 1:23, 4:12ff., 5:36; Col 1:18-24). John Zizioulas observes that this image of the Church cannot be understood outside of the eucharistic experience of the apostolic Church.[27] He notes that the terms "Eucharist" and "church" become interchangeable, as when Paul refers to a eucharistic assembly as a church in 1 Corinthians 11:18: "I hear that when you meet as a church there are divisions among you." Likewise, in verse 22, showing contempt for the eucharistic meaning of the gathering is the same as showing contempt for the Church of God. Zizioulas concludes that in the New Testament the Eucharist appears as the manifestation of the Church itself.

The Body of Christ, the ecclesial body and the Eucharistic body become interchangeable in the text. For example, "discerning the body" (1 Cor 11:29) refers to the recognition of the organic unity of the ecclesial body which should exist.[28] In other words, the Corinthians should attend to the quality of relationships within the ecclesial body before partaking of the eucharistic body identified with the Body of the Lord in verse 24.

Henri de Lubac has shown that in Christian antiquity any kind of theoretical separation between the Eucharist and the Church was unthinkable. For Augustine as well as for the Latin writers of the seventh, eighth, and ninth centuries, "the Eucharist is related to the Church as cause to effect, as means to an end, as a sign to the reality which it signifies."[29] In these early centuries it was the Eucharist that was seen as the "mystical" or sacramental Body of Christ, and the Church was the "real" Body of Christ. Largely as a result of the controversy with Berengar of Tours concerning the Real Presence in the second half of the eleventh century, the Eucharist began to be called *corpus verum,* and the Church assumed the title *corpus mysticum* in contrast to the earlier usage.[30] This weakened the idea of the Church as the Body of Christ and separated the theology of the Church from its christological and sacramental context. As a result, ecclesiology became divorced from a theology of the Eucharist and the Eucharist lost its identity as a sacramental sign of the Church.

Order and Relation within the Body

The sacrament of order finds meaning and signification within the nexus of the Eucharist, the Body of Christ, and the Church. The discussion of the eucharistic assembly in 1 Corinthians 10 is immediately followed by a discussion of the unity and variety of the spiritual gifts with reference to the one Body of Christ and its many members. The various gifts are ordered within the ecclesial body as described in 1 Corinthians 11:28-31. Zizioulas argues that since a body does not exist prior to the existence of the various members that are ordered within it, so too the ecclesial community does not exist prior to assignment to a particular *ordo* in community, but that very ordination to the community is constitutive of the community.[31] The body only exists in terms of ministry, the charismata.[32]

One important conclusion Zizioulas draws from this is that ordination is fundamentally relational in character rather than functional or ontological. He thus tries to avoid two traditional approaches to ministry. In the first approach, ministerial power or grace is transmitted through the ordaining minister as an individual as part of the linear historical line of apostolic succession. The ordained minister, having received power and authority, transmits them in turn to another. Zizioulas modifies this view by noting that a bishop succeeds the apostles not as an individual but as head of his community. In the second approach, a community delegates authority to the ordained person.[33] Both approaches operate within a notion of causality rather than within a network of relationships.

Zizioulas proposes an alternative view of ordination, a view that considers baptism and confirmation as "ordinations" in addition to the ordination of the sacrament of order. Here "ordination" refers to those sacraments that give the recipients of these sacraments a place within the community. Particularly within an Orthodox perspective, this means a "place" within the eucharistic assembly. These "ordinations" order the community. In Zizioulas' view, "there is no such thing as a nonordained person in the Church,"[34] although he does not claim that every person has received the "sacrament of order." Baptism, confirmation, and the sacrament of order are charisms insofar as they are gifts of the Spirit for the upbuilding of the community. The community is understood as "the existential 'locus' of the convergence of the charismata (1 Cor 12)." Ordination "creates" the community in the sense that the unity of the body exists only by virtue of the diversity of the variety of "orders" within it.[35] The community does not exist apart from or prior to the order it receives from the charismata of its members, that is apart from the "ordinations" of its members to their place in the church.

It is essential not to misunderstand Zizioulas' remarks, lest they be interpreted as supporting clericalism. He does not say that the Church is created or constituted by the presbyterate or the episcopacy, but by ordination—the reception of the various charismata through the sacraments of baptism, confirmation, and the sacrament of order. Thus he does not equate the Church with the clerical hierarchy. Furthermore, the highest charism in 1 Corinthians 13 is love, and the ecclesial body is inseparable from the eucharistic body, a body offered for the other. Finally, his whole effort is an attempt to envision ordination as a relationship, which is to say as personal and interpersonal. According to his view, "ministry ceases to be understood in terms of *what it gives* to the ordained and becomes describable only in terms of *the particular relationship* into which it places the ordained."[36] He describes ministry as "a complexity of relationships within the Church and in its relation to the world."[37] The paradigm is nothing less than the interrelationships within the Trinity. The contribution of Zizioulas' thought is that it invites us to consider ordained ministry in its relationship to the Church before we consider specific functions of the minister. Moreover, specific functions may exist by virtue of the ordained minister's relationship to the community, specifically as head of the community.

Within the Eucharist the bishop is not only presider of the eucharistic ritual, but also the focus of the unity of the eucharistic community.[38] This is the bishop's "place" or *ordo* in the community. By virtue of his ordination he is related so profoundly to the community that he can no longer, as ordained, be considered as an individual unto himself.[39] He is so profoundly and so existentially related to the community that "he cannot be any longer, as a minister, conceived in himself."[40] His ministerial existence is determined by *communion* that qualifies and defines both his "ontology" and his "function."[41] The ordained person is consequently not "raised" to a superior ontological level of being, nor does he merely function in the service of the community. Here the "ontology" of the sacramental character of ordination is inseparable from the ordained minister's relationship to the community.

This view of the ontological change effected by ordination, which traditional theology identifies with the sacramental character, is consistent with Thomistic theology if one understands character to be primarily a relationship with Christ and the Church rather than a change within the recipient apart from any such relationship. According to the *Catechism of the Catholic Church,* the three sacraments of baptism, confirmation, and holy orders confer a sacramental character described as an indelible "seal" "by which the Christian shares in Christ's priesthood and is made a member of the Church according to different states and functions."[42] Thus the sacramental character establishes a specific relationship to both Christ and the visible community of the Church. The person who receives the sacramental character receives an "ordination" as a deputation to carry out the priestly acts of Christ in a specifically ecclesial ritual precisely because of this relationship.[43] The metaphors of an indelible "mark" or "seal" may be mistakenly identified as effecting a change in a person apart from the ecclesial and christological relationship when the change effected is precisely that relationship.

Representative Function of the Bishop

The bishop's "place" in the community is a representative one. As the leader of the ecclesial community responsible for its unity, the bishop presides over the Eucharist and represents Christ, speaking the consecratory words on behalf of Christ, who offers himself for his Church. The bishop also represents the Church, offering sacrifice in the name of all. This sacrifice is inseparable from the sacrifice of Christ, because the Church is none other than the Body of Christ. Herein lies the necessary link between the episcopacy, its representation of Christ, and its representation of the Church as the Body of Christ. The pneumatology of the charismata ordaining and thus constituting the community as the Body of Christ in the Eucharist prevents this identification between the Church and the Body of Christ from degenerating into a type of Christomonism that arrogantly appropriates to the Church what is uniquely Christ's. The Church is consequently not a continuation of the incarnation in a literal sense, although it is pneumatologically constituted the Body of Christ in a sacramental sense.

This representative function of the bishop with reference to a local eucharistic community does not significantly differ from that of a presbyter's, with the exception that a bishop is a symbol of unity in his own particular church by presiding over a number of eucharistic assemblies. Historically presbyters assumed the title "priest" when they assumed leadership of the Eucharist. Consequently, it may at first appear that Zizioulas' insight into the relationship character of orders differs little from the traditional view that orders signifies a configuration to Christ, and we still would not have determined the ecclesial content of what is signified in episcopal consecration. The major difference between the two orders consists in the fact that the bishop, in addition to his representative function within the local eucharistic community, represents that community in the college of bishops. We must therefore show the connection between the relational *ordo* of a bishop in his particular church and his *ordo* in the college of bishops.

Just as the *ordo* of the bishop is defined in terms of his relationship with the eucharistic community, so also will his *ordo* within the college of bishops have a eucharistic basis. Since the ecclesial body is constituted according to the charismata, with the result that no member of the body has an existence apart from or independently of other members of the body, so neither does an individual eucharistic community exist independently of the other eucharistic communities. The relationship between the episcopacy and an individual bishop is analogous to that between the universal and the particular church; both relationships reflect the unitary character of the Eucharist despite its manifold celebrations.[44]

The episcopacy is one, the Church is one, and the Eucharist is one, although each subsists in multiple, concrete embodiments. Since the source of this unity is the Eucharist, the structure of the Church derives from its worship, and the episcopacy is the visible manifestation of that structure. The episcopacy, for example, is embodied in each bishop, since the unity of the college of bishops precedes the individual bishop.[45] The college is not the sum of the individual bishops, and the unity of the college does not depend on the moral unity of its individual members, much less on their assembly in the same geographical place. We can say, then, that when a bishop teaches the same creed proclaimed throughout the universal Church, that teaching is a collegial act.

In a similar manner, the universal Church is not the sum total of the particular churches, and a particular church is not a division of the universal Church. The universal Church subsists in each particular church as the Body of Christ is present, whole and undivided, in each eucharistic celebration. The structure of the Church is consequently a union of communions in which the whole exists in each individual part, and each part exists not in isolation from or parallel to the other parts, but in communion with them.

This communion of communions is sacramentalized in the college of bishops. Each bishop is the sacramental sign of the bond between the particular churches, for not only does the bishop function as mediator between Christ and the particular church, but the college of bishops functions as the visible bond between the particular churches. This is reflected in *Lumen gentium*'s statement:

> The individual bishops, however, are the visible principle and foundation of unity in their own particular churches, formed in the likeness of the universal church; in and from these particular churches there exists the one unique catholic church. For this reason individual bishops represent their own church, while all of them together with the pope represent the whole church in the bond of peace, love and unity.[46]

Thus the "fullness of orders" within episcopal consecration represents membership in the episcopal college, the result of episcopal consecration and hierarchical union with the other bishops and the Bishop of Rome. This union within the Church is the ecclesial reality manifested in the episcopal sacrament of order.

Karl Rahner attributes the power of the bishop as an individual, his threefold office of sanctifying, teaching, and governing to his membership within the college of bishops.[47] The power of a bishop, then, derives from the authority and power of the college. The authority of the college does not equal the sum of the authorities of the individual members, since the episcopacy is not the sum of individual bishops. Furthermore, since the college is constituted by sacramental episcopal consecration, this is a sacramental, rather than a juridical, basis of authority. From this we can see that for two reasons the sacrament of order is fundamentally relational rather than a conferral of power on the recipient apart from his *ordo* within the community: (1) orders, when accompanied by union with the bishops and head of the college, confers membership in the college; and (2) a bishop loses his authority to teach and govern if he breaks union with the college and its head.[48]

There are two inadequately differentiated sources of supreme authority in the Church: the college of bishops in union with their head, the Roman pontiff, and the Roman pontiff by reason of his office as the Vicar of Christ.[49] It remains an open theological question whether the Bishop of Rome, when speaking officially in his own name, does not speak as the head of the college, and therefore speaks at least in an implicitly collegial manner.[50] This is especially true if the Bishop of Rome, as the focus of unity for the universal Church, is envisioned as functioning representatively much like a corporate personality.[51] The nature of the ecclesial community is concentrated within the ecclesial leader in such a way that the community recognizes itself in that person. Since this function is as true of a bishop with respect to a particular church as, at another level, of the Bishop of Rome with respect to the universal Church, the particular church is a microcosm of the universal Church.

Problem of the Recognition of Orders

The relational view of ordained ministry as presented here poses new problems regarding the recognition of orders (1) of an individual bishop who breaks unity with the college of bishops, and (2) for those churches such as the separated churches in the East, which are not in full union with the Roman Catholic Church but which the Church recognizes as possessing valid orders. If sacramental consecration to the episcopacy confers membership in the episcopal college on those bishops in union with each other and the Bishop of Rome, and if their authority to teach, sanctify, and govern derives from their membership in the college, then it would appear that a person would remain a bishop in the full and proper sense only as long as that person maintains communion with the head and members of the college.[52]

Unitatis redintegratio, the Decree on Ecumenism, describes ecclesial communities as being either in "imperfect" or "full" communion with the Catholic Church. This allows for different degrees of communion and provides more flexibility than does the concept of membership wherein one is either a member or not. Since the theology of the episcopacy presented here is integral to an ecclesiology of communion, it may be more appropriate to speak of "communion" with the college of bishops rather than "membership" in the college. *Lumen gentium* actually uses both expressions: "A person is constituted a *member* of the episcopal body by virtue of sacramental consecration and by hierarchical *communion* with the head and members of the college."[53] Just as there are varying degrees of communion between ecclesial communities, there are varying degrees of communion among bishops. Since the bishop functions as the representative of the ecclesial community, one would expect these two relationships to be parallel.

Recent discussions of the ecumenical recognition of ministry point out that recognition of ecclesial communities leads to the recognition of ministry rather than the other way around. Zizioulas, for example, calls validity a juridical term that implies that ministry can be isolated from the rest of ecclesiology and can be judged in itself according to objective criteria.[54] He argues that the ecclesial reality of a given community, rather than isolated and objectified norms, is what validates a certain ministry. Therefore, recognition of communities, of their beliefs and sacramental practice, leads to recognition of their ministry. This, of course, entails a reinterpretation whereby the community rather than the minister is in apostolic succession.

A theology of the episcopal college, however, suggests an alternative possibility, that of the bishops as a college succeeding to the apostolic college.[55] Recognition of communion in the college would constitute recognition of apostolic succession. In this instance apostolic succession remains personal but avoids an overly physical and linear-historical in-

terpretation of succession as a succession of laying on of hands, which
cannot historically be substantiated for the earliest historical period.
The college, as the mediating bond between the particular churches
and the larger communion of these churches, represents both the apostolic succession of local communities and the succession of the individual bishops insofar as they are in communion with the college.

Conclusions

1. It is of the essence of the sacrament of order to create a relationship
   bond between a bishop and a particular eucharistic community, as
   well as one between a bishop and the other bishops, including the
   Bishop of Rome. What is signified in the sacrament of order is these
   relationships which both constitute and manifest the order of the
   Church as a communion of communions. The bishops are the visible source and foundation of unity in their own particular churches,
   and as a college they visibly represent the unity among the particular
   churches. Thus they not only sacramentalize this unity in their person and relationships, but their first pastoral concern is to preserve
   and promote that unity both in their own particular church and
   within the communion of churches. The "fullness" represented in
   the episcopacy is none other than this communion within the episcopal college.
2. This ecclesial signification of the sacrament of order is inseparable
   from the more traditional view of orders as signifying configuration
   to Christ, with the difference that this configuration does not occur
   within an ordained minister in isolation from that minister's *ordo*
   within an ecclesial community. The primary configuration to Christ
   is that of the ecclesial community according to the ordering of the
   charismata and the participation of that community in the Body of
   Christ through baptism and the Eucharist.
3. If one understands the Church as ordered according to the charismata in 1 Corinthians 12, Galatians 3:28 cannot be interpreted to
   mean that there is no differentiation within the charismata of the
   ecclesial body. The Church is indeed the People of God, but a charismatic people. Since office within the Church is itself a charism, it
   would be false to dichotomize the leadership in the Church and its

charismatic elements.[56] Eucharistic presidency will remain an *ordo* within the Church, since it is related to the role of leadership and the responsibility for maintaining communion within the body.

4. The distinction between the priesthood of the laity and the ordained minister does not lie in the fact that one is more configured to Christ than the other, but in their role in relation to the community. This relationship to the community specified how each is configured to Christ, the bishop configured to Christ as head of the community and the faithful configured to Christ as members of his body. The ordained minister, charged with preserving the unity of the ecclesial body, represents it and speaks on its behalf in the name of Christ. Even though this means that the priesthood of the faithful is not the basis for eucharistic presidency, this does not preclude the fact that the entire assembly celebrates and offers the liturgy. The ordained minister as representative of the assembly does not function apart from it, but unifies, sums up, and represents both the assembly and its offering. Thus the function of the ordained minister in relation to the worshiping assembly is analogous to that person's function in relationship to the sacrifice of Christ. Both assembly and Christ are "represented" rather than "offered in the place of" or "repeated."

5. The episcopacy is not strictly monarchical in the sense that a bishop functions independently of the college of bishops or in isolation from his college of presbyters. While it is true that episcopal consecration confers a fullness of sacramental power in the bishop's role of teaching and ruling, it can by its very nature be exercised "only in hierarchical communion with the head and members of the college."[57] The supreme exercise of this power is collegial within an ecumenical council, although collegiality is manifested formally and informally in many other ways such as synods, national episcopal conferences, and mutual consultation and support.

6. According to the relational and representational view of the episcopacy presented here, the practice of ordaining titular bishops needs reexamination, since it seems to be of the essence of the episcopacy to preside over a church. The question is whether each bishop must be entrusted, in a one-to-one relationship, with a particular church within the universal Church. Karl Rahner argues to the contrary, but his position seems to be limited by an overly territorial identification of particular churches, as well as by the idea that bishops can be ordained for leadership in the universal Church without having direct responsibility for a particular church. This creates a tension between

a view of the Church conceived as a "communion of communions," wherein the universal Church is present in each particular church, and a view of the Church as having an existence over and apart from particular churches.[58] More work needs to be done on the various types of oversight proper to the episcopacy and the theological reasons why such oversight currently exercised by titular bishops is necessarily episcopal.

Notes, Chapter Three

[1] This chapter was first published in substantially the same form as "The Sacramentality of Episcopal Consecration," *Theological Studies* 51 (1990) 479–96. For commentaries on the sacramentality of episcopal consecration see Karl Rahner, "The Hierarchical Structure of the Church, with Special Reference to the Episcopate," *Commentary on the Documents of Vatican II*, vol. 1 (New York: Herder and Herder, 1967) 193; J. Lécuyer, "Orientations présentes de la théologie de l'épiscopat," in Y. Congar and B. D. Dupuy, eds., *L'Episcopat et l'église universelle* (Paris: Cerf, 1962) 781–811. G. Nicolussi summarizes the doctrinal evolution of Vatican II's statement on the sacramentality of episcopal consecration through the 1962, 1963, and 1964 texts in "La sacramentalità dell'episcopato nella 'Lumen gentium,' Cap. III," *Ephemerides theologicae Lovanienses* 47 (1971) 7–63. His footnotes give the preconciliar literature on the subject.

[2] James Moudry, "Bishop and Priest in the Sacrament of Holy Orders," in *Who Decides for the Church?*, ed. James A. Coriden (Hartford, Conn.: The Canon Law Society of America, 1971) 177.

[3] There is some question today whether or not jurisdiction and the power of governance are the same even though both the 1983 and the 1917 codes of canon law equate them. An older view distinguished between two sources of power in the Church, one originating from holy order and the other from jurisdiction received from a canonical mission. Pope Pius XII asserted in *Mystici corporis* (1943) that jurisdiction comes to bishops through the intervention of the Roman pontiff. Since Vatican II the power of jurisdiction is based in sacramental ordination and activated by being chosen for office. See John F. Lahey, "Jurisdiction" in *The HarperCollins Encyclopedia of Catholicism*, ed. Richard P. McBrien (San Francisco: HarperSanFrancisco, 1995) 725–26. Early scholastics generally did not consider episcopal consecration to be sacramental and attributed the power of governance to jurisdiction.

[4] George Dolan notes that "for St. Thomas the words 'character,' 'ordo,' and 'sacramentum' were all interchangeable, and where one was missing the other two were necessarily absent. It was for this reason that he could not consider episcopal

consecration as a distinct sacrament, although he recognized that in this ceremony an additional power was conferred upon the bishop-elect, a power that he did not have as a simple priest. . . .The episcopate is not a sacrament because it is not an order, and it is not an order because it does not impress a character; and it does not impress a character because 'through it the bishop is not ordinated directly to God, but to the Mystical Body of Christ.' (*Comment. In Sententias*, IV, d. 24, q. 3. A. 2; *Summa Theologiae*, Suppl. Q. 40, a. 5, ad 2)" *The Distinction between the Episcopate and the Presbyterate according to the Thomistic Opinion* (Washington, D.C.: The Catholic University of America Press, 1950) 82–83. For additional history see Seamus Ryan, "Episcopal Consecration: The Legacy of the Schoolmen," *Irish Theological Quarterly* 22 (1966) 3–38.

⁵ This question is asked with the awareness that the terms "bishop" and "presbyter" were synonymous in the early Church and were sometimes interchangeably applied to the same individuals. See Raymond Brown, "*Episkopé* and *Episkopos:* The New Testament Evidence," *Theological Studies* 41 (1980) 322–38. The present point of departure is the contemporary division of ordained ministry as we know it and the contemporary understanding of the ecclesial dimension within sacramental theology.

⁶ For a history of the terms *in persona Christi* and *in persona ecclesiae* see B.-D. Marliangeas, *Clés pour une théologie du ministère* (Paris: Beauchesne, 1978).

⁷ *Presbyterorum ordinis* 2.

⁸ Dolan, *Distinction*, 85.

⁹ "The Area Bishop: Some Theological Reflections," *Theological Investigations* 17 (New York: Crossroad, 1981) 166.

¹⁰ Ibid., 161. For the date and history of the question, see P. Fransen, "Ordo," in *LTK* 7, 1212–20, esp. 1215–17; also Seamus Ryan, "Vatican II: Re-Discovery of the Episcopate," *Irish Theological Quarterly* 33 (1966) 211–17.

¹¹ Karl Rahner, *The Church and the Sacraments* (New York: Herder and Herder, 1963); Otto Semmelroth, *Church and Sacrament* (Notre Dame, Ind.: Fides, 1965). William Van Roo criticizes Rahner's position for not giving sufficient attention to the christological basis of the sacraments: "Reflections on Karl Rahner's 'Kirche und Sakramente,'" *Gregorianum* 44 (1963) 493–98.

¹² Karl Rahner, "The Theology of the Symbol," *Theological Investigations* 4 (New York: Crossroad, 1966) 221–52.

¹³ See especially sermons 3, 6, 226, and 227.

¹⁴ Sermon 6 (Den.) Translation from *Selected Easter Sermons of Saint Augustine* by Philip T. Weller (St. Louis, Mo.: B. Herder Book Co., 1959) 109.

¹⁵ Sermon 3 (Den.), translated in Weller, 113.

¹⁶ For an earlier attempt to identify the ecclesial dimension of episcopal consecration, see Seamus Ryan, "Episcopal Consecration: Fullness of Order," *Irish Theological Quarterly* 32 (1965) 295–324.

¹⁷ Karl Rahner, "Theological Reflections on the Priestly Image of Today and Tomorrow" *Theological Investigations* 12 (New York: Seabury, 1974) 45.

¹⁸ "Apostolic Office: Sacrament of Christ," *Theological Studies* 36 (1975) 243–64. Kilmartin does not distinguish between the representative function of priests and bishops, even from an ecclesial perspective. So, too, Michael Lawler in *Symbol and*

Sacrament: A Contemporary Sacramental Theology (New York: Paulist 1987) 237–45; and Bernard Cooke, "'Fullness of Orders': Theological Reflections," in *Official Ministry in a New Age,* ed. James H. Provost (Washington, D.C.: Canon Law Society of America, 1981) 151–67.

[19] David Power notes that "the history of the ordination rite, beginning with the *Apostolic Tradition,* indicates that it was increasingly the eucharistic ministry of the ordained that was highlighted in the ritual" ("The Basis for Official Ministry in the Church," in *Official Ministry,* 78). Karl Rahner argues against absolute ordination, but from the perspective that all episcopal ordination, including that of titular bishops, is relative to an office whether or not it is relative to a territory. The present chapter agrees with his position that episcopal ordination confers membership in the episcopal college, but would argue that the episcopacy is indissociable from a eucharistic community, however this is conceived (*Bishops: Their Status and Function* [Baltimore: Helicon, 1963] 27–34).

[20] A bishop is ordained to the order of bishops (plural) rather than to the order of bishop (singular). The language indicates that he enters into a network of relationships rather than is elevated to a power in and of himself.

[21] See Bernard Botte, "Collegial Character of the Priesthood and the Episcopate," *Concilium* 4 (New York: Paulist, 1965) 177–83; "L'Ordre d'après les prières d'ordination," in *Etudes sur le sacrement de l'ordre,* ed. J. Guyot (Paris: Cerf, 1957) 13–25; "Caractère collégial du presbytérat," ibid., 97–124. Also J. Lécuyer, *Etudes sur la collégialité épiscopale* (Le Puy: X. Mappus, 1964) 57–79.

[22] *Lumen gentium* 22.

[23] Cooke, "Fullness of Orders," 164.

[24] Power, "Basis for Official Ministry," 66. On p. 78 Power explains that the roles of bishop, presbyter, and deacon in the Eucharist represent "the primary sacramentalization of their role in the community." See also H. M. Legrand, "The Presidency of the Eucharist according to the Ancient Tradition," *Worship* 53 (1979) 407.

[25] *Lumen gentium* 23.

[26] Legrand, "Presidency of the Eucharist," 413–38.

[27] Jean Zizioulas, *L'Eucharistie* (Paris: Mame, 1970) esp. 35–51.

[28] Jerome Murphy-O'Connor, *1 Corinthians* (Wilmington, Del.: Michael Glazier, 1979) 112.

[29] Henri de Lubac, *Corpus Mysticum* (Paris: Aubier-Montaigne, 1944) 24.

[30] Ibid., 39–46.

[31] John Zizioulas, *Being as Communion* (Crestwood, New York: St. Vladimir's Seminary Press, 1985) 216. Note that Zizioulas considers baptism and confirmation to be ordinations inseparably linked with the Eucharist. See also his article "Some Reflections on Baptism, Confirmation, and Eucharist," *Sobernost* 5 (1969) 644–52. Yves Congar also argues that ministry should not be divorced from charismatic gifts and function within a community: "Ministères et structuration de l'église," *Ministères et communion ecclésiale* (Paris: Cerf, 1971) 31–49.

[32] *Being as Communion,* 212. J.-M.-R. Tillard also interprets the order of the eucharistic community according to the charisms of the Spirit and sees the function of the ordained minister as inseparable from his place within the community:

Eglise d'églises: L'Ecclésiologie de communion (Paris: Cerf, 1987) 220ff. So also Edward Schillebeeckx, *Ministry* (London: SCM, 1981) 70.

[33] *Being in Communion,* 215. Zizioulas comments that contemporary biblical studies which stress the absence of "bishop" in the NT have inevitably pushed theology towards the second option.

[34] Ibid., 215–16.

[35] Ibid.

[36] Ibid., 219–20.

[37] Ibid., 220.

[38] Tillard argues that the bishop presides over the Eucharist precisely because he is the person charged with ecclesial communion. Thus his liturgical role evolves from his ecclesial role (*Eglise d'églises,* 238).

[39] Zizioulas, *Being as Communion,* 226–27.

[40] Ibid., 226.

[41] Ibid.

[42] *Catechism of the Catholic Church,* 1121.

[43] See Edward Schillebeeckx, *Christ the Sacrament of the Encounter With God* (Kansas City, Mo.: Sheed and Ward, 1963) 156–72.

[44] For the Eucharistic foundation of episcopal collegiality see Susan Wood, "The Theological Foundation of Episcopal Conferences and Collegiality," *Studia canonica* 22 (1988) 327–38.

[45] Rahner, "Hierarchical Structure of the Church," 198.

[46] *Lumen gentium* 23.

[47] Rahner, "Hierarchical Structure of the Church," 198; "Aspects of the Episcopal Office," in *Theological Investigations* 14 (New York: Seabury, 1976) 191–92; and "On the Divine Right of the Episcopate," in *Episcopate and Primacy* (New York: Herder and Herder, 1962) 75–135.

[48] He does not, however, lose his power to sanctify. This dates from Augustine's controversy with the Donatists. The sacraments administered by someone who had broken ecclesial communion by handing over the Scriptures during persecution were still valid because Christ acts in the sacraments, not the minister.

[49] *Lumen gentium* 22.

[50] Rahner, "Divine Right of Episcopate," 102.

[51] Tillard, *Eglise d'églises,* 243–51; Zizioulas, *Being as Communion,* 230.

[52] This is also the deduction of Seamus Ryan in "Episcopal Consecration: Trent to Vatican II," *Irish Theological Quarterly* 33 (1966) 123. Related to this see C. Vogel, "Laica communione contentus: Le retour du presbytre au rang des laics," *Revue des sciences réligieuses* 47 (1973) 56–122.

[53] *Lumen gentium* 22.

[54] Zizioulas, *Being as Communion,* 243.

[55] This is Karl Rahner's position in "On the Divine Right of the Episcopate," 75, 83–108.

[56] Karl Rahner, *The Dynamic Element in the Church* (New York: Herder and Herder, 1964) 13–83. See also Carolyn Osiek, "Relation of Charism to Rights and Duties in the New Testament Church," in *Official Ministry in a New Age,* 41–59.

[57] *Lumen gentium* 51.

[58] Karl Rahner argues to the contrary in *Bishops: Their Status and Function,* 27–34. His position seems to be limited by an overly territorial identification of particular churches, as well as by the idea that bishops can be ordained for leadership in the universal Church without having direct responsibility for a particular church. This creates a tension between a view of the Church conceived as a "communion of communions," wherein the universal Church is present in each particular church, and a monolithic view of the Church as having an existence over and apart from particular churches.

Chapter Four

The Liturgical Rite
of the Ordination of Presbyters

B oth the theology and rites of the presbyterate have undergone considerable historical change.[1] In the early Roman church the collegial character of the presbyterate as counselors to the bishops predominated. Presbyters concelebrated according to their rank with the bishop at the Eucharist. Some of them prepared the catechumens for baptism, and the presbyterate assisted the bishop during the liturgy of baptism. The bishop consulted with them for pastoral or administrative decisions. They replaced him during his occasional absences.

Later Eastern and Gallican liturgies of ordination emphasized the ministerial functions of "teaching, offering, baptizing and blessing the people"[2] over the presbyter's relation to the bishop's presbyterate. The primary ministry of the priest was to transform bread and wine into the Body and Blood of Christ. He had the responsibility for a rural parish assigned to his care. By the thirteenth century, detailed sacerdotal functions are enumerated in the pontifical: "The priest must offer, bless, preside, preach and baptize."[3]

The two primary meanings of the presbyterate received from the tradition are thus: (1) the presbyterate is a college in service of the bishop; and (2) the priesthood exists for the sanctification of the people of God through sacramental ministry. The 1968 rite restored the balance between these two meanings by stressing the role of the priest as a helper of the bishop in building up the Church.

As was the case for the rite of episcopal ordination, the rite of presbyteral ordination accumulated a number of secondary rites, which obscured the ordination prayer. Many considered the handing over of the paten of bread and chalice of wine as comprising the essential rite of ordination. Whether or not the ritual of ordination consisted in the laying on of hands, or the presentation of the objects characteristic of the powers conferred, or both, had been disputed for centuries. Pius XII's apostolic constitution *Sacramentum Ordinis* (1947) settled this dispute by decreeing the sign of the sacrament to be the imposition of hands and the form to be the prayer of ordination. Paul VI confirmed this in his apostolic constitution *Approving New Rites for the Ordination of Deacons, Presbyters and Bishops* (June 18, 1968).

From the 1968 Rite to the 1990 Rite

The 1968 rite only slightly modified the ordination prayer of priests: the ending was changed to include a larger missionary perspective: "May he be faithful in working with the order of bishops, so that the words of the Gospel may reach the ends of the earth, and the family of nations made one in Christ may become God's one, holy people."[4] After its publication, the prayer of ordination received a number of criticisms: for not reflecting the conditions of actual ministry where the priest often functions alone in a parish, for emphasizing the priesthood as a "second rank," perhaps devaluing it in the eyes of the faithful, and for not enumerating the functions of a priest.[5] In response to these criticisms, the greatest change in the revisions of the 1990 rite of ordi-nation of presbyter occurs in the prayer of ordination.

A Question of Vocabulary

The confirmed translation of the 1968 rite frequently uses "priest" and "priesthood" to translate both *presbyter* and *sacerdos, presbyteratus* and *sacerdotium*, respectively, except where the Latin text clearly differ-entiated the Latin alternatives or where the context seemed to require the distinct reference to the presbyteral order. The introductory mater-ial given in the United States publication of the rites seems to give a practical rather than a theological reason for the hesitancy to use the term "presbyter" consistently, noting that the words "presbyter" and "presbyterate" are not so commonly used.[6]

The Latin text distinguishes between *presbyter* and *sacerdos*. Because both presbyters and bishops are ordained to be priests, the term "presbyter" distinguishes the order of presbyters from the order of bishops. Both orders share the ministerial priesthood and are *sacerdos,* that is, priests. This is consistent with the ordination rite in the 1962 *Pontificale Romanum* which entitles the rite "De ordinatione presbyterorum," a practice at least as ancient as the Latin translation of the *Apostolic Tradition,* usually dated at the beginning of the third century, in its section, "De presbyteris."[7] "Most recently, the *Catechism of the Catholic Church* speaks of the sacrament of apostolic ministry as including three degrees: episcopate, presbyterate, and diaconate" (no. 1536), and of ordination as integrating a person into "the order of bishops, presbyters, or deacons" (nos. 1538 and 1593). Nevertheless, usage is not absolutely consistent since the catechism in no. 1542 states: "At the ordination of priests, the Church prays . . ." where it is clearly a case of presbyters as distinct from bishops. In order to obtain confirmation by the Vatican, the International Commission on English in the Liturgy changed from its use of "presbyter" and "presbyterate" in the 1993 translation to "priest" and "priesthood" in the 2000 translation. The translation of the Latin *"presbyter"* has become a linguistic, theological, and political issue, compounded by the fact that, although the English word "priest" has etymological roots in *presbyter,* it inadequately distinguishes the second degree of the sacrament of order from the first since both presbyters (priests) and bishops are priests *(sacerdos).* Since the present study of the three rites endeavors to distinguish theologically between bishops and presbyters, "presbyter" will designate a member of the presbyterate, the second degree of the sacrament of order. "Priest" will generally be used where it is appropriate to speak of either a bishop or a presbyter in their common priesthood, particularly in their liturgical role. Liturgical texts will be cited according to their most recent translation, pending confirmation by the Vatican. The reality is that a candidate is ordained a priest within the order of the presbyterate. This person can be called either a "priest" or a "presbyter."

The outline of the 1990 rite is as follows:

Introduction to the Rite of Ordination of Presbyters

Importance of the Ordination

Duties and Ministries

Celebration of the Ordination
Requisites for the Celebration

Outline of the Rite of Ordination of Presbyters

Introductory Rites
Liturgy of the Word
Liturgy of Ordination
    Preparatory Rites
        Election
            Calling of the Candidates
            Presentation of the Candidates
            Election by the Bishop and Assent of the People
        Homily
        Promises
            Promises of the Elect
            Promise of Obedience
        Litany of Supplication
            Invitation to Prayer
            Litany
            Concluding Prayer
        Laying on of Hands and Prayer of Ordination
            Laying on of Hands
            Prayer of Ordination
        Explanatory Rites
            Investiture with Stole and Chasuble
            Anointing of Hands
            Presentation of the Bread and Wine
            Kiss of Peace
    Liturgy of the Eucharist
    Concluding Rite
        Solemn Blessing

The Rite of Ordination of Presbyters

Introduction

Section I presents a short doctrinal synthesis of the importance of the ordination largely taken from *Lumen gentium* 28. It emphasizes the presbyter's reception of a distinct sacramental character which so configures the ordained person to Christ that he acts in the person of Christ the Head. Presbyters constitute one priestly college with their bishop, cooperate with the episcopal order, and share in the bishop's priesthood and mission. Christ is the sole Mediator, but presbyters share in this function above all in eucharistic worship, in exercising the ministry of reconciliation, and by presenting the prayers of the faithful to God the Father. Within the limits of their authority they exercise the function of shepherd by gathering together God's family as a community all of one mind and lead them in the Spirit through Christ to God the Father. Finally they labor in preaching the word and teaching.

Even though there is a close correspondence between this section of the introduction and the suggested homily, the introduction fails to situate the ordained priesthood in relationship to the priesthood of the People of God as does the homily. The introduction stresses the priest's configuration to Christ, but not his function of representing the Church other than "presenting the prayers of the faithful to God." It notes that he represents Christ the Head, but does not develop the point that headship always entails a community. The sacramental character has been traditionally interpreted as having three effects: (1) it configures the ordained person to Christ; (2) it distinguishes the ordained person from other nonordained persons among the People of God; and (3) once validly conferred, the sacrament cannot be repeated.[8] More contemporary studies in this century, however, stress the ecclesial relationship that it creates.[9] Sacramental character is a participation in the priesthood of Christ, but this priesthood is related to the priesthood of the People of God, the reason why the sacramental character is configuration to Christ specified as Head, and not simply just configuration to Christ. The character constitutes the priest in a relationship with the ecclesial community.

Section I stresses the collegial nature of the presbyterate and the threefold office of pastoral leadership, teaching, and sanctifying, although the sanctifying function receives more emphasis than the other two offices. It makes a point of the limited authority of the presbyter, citing here *Lumen gentium* 28. Their authority is limited because it is subordinated to the fullness of office present in the episcopal office.

Section II outlines the duties and ministries of participants in the ordination rite, beginning with the role of the faithful who assist the candidates for ordination by their prayers. Since a presbyter is appointed for the sake of the entire local church, the clergy, especially all the presbyters, and the faithful are invited to the ordination so that great numbers may take part in the celebration. This section remains incomplete, however, for it does not specifically name the active role of the faithful in the ordination rite itself: the assent of the people following the election by the bishop, their active prayer in the litany of supplication, and their silent prayer during the laying on of hands and the consecratory prayer.[10] As in the ordination of a bishop, the people's prayer during the laying on of hands and the prayer of ordination should be included as a rubric in the worship aids to inform them of their active role lest they become passive spectators during the most important moment of the rite.

The desirability of strengthening the legitimate and active presence and participation of the laity at ordinations is highlighted in various proposals for territorial adaptation of the United States Bishops' Committee on the Liturgy. Possibilities for adaptation include: (1) questioning the people whether they are willing to support the candidates, and (2) asking the elect regarding their willingness to consult or work with the laity.[11] The second possibility underscores the collaborative relationship between pastors and the laity described in *Lumen gentium* 37:

> The pastors . . . should recognize and promote the dignity and responsibility of the laity in the Church. They should willingly use their prudent advice and confidently assign duties to them in the service of the Church, leaving them freedom and scope for acting. Indeed, they should give them the courage to undertake works on their own initiative. They should with paternal love consider attentively in Christ initial moves, suggestions and desires proposed by the laity. Moreover the pastors must respect and recognize the liberty which belongs to all in the terrestrial city.

Such a promise also supports the rights of the lay Christian faithful outlined in canon 228, to assist pastors as experts or advisors according to their knowledge, prudence and uprightness, and canon 212.3, to manifest to pastors their opinion on matters which pertain to the good of the Church in accord with the knowledge, competence, and preeminence which they possess. *Lumen gentium* 37 states this even more strongly, saying the laity are not only empowered, but indeed sometimes obliged, to manifest their opinion on those things which pertain to the good of the Church.

Presbyters participate in the ordination by laying hands on the candidate with the bishop, by assisting in vesting the newly ordained, by greeting the newly ordained with the kiss of peace as a sign of reception into the presbyterate, and by concelebrating the Liturgy of the Eucharist. One of the bishop's assistants charged with the formation of the candidates requests, in the name of the Church, the conferral of ordination and responds to the bishop's question on the worthiness of the candidates. The various roles of the presbyters symbolize the collegial presbyteral order to which the newly ordained is admitted.

The request for ordination in the name of the local church, ordination by the diocesan bishop, the presence of the people of the local church, and the participation of the presbyters clearly indicate that a candidate is ordained for a local church. They are not ordained for service to the universal Church at large, but only serve the universal Church in and through service to particular churches inasmuch as the universal Church is formed in and from the particular churches.[12] Both the First Council of Nicaea (325), Can. 15, and the twenty-third session of the Council of Trent (1563), Can. 16, prohibited absolute ordinations, that is, ordinations not tied to a particular church. The purpose of this prohibition was to assure sufficient clergy to meet the needs of the community and to preclude the undisciplined wandering of vagrant clerics. In current practice much of the discipline of this canon is provided by the canonical laws on incardination, which, in addition to tying a priest to a local church, assure his financial support.

The rite presupposes the diocesan clergy and a theology of the local church. The case of presbyters belonging to exempt religious communities raises theological questions about the relationship of these presbyters to a local church that have yet to be completely worked out. In the 1990 rite, religious clerics also make a promise of obedience to the bishop in addition to the promise of obedience to their legitimate superior, which reinforces their relationship to the local church. The ordinations of religious clerics are not "absolute ordinations." If religious presbyters leave their religious community they immediately lose faculties until they are incardinated in a diocese. Religious presbyters receive support from the "common table" of their community and are ordained to serve the charism of their institute, which involves service to particular churches, even though these institutes transcend any one particular church.[13]

Section III gives directives for the celebration of the ordination—the required five-day retreat, where and when the celebration may take place, which ritual Mass may be used—and describes much of the rite. Section IV lists the requisites for the celebration.

Preparatory Rites

Election

The deacon calls the names of those to be ordained who then come forward answering, "Present." Then a presbyter designated by the bishop, one usually charged with the formation of the candidates, asks the bishop in the name of "holy mother Church" to ordain the candidates. The bishop asks whether the presbyter judges them to be worthy. The presbyter responds: "After inquiry among the Christian people and upon the recommendation of those concerned with their formation, I testify that they have been found worthy." The bishop then elects the candidates by saying: "We rely on the help of the Lord God and our Savior Jesus Christ, and we choose these, our brothers, for the Order of the presbyterate." All present give their assent by saying "Thanks be to God" or in some other way according to regional customs.[14] In the United States this is frequently accompanied by applause.

The candidates are called and elected. They do not assume the office of presbyter on their own, but on the invitation of the Church and by the election of the bishop. When the presbyter requests ordination in the name of "holy mother Church," clearly the Church is the whole People of God, not exclusively the hierarchy. The Church requests that the hierarchy ordain the elect. The three groups who attest to the worthiness of the candidate—the Christian people, those charged with their formation, and the presbyter who speaks on behalf of these groups—show that those who know the candidates and who present them for ordination are willing to receive them as priests. This presupposes that some kind of consultation with the Christian people has occurred. This testimony, along with the ritualized assent of the assembly, constitutes a moment of ecclesial reception of the candidates.

Homily

The suggested homily instructs the assembly on the nature of the ministerial priesthood from the teaching of Vatican II. The point of departure is the universal priesthood of the People of God deriving from its participation in the priesthood of Christ. The presbyter carries out his priestly ministry in the name of Christ on behalf of all humanity. The work of Christ as Teacher, Priest, and Shepherd continues through the ministerial priesthood. Presbyters are coworkers of the order of bishops with whom they are joined in the priestly office and service of the people of God.

The bishop then addresses the elect on their duties to carry out Christ's threefold ministry of teaching, sanctifying, and pastoral leadership. Teaching includes meditating on and joyfully sharing the word of God. He instructs the elect to "believe what you read, teach what you believe, and put into practice what you teach."

The mission of sanctifying includes perfecting the spiritual sacrifice of the faithful by uniting it to Christ's sacrifice in the Eucharist, bringing men and women into the People of God through baptism, forgiving sins in the name of Christ and the Church, relieving and consoling the sick through anointing, and praying for the whole world throughout the day. The bishop exhorts the elect to "know therefore what you do and imitate what you celebrate."

Finally the bishop instructs the elect to bring the faithful together into a unified family and to lead them through Christ in the Holy Spirit to the Father.[15] He tells them to remember the Good Shepherd "who came not to be served but to serve, and to seek out and save what was lost." In every instance, the presbyter's personal life must correspond to his public ministry. The threefold structure of ministry is much more developed in the homily for the presbyter than in the one for the bishop. The presbyter's sanctifying role is the most developed, while his duties for pastoral governance are not developed in any detail. The homily exhorts the presbyter to share the word of God, but does not specifically name his responsibility to preach. The homily stresses the relationship between bishop and presbyter, but no mention is made of collaboration with the laity or deacons, who also participate in the function of Christ, priest, prophet, and king.[16] References to the collegial character of the presbyterate are also absent.

Promises

The promises express the values embedded in priestly ministry: to work with the bishop, to preach, celebrate the sacraments, pray, and imitate Christ. The ritual formalizes the discernment and commitment that have already occurred before the ritual. The elect declare their intention to undertake the office of presbyter through the following promises:

1. Promise to discharge the office of priesthood in the presbyteral rank as worthy fellow workers with the Order of Bishops.

2. Promise to exercise the ministry of the word worthily and wisely, preaching the gospel and teaching the Catholic faith.

3. Promise to celebrate faithfully and reverently the mysteries of Christ handed down by the Church, especially the sacrifice of the Eucharist and the sacrament of Reconciliation, for the glory of God and the sanctification of the Christian people.

4. Promise to implore God's mercy upon the people entrusted to their care by observing the command to pray without ceasing.

5. Promise to be united more closely every day to Christ the High Priest, who offered himself for us to the Father as a pure sacrifice and to consecrate themselves to God for the salvation of all.

These promises emphasize the collegial nature of the presbyterate in union with and service to the bishop. Preaching and sacramental ministry have priority of place among the duties of the presbyterate. The 1990 revised rite reverses the order of the second and third promises, placing the promise about the ministry of the word before that concerning celebrating the liturgy. This emphasizes the "prophetic" dimension of presbyteral ministry, correcting the former almost exclusive emphasis on this ministry's ability to "confect the sacraments."[17] The explicit naming of the ministries of reconciliation and the Eucharist as the "mysteries of Christ" to be celebrated by the new presbyters is a substantive change in the 1990 rite. The reference to penance, in particular, is an attempt to balance the almost exclusive reference to the Eucharist in the explanatory rites by naming other sacramental ministries.[18] Since the presbyter unites himself with Christ as High Priest rather than Christ as Teacher or Shepherd, the priestly and sanctifying roles of the presbyterate still seem to take precedence over the teaching and governing roles, despite the reversal in the order of promises which places the ministry of the word first.

The promise to pray without ceasing for God's people is another innovation. The two are related: the emphasis on the essential sacramental ministry of the priest requires a fidelity to prayer. One observes, however, that this prayer for God's people occurs where one would expect a reference to pastoral governance if the promises followed the rhythm of the threefold office so prominent in the introduction and the homily. This is true not only in the promises, but also in the ordination prayer itself in the section which follows the reference to preaching and stewardship of mysteries. This suggests that a presbyter's leadership is preeminently a spiritual one.[19]

The sacerdotal character of the presbyterate is more evident than its teaching and governing functions. Since the introduction to the second typical edition (1990) allows for additional questions and promises to ascertain the worthiness of the candidate and to express the needs of the local church, it would be good to include a promise of the candidate's resolve to exercise pastoral leadership, particularly when the presbyter is to be assigned to a parish.

Promise of Obedience

The candidate for ordination makes a promise of respect and obedience to the diocesan bishop while kneeling before him and placing his joined hands between those of the bishop, a gesture originating in the feudal relationship between a lord and vassal. The promise of obedience to the bishop originated at the time of the lay investiture controversy when clerics were subject to lay authority and considered as serfs subject to a feudal landlord. The promise to the bishop opposed lay investiture by emphasizing that the priest is subject to the bishop and him alone.[20]

The General Introduction, no. 11c, allows national conferences of bishops to specify the form by which the elect for the diaconate and the presbyterate are to promise respect and obedience. In this day and age, a gesture less linked to a feudal relationship would be more appropriate. The traditional gesture sometimes results in strange inconsistencies. The 1968 rite resulted in the anomaly of a religious presbyter placing his hands in those of the diocesan bishop while promising obedience to his ordinary who was his religious superior. In the case of an elect who belongs to a religious community, the problem continues to exist in 1990 rite where he places his hands in those of the bishop, but promises respect and obedience to both the bishop and his legitimate superior.

Litany

The litany, a prayer of the universal Church, is sung over the elect while they lie prostrate on the floor. The litany differs from the litany used in the rite of episcopal ordination in that it does not list all the apostles. The names of other saints such as the patron saint, the titular or founder of the church, the patron saints of the ones to be ordained or other petitions suitable to the occasion may be added at the proper place in the litany.

Laying on of Hands and Prayer of Ordination

The gift of the Holy Spirit for the office of presbyter is conferred by the laying on of hands and the prayer of ordination. The laying on of hands has the same significance and occurs in the same manner as in the ordination of a bishop. After the bishop has laid on hands in silence, all the presbyters present lay hands on each of the elect in silence. Hippolytus' *Apostolic Tradition* explains this gesture: "They all have a common and similar spirit." By this gesture the presbyters receive the elect into the presbyteral college.

The prayer of ordination of a presbyter is significantly altered in the 1990 rite. The title of the prayer in the 1990 rite is "prayer of ordination," a change from the 1968 title, "prayer of consecration."

Prayer of Ordination of a Presbyter (1990)

1 Be with us, Lord, holy Father;
2 be with us, almighty and eternal God,
3 author of human dignity and bestower of every grace.
4 Through you all things progress,
5 through you all things stand firm.
6 To form a priestly people
7 you appoint ministers of Christ your Son
8 by the power of the Holy Spirit,
9 arranging them in different orders.

10 Already in the earlier covenant
11 a diversity of offices flourished
12 established by sacred rites:
13 when you set Moses and Aaron over your people
14 to govern and sanctify them,
15 you chose men next in rank and dignity
16 to accompany them and assist them in their task.

17 So too in the desert
18 you implanted the spirit of Moses;
19 in the hearts of seventy wise men
20 with their help he ruled your people with greater ease.

21 So also you gave to the sons of Aaron
22 an abundant share of their father's plenty,
23 that the number of the priests prescribed by the Law
24 might be sufficient for the sacrifices of the tabernacle,
25 which were a foreshadowing of the good things to come.

26 But in these last days, holy Father,
27 you sent your Son into the world,
28 Jesus, who is Apostle and High Priest of our faith.

29 Through the Holy Spirit
30 he offered himself to you as a spotless victim;
31 to his Apostles, consecrated in the truth,
32 he gave a share in his mission.
33 You provided them also with companions
34 to proclaim and carry out the work of salvation
35 throughout the whole world.

36 And now we ask you, Lord:
37 in our weakness give us also the helpers that we need
38 to exercise the priesthood that comes from the Apostles.

39 Almighty Father,
40 grant, we pray, to these servants of yours
41 the dignity of the priesthood.
42 Renew deep within them the Spirit of holiness.
43 May they safeguard this office,
44 next in rank to our own,
45 which they receive from you, O God,
46 and by their manner of life
47 may they be examples of right conduct.

48 May they be worthy coworkers with the Order of Bishops,
49 so that by their preaching
50 and through the grace of the Holy Spirit
51 the words of the Gospel may bear fruit in human hearts
52 and reach even to the ends of the earth.

53 Together with us,
54 may they be faithful stewards of your mysteries,
55 so that your people may be renewed in the waters of rebirth
56 and nourished from your altar.
57 And so that sinners may be reconciled,
58 and the sick raised up.

59 May they be joined with us, Lord, to implore your mercy
60 for the people entrusted to their care and for all the world.

61 And so may all nations,
62 gathered together in Christ,
63 be transformed into your one people
64 and be brought at last to the fullness of your kingdom.

65 We ask this through our Lord Jesus Christ, your Son,
66 who lives and reigns with you in the unity of the Holy Spirit,
67 God for ever and ever.

       All answer:
68 Amen.

Summary of changes in the 1990 text of the prayer of ordination:[21]

1968 Prayer of Consecration	*1990 Prayer of Ordination*
"You are the source of every honor and dignity"	"author of human dignity and bestower of every grace." Eliminates language of status elevation.
"You watch over the growing family of man by your gift of wisdom and your pattern of order."	"To form a priestly people you appoint ministers of Christ your Son by the· power of the Holy Spirit, arranging them in different orders." Additions include the identification of the "priestly people" rather than the "family of man."
"and so there grew up the ranks of priests and the offices of levites, established by sacred rites."	Phrase omitted. Old Testament ministries are no longer direct antecedents of Christian ordained ministry. The typology of levitical priesthood remains, but reference to a hierarchically ranked office is removed.
"When you had appointed high priests to rule your people"	"when you set Moses and Aaron over your people to govern and sanctify them" Moses and Aaron are mentioned by name. The reference to "high priests" is omitted.
"In the desert you extended the spirit of Moses to seventy wise men to help him to rule the great company of his people."	"So too in the desert you implanted the spirit of Moses in the hearts of seventy wise men; with their help he ruled your people with greater ease." The people are identified as God's people rather than as Moses' people.

1968 Prayer of Consecration (cont.)	*1990 Prayer of Ordination* (cont.)
"You shared among the sons of Aaron the fullness of their father's power to provide worthy priests in sufficient number for the increasing rites of sacrifice and worship."	"So also you gave to the sons of Aaron an abundant share of their father's plenty that the number of the priests prescribed by the Law might be sufficient for the sacrifices of the tabernacle, which were a foreshadowing of the good things to come." The reference to "worthy priests in sufficient number" is omitted. The former rites of sacrifice foreshadow future blessings. There is no longer a direct correspondence between the Old Testament rites of sacrifice and worship and Christian worship.
	"But in these last days, holy Father, you sent your Son into the world, Jesus, who is Apostle and High Priest of our faith. Through the Holy Spirit he offered himself to you as a spotless victim; to his Apostles, consecrated in the truth, he gave a share in his mission." The 1968 text made no reference to Jesus' ministry.
"Lord, grant also to us such fellow workers, for we are weak and our need is greater."	"And now we ask you, Lord: in our weakness give us also the helpers we need to exercise the priesthood that comes from the Apostles." Presbyters are necessary coworkers with bishops, not a concession to their weakness.
	"Together with us, may they be faithful stewards of your mysteries, so that your people may be renewed in the waters of rebirth and nourished from your altar, and so that sinners may be reconciled and the sick raised up." This addition to the prayer specifies the sacramental activities and intercessory prayer of presbyteral ministry.
"May he be faithful in working with the order of bishops, so that the words of the Gospel may reach the ends of the earth, and the family of nations, made one in Christ, may become God's one, holy people."	"And so, may all nations, gathered together in Christ, be transformed into your one people and be brought at last to the fullness of your kingdom." Presbyteral ministry not only serves the Church, but the reign of God.

The changes in the 1990 prayer of ordination de-emphasize language of status elevation although they retain hierarchical ranking. They present Old Testament typology in a more restrained manner. The sons of Aaron and the seventy elders prefigure presbyters as co-workers of bishops, but the sacrifices of the two Testaments no longer directly correspond. The prayer presents ordained priesthood more explicitly in reference to the priesthood of Christ. The tasks of ministry emphasize the sacramental ministry of the presbyterate in more specific detail extending beyond the Eucharist to baptism, reconciliation, and the sacrament of the sick. In terms of balance, sacramental ministry receives more weight than governing or preaching. Finally, the prayer situates ordained priesthood within the eschatological completion of the kingdom of God. The intercessory petitions in the prayer of ordination are formulated to correspond to the content of the questions the bishop has just asked the presbyteral candidates.

The general structure of the prayer is invocation, anamnesis, epiclesis, intercessory, prayer related to the tasks of ministry, and doxology:

Invocation:
ll. 1–5   Prayer for the presence of God
ll. 6–9   Statement of the purpose of ministry: to shape God's priestly people.

Anamnesis:
ll. 10–25   Old Testament typology of presbyteral ministry
ll. 26–35   New Testament typology of presbyteral ministry in Christ

Epiclesis:
ll. 36–38   Prayer for helpers to fulfill the apostolic priesthood
ll. 39–47   Essential form of the sacrament:
              Prayer for co-workers with the order of bishops
              Prayer for the Spirit of holiness

Intercessory prayer related to the tasks of ministry:
ll. 48–60   Tasks of presbyteral ministry:
              working virtuously with the order of bishops
              preaching (teaching role)
              being stewards of sacramental mysteries (sanctifying role)
              imploring mercy on the people (governing role in spiritual leadership)

Eschatological completion of ministry:
ll. 61–64   Prayer for unity and fullness of the kingdom.

Doxology:
ll. 65–68   Concluding doxology

The prayer of ordination situates ministry within a trinitarian context. The prayer is directed to the Father who by the power of the Holy Spirit provides various forms of ministry within the Church of Christ, the Son. A second trinitarian dynamic occurs in the fifth paragraph which recalls that Jesus, God's Son, is the Apostle and High Priest who offered himself through the Holy Spirit to the Father as a spotless victim. Finally, the prayer ends with a doxology.

The prayer does not focus immediately or exclusively on presbyteral ministry, but acknowledges various forms of ministry whose purpose is to shape God's priestly people. This roots presbyteral ministry in its ecclesiological foundations, reflecting the teaching of *Lumen gentium* 10 and 28, and *Presbyterorum ordinis* 12, that the ministerial priest "forms and rules the priestly people," "shepherds the faithful," and "builds up the Body of Christ, the Church."

The reference to God as "author of human dignity and bestower of every grace" modifies the 1968 reading, "source of every honor and dignity." The 1990 text moves away from suggesting that ordination to the presbyterate represents an elevation in honor and dignity. The term "dignity of the priesthood" occurs only in the central petition of the prayer where it is joined with a description of the ordained as God's servants. This sentence, taken from the text for the consecration of presbyters in the ancient Roman Sacramentaries, reflects the civic terminology characteristic of late antiquity in Roman culture.[22]

The prayer text then compares presbyters with three kinds of helpers in the Old and New Testament through the use of typology. In the Old Testament Moses represents governance, and Aaron, priesthood. Other men were chosen, next to them in rank and dignity, to help them: seventy elders helped Moses rule the Israelites, and the sons of Aaron provided priests for the former rites of sacrifice that foreshadowed the sacrifice of the New Covenant. The apostles are the third group who shares the mission of Christ to proclaim and carry out the work of salvation throughout the whole world. This group teaches and preaches. Here we see a diversity of offices foreshadowing what would develop as the threefold office of ruler, priest, and teacher.[23] We also have the tradition of Moses, Aaron, and Christ gathering helpers around them who are "next to" but not equal to them in rank and dignity.[24]

Contemporary ministry differs from its typological figures in that all three functions are embodied in one office holder. Christ was Priest, Prophet, and King, but the elders around Moses and the sons of Aaron did not exercise all three offices. The idea of a threefold office in contemporary ministry reflects christology more than it does Old Testament typology.

Within the ordination rites and the theology of ministry in *Lumen gentium,* the priestly people have a kingly, priestly, and prophetic role as do bishop and presbyter. Deacons are an exception since they are not ordained to the priesthood. Nevertheless, the offices do not exercise the three functions equally. In the last chapter we found the governing role of the bishop to be predominant despite *Lumen gentium*'s teaching that "among the more important duties of bishops that of preaching the Gospel has pride of place."[25] Among the duties of presbyter, the sanctifying role predominates. References to a presbyter's governing role are either explicitly limited, subordinated to that of the bishop, or indirect and oblique, inferred from spiritual leadership. As ministries become more diversified in the Church, different people will exercise various charisms for ministry. They will not be assumed into one office although the bishop will retain oversight of all offices.

The typology of the Old Testament is fulfilled in Jesus, God's Son, sent into the world as "Apostle and High Priest of our faith." He offered himself to the Father as a spotless victim and gave a share in his mission to the apostles. Christ is not named "Apostle" in the 1968 text. The addition here is a reference to Hebrews 3:1: "Therefore, brothers and sisters, holy partners in a heavenly calling, consider that Jesus, the apostle and high priest of our confession, was faithful to the one who appointed him, just as Moses also 'was faithful in all God's house.'" Christ is apostle in the sense that he was sent by the Father (John 20:26) to fulfill his mission to the world, although the word "apostle" is not commonly attributed to Christ. The reference to Jesus as High Priest and spotless victim echoes Hebrews 3:1 and Hebrews 9:14.

The text clearly states that the apostles share in Christ's mission. The apostolic priesthood, exercised by bishops, is an extension of the high priesthood of Christ. Presbyters, the companions of the bishops representing the companions of the apostles, help the bishops fulfill that priesthood. The dynamic is Christ–apostles–bishops–presbyters: presbyters represent and extend the mission of the bishops who represent and extend the mission of the apostles who represent and extend the mission of Christ.

Lumen gentium 20 develops this relationship between the bishop and Christ: "The sacred synod teaches that by divine institution the bishops have succeeded to the place of the apostles as shepherds of the Church: and the one who hears them hears Christ but whoever rejects them rejects Christ and him who sent Christ (see Luke 10, 16)." Here the ability of the bishops to represent Christ is mediated by their relationship to the apostles.

The theme of presbyters as coworkers with the bishops occurs twice in the middle of the ordination prayer. In the introduction to the essential form of the prayer, the Church asks God for helpers to fulfill the apostolic priesthood. The ordaining bishop prays that they "be worthy coworkers with the Order of Bishops." The relationship to the bishops grounds and precedes any presbyteral ministry.

The section of the ordination prayer identified by Paul VI as belonging to the form of the sacrament and essential for its validity makes four petitions of the Father: the dignity of the priesthood, a renewal of the Spirit of holiness within the elect, fidelity to the ministry, and right conduct. The Spirit petitioned in this part of the prayer specifies the primary task of the office. In the ordination of a bishop, the prayer asks for a governing Spirit. In the ordination prayer for a deacon, it will be the Holy Spirit and the gift of sevenfold grace. Here the prayer is for a Spirit of holiness, underscoring the sanctifying role of the presbyter and naming the quality needed for configuration to Christ, the "spotless victim." Themes of holiness and sanctification are present at other points in the rite for presbyters: in the promise to consecrate one's life to God for the salvation of his people, in the prayers for holiness in the litany, in the exhortation of the homily, and in the symbolism of the anointing of hands. A presbyter carries out Christ's mission of sanctifying, a task that cannot be, or should not be, undertaken apart from his own sanctification and relationship to God. He is to be a model of right conduct to others.

The pneumatological emphasis in the prayer over a christological one reflects its epicletic nature and corrects a frequently perceived neglect of the Spirit within the Roman Rite. The Holy Spirit is named five times within the prayer of ordination. The Holy Spirit provides the Church with different orders of ministry to form God's priestly people (ll. 6–9). Through the Holy Spirit Jesus offered himself to the Father as a spotless victim (ll. 29–30). The prayer of ordination asks the Spirit of holiness to renew the new presbyters (l. 42). Through the Holy Spirit the words of the gospel take root in human hearts and bear fruit to the ends of the earth (ll. 50–52). The final mention of the Holy Spirit occurs in the final doxology (l. 66). In contrast, reference to Jesus Christ occurs only three times in the prayer: where Christ is described as Apostle and High Priest who offered himself as a spotless victim (ll. 27–30), in the eschatological reference to all nations of the earth being gathered together in Christ (ll. 61–64), and in the final doxology (l. 66).

The second half of the prayer, enumerating the tasks of presbyteral ministry, directly corresponds to the promises made by the elect during the preparatory rites: working with the bishops, preaching, being stewards of God's mysteries through sacramental ministry, and imploring the mercy of God on the people entrusted to their care and for the whole world.[26] These tasks correspond to the threefold office of teaching, sanctifying, and pastoral leadership. The final section ends with an eschatological reference. Presbyteral ministry extends beyond the Church to the kingdom of God as it gathers all nations into one holy people in Christ to fulfill the kingdom.

Explanatory Rites

The visual symbols and accompanying prayers of the explanatory rites express what has taken place during the sacramental rite and are visual signs of the tasks of office. All the symbols of office, however, pertain to the sacerdotal function of the priest. None of the symbols represent his teaching or pastoral functions for the new presbyter has already received the Book of the Gospels when he was ordained a deacon, and we have no symbol for his participation in the governing function of the bishop.[27] The lack of explanatory rites pertaining to pastoral leadership or teaching at this point in the rite has the unfortunate effect of restricting the presbyteral office symbolically and visually to the functions of sanctifying. At a moment in history when issues of presbyteral identity are particularly acute, this is particularly regrettable.

Investiture with Stole and Chasuble. Some of the presbyters help the newly ordained arrange the stole in the manner proper to presbyters and to put on the chasuble, the outermost garment worn by the bishop or the presbyter presider of the Eucharist. The stole, the major indispensable sign of ordination, is a band of material worn by bishops, priests, and deacons for all liturgical services. Bishops and priests wear it around their neck with the ends dropping down in front. Deacons wear it across their chest from left shoulder to right hip. No formula accompanies this action, nor are the vestments allegorized, that is, given symbolic meanings, as they were in the medieval rites.

Anointing of Hands. The bishop anoints the palms of each new presbyter with chrism and says: "The Lord Jesus Christ, whom the Father anointed with the Holy Spirit and power, guard and preserve you, that you may sanctify the Christian people and offer sacrifices to God." The anointing with oil is a sign of anointing by the Holy Spirit, which has taken place through the imposition of hands and the prayer of ordination. It also symbolizes the presbyters' distinctive participation in Christ's priesthood.[28]

The 1968 rite simplified this gesture by abolishing the practice of tying the priest's hands together with a white strip of linen cloth.[29] The purpose of the simplification of the rite is to show the centrality of the laying on of hands and the ordination prayer of consecration. In the former rite, the priest touched the chalice and host with the tips of his fingers, his hands being bound together, while the bishop said: "Receive the power to offer sacrifice to God and to celebrate Mass for the living as well as for the dead in the name of the Lord." This gave the appearance of being the moment of ordination and identified ordination to the presbyterate rather exclusively with the power to celebrate Mass. The 1990 rite further clarified the gesture by omitting the suggestion that the hymn *Veni, Creator Spiritus* may be sung while the new priest is being vested and the bishop is anointing his hands. The former rites gave the mistaken impression that the action was epicletic rather than signifying an epiclesis that had already occurred in the imposition of hands and the prayer of ordination. The rite recommends Psalm 110 or a similar song. When Psalm 110 is the responsorial psalm in the Liturgy of the Word, the antiphon is: "Christ the Lord, a priest forever in the line of Melchizedek, offered bread and wine [alleluia]."

Presentation of the Bread and Wine. Some of faithful bring the plate holding the bread and a cup containing the wine mixed with water for the celebration of the Eucharist. These are symbols of the presbyter's duty to preside at the eucharistic celebration and to follow

Christ crucified.[30] The deacon receives them and gives them to the bishop who hands them to each of the newly ordained saying: "Receive from the holy people the gifts to be offered to God. Know what you do, imitate what you celebrate, and conform your life to the mystery of the Lord's cross." This ritual ties the rite of ordination directly to its eucharistic context and to the presbyter's service on behalf of the People of God. The 1968 rite removed all references to "the power of offering to God the sacrifice of the Mass for the living and for the dead" which had given the impression that the giving of the paten and chalice constituted the sacramental rite.

The close connections between ordination and the celebration of the Eucharist is also made by the celebration of the rite within Mass, the interpolations within the Eucharist Prayer mentioning the newly ordained, special texts for the solemn blessing at the end of the Eucharist, and the use of the ritual Mass proper to the conferral of the various orders.[31]

Kiss of Peace. The bishop and all, or at least some, of the presbyters present give the kiss of peace to the newly ordained. The bishop's kiss of peace seals the admittance of his new coworkers into their ministry. By the kiss of peace the presbyters welcome the newly ordained to a shared ministry in the order of presbyters.[32] This does not replace the kiss of peace during the Communion Rite.

Special Questions

For religious presbyters, the greatest innovation in the 1990 rite is the promise of obedience to the local bishop. This innovation was included in the new rite without the consultation with either the Union of Superiors General of Men or the Congregation for Institutes of Consecrated Life.[33] The lack of consultation, extensive theological reflection on the question, and education on the theological and canonical implications has the potential of causing serious misunderstanding and tensions between religious presbyters and bishops. Several goods are apparently in conflict: an ecclesiology of communion, which begins with reflection on the particular church and considers the universal Church as existing in and through the particular churches, on the one hand, and the principles and practice of autonomy and exemption in religious institutes, on the other hand. Many religious consider themselves to be ordained for service to the universal Church and have little or no experience of a particular church. Yet the universal Church only has concrete, practical existence in particular churches. Furthermore, since the clear teaching on the sacramentality of the episcopacy as having the fullness of orders, including the fullness of the priesthood, religious presbyters now must consider how their priesthood is related to the priesthood of the episcopacy. This is a theological, rather than a purely juridical question.

The promise of obedience to the local bishop is not merely a question of the exercise of priestly power being dependent on the bishop or even on ministerial good order within a diocese. Beyond that, the promise of obedience to the local bishop represents a development in the ecclesiology of a local church and in the theology of the episcopacy as the fullness of holy order. As we saw in the last chapter, the bishop in the fullness of the sacrament of order represents the particular church within the communion of churches. The communion of bishops in the episcopal college represents the communion of churches. The particular church is defined as an altar community around the bishop. One of the principal duties of the presbyter is to preside at the Eucharist, the sacrament of unity. Every Eucharistic Liturgy is an extension of the bishop's Eucharist just as a presbyter's ministry represents an extension of the bishop's personal presence. Within a theology of the episcopacy as the fullness of order, the presbyter participates in the fullness of priesthood of the bishop, which is to say that his priesthood does not exist apart from that of the bishop: "All priests, whether diocesan or religious, together with the bishop share in and exercise the one priesthood of Christ and are, therefore, ordained to be prudent cooperators of the episcopal order."[34]

The presbyter's promise of obedience to the bishop also connects him to the local church. In committing himself to serve the bishop obediently, he thereby commits himself to serve the people of that diocese, to make the objectives of the diocesan church his own, and to commit himself to furthering its mission. The promise of obedience to the diocesan bishop by religious emphasizes the connection between religious and the pastoral life of the diocese where they reside and the oversight the bishop exercises with regard to the exercise of priesthood in his diocese. Religious are subject to the local bishop in all aspects of their public ministry and worship.[35]

The relationship between presbyter and bishop is more than jurisdictional regulation, but is also personal representation. The presbyter represents the bishop who represents the local church. There is no genuine priestly ministry except in communion with the supreme pontiff and the episcopal college, especially with one's own diocesan bishop.[36] A religious superior who is the ordinary of his subject does not have the representational link with the local church that a bishop does. Hence the need for a personal relationship with the bishop expressed in filial obedience.

The problems with the promise of obedience for a religious presbyter are: (1) the conflict between his potential mobility and the original purpose of such a promise; (2) the normativity of diocesan parish life for our understanding of presbyteral ministry which is not the pastoral experience of many religious presbyters; and (3) the conflict between obedience to a diocesan bishop and religious autonomy and exemption.

Jungmann has traced the promise's origins to a High German "priest's oath" of the ninth century. The oath created a feudal relationship between priest and bishop and bound the priest to remain in the bishop's service and not to move to another diocese.[37] The anomaly in the instance of a religious is that he may be subject to transfer to another diocese to serve a bishop to whom he has not promised obedience. Here the contemporary ritual belies its historical origins.

James O'Malley argues that the documents *Presbyterorum ordinis, Christus Dominus,* and *Optatam totius* presuppose that presbyteral ministry serves a stable community in which a regular rhythm of liturgies of word and sacrament will be celebrated and a stable community composed of the faithful. They also presuppose that a priest-minister is in hierarchical communion with his bishop.[38] Here the parish is normative for ministry. This, however, is often not the experience of religious. The instance of a religious presbyter's relationship to a local church is analogous in some ways to the problem of titular bishops. Both may have a more immediate relationship with the universal Church than with the local church, even though the local church, a residential diocesan bishop, and diocesan presbyters remain the norm for understanding ordained ministry. Other ministries in the diocese represent exceptions to the norm even though they are necessary and serve the good of the Church.

This forces the question: when and why is ordination necessary? The answer: for sacramental, teaching, and governing ministry that requires official and public representation of the ecclesial community in the name of Christ whose body the Church is. Priests were originally ordained in many communities to serve the sacramental needs of their community. The proliferation of ordained ministers in many religious communities dates to the practice of private Masses. Here the connection between ordained ministry and a faith community was generally reduced to the presence of a lone acolyte. The practice of ordaining members who minimally exercise their priesthood is questionable.

Many religious communities, however, often minister to specialized populations such as students, missionary areas, retreat centers, and hospitals, which, although not parishes, are segments within the particular church. It is important for these groups to maintain their ties with the local church. Here the link between ordained ministry and the local bishop reinforces the tie between these groups and the local church.

Lumen gentium 45 sets out the principle of exemption: "With a view to providing better for the needs of the whole of the Lord's flock and for the sake of the general good, the Pope, as primate over the entire Church, can exempt any institute of Christian perfection and its individual members from the jurisdiction of local ordinaries and subject them to himself alone."[39] The exemption of a religious community, wherein the internal affairs of a religious community are not subject to the authority of a diocesan bishop, has proven to be a beneficial arrangement for ministry within the universal Church.[40] *Christus Dominus* 35 explains the relationship between religious exemption and episcopal jurisdiction thus:

> The privilege of exemption . . . has in view principally the internal order of the institutes. The object is that everything in these institutes should be well coordinated and in the interest of the growth and perfection of religious life. The purpose of exemption is also that the supreme pontiff may be able to use these religious for the good of the whole church, or indeed that some other competent authority may be able to use them for the good of churches under its own jurisdiction. This exemption, however, does not stand in the way of religious in their respective dioceses coming canonically under the jurisdiction of the bishops, in so far as is required for the fulfillment of their pastoral duties and the well ordered care of souls.

The purpose of exemption, as expressed here, is twofold: for the internal order of institutes and service of the universal Church. It is not absolute insofar as pastoral work comes under the jurisdiction of the bishops.

Autonomy, distinct from exemption, is the principle which allows an institute to be faithful to its distinctive charism and way of life free from unauthorized external controls.[41] Canons 573, 576, and 578 address the issue of autonomy, emphasizing that an institute, once ratified by competent ecclesiastical authority, is to "grow and flourish according to the spirit of the founders and wholesome traditions."[42] In other words, autonomy prevents interference from the bishop which might deflect an institute from its proper purpose and manner of life. The history of the Church, however, chronicles numerous attempts by bishops to bring religious communities more closely under their control.[43] In reality, the situation is one of checks and balances. Autonomy is not absolute: a religious institute must be ratified by competent ecclesiastical authority. Its charism must be tested by the Church. Yet, once approved, it must be allowed to operate according to its proper identity.

The danger in a double promise of obedience is, of course, the possibility of divided loyalty to two masters. The character of a promise of obedience must necessarily differ between a diocesan and a religious presbyter. The bishop must respect the exemption, thereby acknowledging limitations to his authority. He cannot require, for example, that a religious presbyter be assigned to his diocese rather than to another one. He can accept or reject a presbyter's assignment to the diocese in a parish staffed by a religious community, but cannot arbitrarily reassign that presbyter to another ministry.

Obedience is a two-way street. It does not mean mere submission to the decrees of another, but a mutual relationship of respect and responsibility toward the other. The presbyter promises obedience and must cultivate a sense of belonging to a local church. The bishop "is to consider the priests his cooperators as sons and friends."[44] However, as Kevin Seasoltz notes, the conciliar texts do not provide a clear statement of the rights of religious with respect to the local bishop.[45]

The heart of the matter lies less in jurisdictional legislation than in the respectful listening intrinsic to obedience. As Alois Müller notes, "obedience" should not be understood in a positivistic sense as in "There is the rule—now obey it." It is rather "an acceptance of and attention to the universal norm of what it is to be the Church, which is always in the background and of which the bishops are only representatives."[46] He cautions that obedience to the bishop is seriously misrepresented if it is seen only as "authoritarian centralism." The bishop's claim to obedience derives from his relationship to the Church rather than the reverse relationship. Obedience is conditioned by the nature of the authority exercised, while the authority is in turn conditioned by the particular relationship. The diocesan bishop and the religious superior have different relationships to the religious presbyter and thus exercise authority differently, neither being absolute.

The danger with the innovation in the 1990 rite is that neither bishop nor religious presbyter will understand the nature and limitations of the authority exercised, the obedience required, or the ecclesiological foundations of the change. This has the potential of contributing to strained relationships between bishops and religious. The lack of theological preparation and dialogue prior to the change in the rite only compounds the problem. It is important that any presbyter's relationship to the local bishop be evident in the rite. Given the complications with respect to the exemption and autonomy of religious communities, we might question, however, whether a promise of obedience is the best vehicle with which to express this relationship. It does not add anything new to a religious presbyter's obligation to submit to the jurisdiction of the local bishop with respect to his pastoral and liturgical duties, and it has the potential of creating misunderstandings regarding the appropriate exercise of authority with respect to exempt communities. Some other sign of communion with the local church might be more appropriate.

Conclusion

This close study of the ordination rite for presbyters reveals the essence of ordination to the presbyterate to lie in the constituting of coworkers for the order of bishops to assist in the threefold office of governing, sanctifying, and teaching. The rite places more emphasis on the sanctifying role of the presbyter than on the roles of teaching and governing even though the threefold office constitutes a major structuring device within the suggested homily, the promises of the elect, and the ordination prayer. In fact, attention to the threefold office is more consistent in the ordination rite for presbyters than it is in the rite for bishops. The emphasis on sanctification suggests that presbyters are called to be holy persons who lead the People of God to holiness. The comparatively lesser emphasis on pastoral governance and teaching, however, makes it less clear that ordination exists for building up and presiding over the Church. Sanctification, in and of itself, can be subject to an individualistic interpretation apart from more explicit ecclesial references.

The ordination rite for presbyters exhibits a certain sobriety with respect to a presbyter's relationship to Christ. Presbyters are "stewards" of Christ's mysteries. They neither own nor possess them. They participate in the mission of Christ and consecrate their lives to God and imitate Christ's holiness in order to accomplish that mission. The emphasis is on service, not on dignity or honor. They imitate Christ victim, not conqueror or Lord.

Finally, presbyteral ministry exists for the Church and, ultimately, for the kingdom. Ordained priesthood exists for the service of a priestly people.

Notes, Chapter Four

[1] This present study does not intend to retrace these histories in detail. For a history of ordination rites see Paul F. Bradshaw, *Ordination Rites of the Ancient Church of East and West* (Collegeville: The Liturgical Press, 1990); Bruno Kleinheyer, *Die Priesterweihe im römanischen Ritus. Eine liturgiehistorische Studie.* Coll. Trierer Theologische Studien, vol. 12 (Trèves, 1962); James F. Puglisi, *The Process of Admission to Ordained Ministry: Epistemological Principles and Roman Catholic Rites,* volume I, trans. Michael S. Driscoll and Mary Misrahi (Collegeville: The Liturgical Press, 1996); and A. Santantoni, *L'ordinazione episcopale. Storia e theologia dei riti dell'ordinazione nelle antiche liturgie dell'Occidente.* Coll. Studia Anselmiana, 69, Analecta Liturgica, 2 (Rome: Ed. Anselmiana, 1976). For a history of the sacrament of order see Nathan Mitchell, *Mission and Ministry: History and Theology in the Sacrament of Order,* Message of the Sacraments, vol. 6 (Collegeville: The Liturgical Press, 1982); and Kenan B. Osborne, O.F.M., *Priesthood: A History of Ordained Ministry in the Roman Catholic Church* (Mahwah, N.Y.: Paulist Press, 1988).

[2] *Les Constitutions apostoliques* 8.16, ed. Bernard Botte (Münster Wesfalen, Aschendorf, 1963) 20–23. Cited by Pierre Jounel, "La nouvelle édition typique du rituel des ordinations," *La Maison-Dieu* 186 (1991) 14.

[3] Pierre Jounel, "La nouvelle édition typique du rituel des ordinations," 16.

[4] *The Rites of the Catholic Church,* Volume Two, Prepared by the International Commission on English in the Liturgy, Study Edition (Collegeville: The Liturgical Press, 1991) 45.

[5] Pierre Jounel, "La nouvelle édition typique du rituel des ordinations," 18.

[6] Bishops' Committee on the Liturgy, *Newsletter 1965–1975* (Washington, D.C.: Bishops' Committee on the Liturgy) 175.

[7] *Apostolic Tradition*, 7. The *Apostolic Tradition* is probably of composite authorship and may not be of Roman origin. For authorship and dating of the *Apostolic Tradition*, see Paul F. Bradshaw, "Redating the *Apostolic Tradition:* Some Preliminary Steps" in *Rule of Prayer, Rule of Faith: Essays in Honor of Aidan Kavanagh, O.S.B.* (Collegeville: The Liturgical Press, 1996) 3–17, and Marcel Metzger, "Novvelles perspectives pour la prétendue Tradition Apostolique," *Ecclesia Orans* 5 (1988) 241–59; "Enquêtes autour de la prétendue Tradition apostolique," *Ecclesia Orans* 9 (1992) 7–36; "A propos des règlements écclesiastiques et de la prétendue Tradition apostolique," *Revue des sciences religieuses* 66 (1992) 249–61.

[8] *The Code of Canon Law: A Text and Commentary*, commissioned by the Canon Law Society of America, eds. James A. Coriden, Thomas J. Green, and Donald E. Heintschel (New York: Paulist Press, 1985) 717.

[9] See Edward Schillebeeckx, *Christ, the Sacrament of the Encounter with God* (New York: Sheed and Ward, 1963) 154–79; Eliseo Ruffini, "Character as a Concrete Visible Element of the Sacrament in Relation to the Church," in *The Sacraments in General: A New Perspective*, eds. Edward Schillebeeckx and Boniface Willems, *Concilium* 31 (New York: Paulist Press, 1968) 101–14; Karl Rahner, *The Church and the Sacraments*, Questiones disputatae 10 (Freiburg, Herder and Herder, 1963) 90–93; Aubert Roguet, "La théologie du charactère et l'incorporation à l'Eglise," *La Maison-Dieu* 32 (1952) 74–89.

[10] *De Ordinatione Episcopi, Presbyterorum et Diaconorum*, Praenotanda Generalia, no. 7.

[11] Bishops' Committee on the Liturgy, *Newsletter* 28 (September 1992) 34.

[12] *Lumen gentium* 23.

[13] See the essays in *A Concert of Charisms: Ordained Ministry in Religious Life*, ed. Paul K. Hennessy, C.F.C. (New York: Paulist Press, 1997) and Paul J. Philibert, "Priesthood Within the Context of Religious Life," in *Being a Priest Today*, ed. Donald J. Goergen (Collegeville: The Liturgical Press, 1992) 73–96.

[14] General Introduction, 11, a.

[15] This section of the homily repeats the material in no. 107 of the introduction, which presents the importance of the ordination.

[16] *Apostolicam actuositatem*, 10.

[17] Jan Michael Joncas, "The Public Language of Ministry Revisited: *De Ordinatione Episcopi, Presbyterorum et Diaconorum* 1990," *Worship* 68 (1) (1994) 396.

[18] Maurice Vidal, "La Nouvelle prière d'ordination des prêtres," *La Maison-Dieu* 186 (1991) 25.

[19] In addition to a similar interpretation to this, Michael Joncas suggests the possibility that this promise is the counterpart of the new promise in the OEPD 1990 diaconal ordination rites concerning the fostering of a life of prayer with a pledge to celebrate the Liturgy of the Hours. "Naming the Tasks of Presbyteral Ministry: A Comparison of the *Promissio Electorum* in the 1968 and 1990 Roman Rite Ordination Ritual," in *In Service of the Church: Essays on Theology and Ministry Honoring Reverend Charles L. Froehle*, eds. Victor J. Klimoski and Mary Chris-

tine Athans, B.V.M. (St. Paul, Minn.: The Saint Paul Seminary School of Divinity, University of St. Thomas, 1993) 106.

[20] Puglisi, 166.

[21] These are enumerated by Jan Michael Joncas, in "The Public Language of Ministry Revisited: *De Ordinatione Episcopi, Presbyterorum et Diaconorum* 1990," *Worship* 68 (1) (1994) 398–400. I differ somewhat in some of my interpretations of these changes.

[22] Michael Joncas, "New Roman Rite Prayer of Ordination of Presbyters," *Priest* 48 (May 1992) 41.

[23] Maurice Vidal makes this observation in "La Nouvelle prière d'ordination des prêtres," *La Maison-Dieu* 186 (1991) 26.

[24] The 1990 prayer removes explicit reference to "grades of priests and offices of Levites." It mentions Moses and Aaron by name rather than referring to them as "high priests."

[25] *Lumen gentium* 25.

[26] This correspondence is noted by Bruno Kleinheyer, "Ordinationsfeiern," *Liturgisches Jahrbuch* 41 (2) (1991) 108–09.

[27] Bruno Kleinheyer, "L'Ordination des prêtres," *La Maison-Dieu* 98 (1969) 106.

[28] *De Ordinatione Episcopi, Presbyterorum et Diaconorum,* 113.

[29] In the ordination rite prior to 1968 this rite, called the manutergium, served a practical function, that is, keeping the priest from getting oil on his vestments. There is no longer any need to bind the hands together since the new priest washes his hands immediately after they are anointed and before the presentation of the offering of the people. The use of the manutergium has been abolished and no one on his own initiative may reintroduce the practice. See the Bishops' Committee on the Liturgy *Newsletter* 28 (June/July 1992) 27, and 28 (September 1992) 34.

[30] *De Ordinatione Episcopi, Presbyterorum et Diaconorum,* 113.

[31] *De Ordinatione Episcopi, Presbyterorum et Diaconorum,* 10.

[32] *De Ordinatione Episcopi, Presbyterorum et Diaconorum,* 113.

[33] R. Kevin Seasoltz, O.S.B., "Institutes of Consecrated Life and Ordained Ministry: Some Canonical Issues," in *A Concert of Charisms: Ordained Ministry in Religious Life,* ed. Paul K. Hennessy, C.F.C. (New York: Paulist Press, 1997) 159.

[34] *Christus Dominus* 28.

[35] See *Christus Dominus* 35; Code of Canon Law (1983), canons 678 and 681; Apostolic Letter on the Implementation of the Decrees Christus Dominus, Presbyterorum Ordinis and Perfectatae Caritatis, *Ecclesiae Sanctae* (August 6, 1966). These stress the need for the unity of all pastoral ministry within a diocese under the authority of the local bishop.

[36] John Paul II, *I Will Give You Shepherds (Pastores dabo vobis)* (1992) 28.

[37] Alois Müller, "Obedience to the Bishop," in *The Unifying Role of the Bishop,* ed. Edward Schillebeeckx *Concilium* 71 (New York: Herder and Herder, 1972) 80–81, citing J. A. Jungmann, "Das Gehorsamsversprechen nach der Priesterweihe und

der althochdeutche Priestereid," in *Universitas, Dienst an Wahrheit und Leben,* Festchrift für Bischof Dr. Albert Stohr, vol. I (Mainz, 1960) 430–35.

[38] J. W. O'Malley, "Priesthood, Ministry and Religious Life: Some Historical and Historiographical Considerations," *Theological Studies* 49 (1988) 250.

[39] This is also set out in canon 591.

[40] O'Malley argues, however, that beginning with the thirteenth century, the most impressive privileges of the orders related directly to ministry (253).

[41] For a discussion on autonomy and exemption as well as a discussion on the requirement of a promise of obedience for religious, see R. Kevin Seasoltz, O.S.B., "Institutes of Consecrated Life and Ordained Ministry: Some Canonical Issues," 139–68.

[42] Canon 576.

[43] Kevin Seasoltz recounts some of this in "Institutes of Consecrated Life and Ordained Ministry: Some Canonical Issues." For a more complete treatment see also Leon Strieder, *The Promise of Obedience in Ordination Rites in the West* (Rome: Pontificium Institutum Liturgicum, 1994).

[44] *Lumen gentium* 28.

[45] R. Kevin Seasoltz, O.S.B., "Institutes of Consecrated Life and Ordained Ministry: Some Canonical Issues," 158.

[46] Müller, 84–85.

Chapter Five

Theology of the Presbyterate

For largely historical reasons, the presbyterate is the least theologically defined order. There are presbyter-bishops in some post-Pauline churches. Here presbyters and bishops are essentially the same and share the responsibility for the pastoral care of the churches.[1] Their activity, dating from the 80s if not earlier, is evident in the pastoral epistles, 1 Peter, and Acts. With the possible exception of 3 John, the structure of a single bishop with the council of presbyters as his helpers does not exist as it does in the letter of Ignatius of Antioch (d. ca. 110). Raymond Brown places the emergence of a single bishop in the Roman Church, distinct from the college of presbyter-bishops, well into the second century.[2]

The Ignatian model, the precursor to the "monarchical episcopacy," evinces a threefold ministry of bishop, presbyter, and deacon, each with its distinctive service:

> Hence I urge you to aim to do everything in godly agreement. Let the bishop preside in God's place, and the presbyters take the place of the apostolic council, and let the deacons (my special favorites) be entrusted with the ministry of Jesus Christ.[3]

In this, the Ignatian model, the presbyters form a council like that of the apostles, and the deacons serve. The bishop is responsible for the unity of the church and its maintenance in orthodoxy. He presides over teaching, service, and worship. He or one of the presbyters whom he designates presides over the Eucharist.[4] Presbyters exercise a collegiate and deliberative role in assisting the bishop, as a council community

117

government. However, there is no proof that the Church structure described by Ignatius was universal.

In the early Church, the notion of a Christian priesthood emerges with the understanding of the Eucharist replacing the bloody sacrifices of the Temple.[5] Brown places the emergence of a "full-blown concept of the Christian priest" by the end of the second century. Most references to priesthood refer to the bishop rather than presbyters until the latter assume sacerdotal functions upon the expansion of the Church and its spread into rural areas.[6] Over an extended period of time presbyters took over the sacramental functions of bishops out of necessity. Originally the bishop was not only the ordinary minister of the Eucharist, but also of baptism and penance. Presbyters were primarily sacramental ministers by the fifth and sixth centuries when they rarely functioned as a council of community government,[7] although the presbyter did not become the normal minister of baptism until the eleventh century.[8] With the assumption of priestly functions by the presbyters, bishops were no longer the visible center of most of the eucharistic assemblies, and presbyters became more individualized, losing much of their collegial identity.[9]

Both in the earliest period, when the office is a rather undifferentiated presbyter-bishop,[10] and in a later period, when presbyters assume sacerdotal functions as delegated by the bishop, there is a close correspondence between the pastoral/sacramental roles of bishops and presbyters. The distinction between them was most clear within the Church structure of a monarchical episcopacy assisted by a council of presbyters. Today, the shortage of presbyters is forcing many of them to assume functions of *episcope* or oversight as they find themselves as resident pastors of three or even four parishes, although they remain subordinate to a bishop. The distinctions which remain constant, however, are the supervisory functions of the bishop in his service to the unity of the Church, his responsibility for continuity with the apostolic tradition, and his role as link to the universal Church through the college of bishops.

Since Vatican II, the bishop is seen as having the fullness of the priesthood rather than the presbyter. Prior to this the presbyter had the fullness of the priesthood, and the primary reference to ordained ministry was the priesthood. Additional powers of jurisdiction were added to a bishop. Today, however, the reference for considering the sacrament of order is the episcopacy. The perceptual difference between thinking of a bishop as something more than a priest and thinking of a priest as something less than a bishop may contribute to a feeling of diminishment on the part of some presbyters.

On yet another front, the assumption of many pastoral tasks on the part of the laity leave some presbyters wondering if there will be anything left for them to do despite the fact that most find themselves in fact overworked. The danger of reducing the threefold office of sanctifying, witnessing to the word, and exercising pastoral leadership to the dispensing of sacraments reserved to priests is real as the shortage of priests reduces many to the role of sacramental circuit rider. In this sense, there really is paradoxically less for them to do even as they find themselves more and more busy. The challenge today is to articulate a theology of the presbyterate to address the "identity crisis."

Although a major achievement of Vatican II was the development of a theology of the episcopacy, it did not, however, achieve the same for the presbyterate and the diaconate. Only one section of *Lumen gentium* treats a theology of priesthood. The Decree on the Training of Priests *(Optatam totius)*, predominantly practical in its purpose, addresses the fostering of priestly vocations and the principles and regulations for priestly training. Although the Decree on the Ministry and Life of Priests *(Presbyterorum ordinis)* as well as the Decree on the Pastoral Office of the Bishops in the Church *(Christus Dominus)* present the theology of the episcopacy and presbyterate, much more theological work remains to be done.

The functions of ministry continue to evolve today as they have in the past. Today in some instances the laity are able, through a transfer of jurisdictional authority, to exercise a variety of ministries formerly associated with ordination such as the witnessing of marriages, presiding at burial services, or the ordinary administration of baptism. If a presbyter is identified by what he does, this identity is potentially threatened with the change of activity. More profoundly, however, these functions or ministries become an extension of the general ministry of the congregation, a phenomenon known as congregationalism.[11] In congregationalism ritual forms are regarded as the product, creation, and property of the congregation and lack their own symbolic density, authority, and objectivity.[12] There is no essential difference between a lay and an ordained minister. They are merely differentiated by what they do rather than by what they are. Since what the presbyter does is becoming more and more interchangeable with what the lay people do, this results in an identity crisis for the ordained minister.[13]

An alternative approach is to consider the presbyterate as identified by four relationships: to Christ, to the bishop, to other presbyters, and to the Church. Because both share ministerial priesthood, there is some overlapping between the episcopacy and the presbyterate in some of these relationships.

Relationship between Presbyters and Christ

All Christians are configured to Christ through baptism, for that is the sacrament by which the new people of God are incorporated into the Church, participate in Christ's death and resurrection, and assume the name "Christian." All God's people relate to Christ as his disciples and have the obligation of extending his work and presence in the world today. Some Christians are called to imitate Christ according to certain specific aspects of his life. A presbyter is configured to Christ specifically as "spotless victim," as priest, and as "head."

The first two, "spotless victim" and "priest," are characterizations of Christ in the ordination prayer for presbyters which speaks of Jesus as Apostle and High Priest who offered himself as a spotless victim through the Holy Spirit. The epicletic section of this prayer asks the Father to renew in the candidate the Spirit of holiness, the quality needed for configuration to Christ, the "spotless victim." Christ is both victim, that which is offered by the priest, and priest, the one who offers the victim. This configuration, of course, evokes the sacrificial role of the priest in offering Christ in the Eucharist. This reference also occurs in *Lumen gentium* 28:

> But it is above all in the eucharistic worship or synaxis that they exercise their sacred function, when acting in the person of Christ and proclaiming his mystery, they unite the prayers of the faithful to the sacrifice of their head, and in the sacrifice of the mass make present and apply, until the coming of the Lord (see 1 Cor 11:26), the one sacrifice of the New Testament, that is, the sacrifice of Christ who once and for all offers himself as an unblemished victim to the Father (see Heb 9:11-28).

The reference to the role as "head" does not occur in the ordination prayer for a presbyter, although it does occur in the ordination prayer for a bishop. *Lumen gentium,* however, attributes it to presbyters on account of their relationship to the bishop: "According to their share of authority they exercise the office of Christ the shepherd and head. . . ."[14] *Presbyterorum ordinis* makes the same point: "As it is joined to the episcopal order, the priesthood shares in the authority with which Christ himself constitutes, sanctifies and rules his body. Hence the priesthood of the presbyteral order presupposes the sacraments of Christian initiation, but is conferred by the particular sacrament in which priests are sealed with a special mark by the anointing of the Holy Spirit, and thus are patterned to the priesthood of Christ, so that they may be able to act in the person of Christ, the head of the body."[15] When the presbyter is configured to Christ as Head, this indicates his relationship to Christ's body, the Church. The reference to headship identifies the difference between the Christic representation of the priest and that of the rest of the baptized. Headship is related to the ability to stand in the place of and sacramentally represent the community, as the etymology of the word *recapitulate* indicates. From this sacramental understanding of representation, headship can be understood—not as domination over—but as standing in the place of the community on behalf of the community. A presbyter's relationship to Christ is inseparable from his relationship to the community.

A presbyter's and bishop's relationship to the headship of Christ specifies how an ordained priest functions with respect to the threefold office of teaching, sanctification, and governance.[16] With respect to governance, headship indicates his responsibility for pastoral leadership of the Christian community. Pastoral leadership involves forming the People of God into the Church of Christ through oversight of the parish community and coordination of the various charisms present within it. With respect to sanctification, the people of God are constituted as Church by being constituted as the body of Christ through the sacraments. The priest relates to the priesthood of the people of God through the witness of a holy life, exhortation through the preaching of the gospel, and sacramental ministry. Although the ministry of sanctification involves work with individuals, individual sanctification does not occur apart from a relationship with the holy people of God formed especially in baptism and the Eucharist. An ordained priest exercises headship by representing Christ and his Mystical Body in the administration of the sacraments.

Relationship between Presbyters and Bishop

Both the ordination rite and the documents of Vatican II locate a portion of the presbyter's identity in his relationship to the bishop. The prayer of ordination identifies them as "co-workers with the order of bishops." The presbyter-elect promises to discharge the office of priesthood in the presbyteral order as conscientious fellow workers with the bishops and makes a promise of obedience to his diocesan bishop. *Lumen gentium* 28 locates the association of presbyters with the bishop by reason of their common participation in the priesthood. The suggested homily describes the presbyteral priesthood as joined to the priesthood of the bishop.[17] Presbyters exercise the office of pastoral leadership within their share of the authority that is theirs. They are "prudent cooperators of the episcopal order and its instrument and help."[18] In a certain sense they make the bishop present in the individual local congregations of the faithful, although they also have a responsibility for the whole diocese as well as the whole Church. These texts indicate that the episcopacy is the point of reference for understanding the presbyterate according to the theology of Vatican II. The bishop's priesthood is not something added to the presbyter's, but the presbyter's priesthood is a sharing in that of the bishop.

The decree *Presbyterorum ordinis* likewise teaches the one identical priesthood and ministry of Christ that priests share with bishops and that requires hierarchical union with them.[19] However, it uses stronger hierarchical language to emphasize the subordination of the presbyteral order to the episcopal order: "the bishops' office of service was delegated to priests in a subordinate capacity, men ordained into the presbyteral order to be collaborators with the episcopal order in carrying out the apostolic mission entrusted to them by Christ."[20] They are exhorted to bear in mind the fullness of the sacrament of order given to bishops, respecting in them the authority of Christ the supreme shepherd. They are to be loyal to their own bishop with true love and an obedience permeated with a spirit of cooperation.[21] The reason given for this close union between priests and bishops is the necessity for apostolic initiatives to extend beyond the limits of any one parish or diocese. Presbyters cannot fulfill their mission in isolation, but only with other presbyters under the leadership of those who preside over the Church.[22]

The unity between bishop and presbyters is liturgically symbolized when they concelebrate together.[23] The *Apostolic Constitutions* (fourth century) stipulated that the priests should be with their bishop, particularly on Sunday.[24] However, today when presbyters celebrate the Eucharist apart from the bishop, the Constitution on the Sacred Liturgy treats the presbyter in liturgical actions as representative of the bishop: "Since the bishop himself in his church cannot always or everywhere preside over the whole flock, he must of necessity set up assemblies of believers. Parishes, organized locally under a parish priest who acts in the bishop's place, are the most important of these."[25] Historically, in addition to the practice of concelebration with the bishop on feast days or on the occasion of the ordination of a priest,[26] this unity was symbolized in Rome at the time of Innocent I by the sending of the *fermentum,* a host consecrated by the Pope. When the cardinal-priests celebrated Mass in their own titular churches at Easter, each sent a priest sacristan to the basilica of the Lateran to receive a particle of the host consecrated by the Pope for the Communion for the presbyters presiding over the non-eucharistic services.[27] This custom of the *fermentum* was preserved the longest in the ordination rite to the priesthood. The ninth-century rite stipulates that the bishop take whole eucharistic loaves and distribute them among all the newly ordained priests who communicated from them for eight days in the particular churches for which they were ordained.[28]

The teaching of Vatican II on ordained ministry broadened the theology of the presbyterate at the same time it narrowed it. It broadened it by departing from Trent's identification of the priesthood as "the power to consecrate, offer and administer his body and blood, as also to remit or retain sins."[29] Instead, *Presbyterorum ordinis* defined the presbyterate as instituted for ministry, that is, for service of the People of God.[30] *Lumen gentium* described this ministry as a threefold office of teaching, governing, and sanctifying. It also broadened a theology of the presbyterate by stressing its collegial relationship to the episcopacy. It may also have inadvertently narrowed a theology of the presbyterate through its teaching on the sacramentality of episcopal consecration, for the priesthood of the presbyterate is subordinate to that of the bishop.

As we have seen, prior to Vatican II the distinction between the episcopate and the presbyterate lay primarily in jurisdictional powers. When coupled with a hierarchical, that is, a gradated notion of the relationship of the two orders wherein the presbyterate is seen not only as "coworkers" and "helpers" of the episcopacy within a relationship of communion and collegiality, but in a relationship of subordination to it, the result may be a diminishment, or perceived diminishment, of the presbyterate. In reality, no one would ever argue that the presbyterate and the episcopacy have ever been equal since the time they developed as distinct orders, so at one level there is nothing new here. Certainly, an exercise of *episcope* or oversight entails the ability to direct, lead, and govern. However, the difference between the two is now defined sacramentally and not only jurisdictionally. Furthermore, while the documents describe a bishop's authority as "proper, ordinary, and immediate" because of his sacramental consecration even though the exercise of this authority is "ultimately controlled by the supreme authority of the Church and can be circumscribed within certain limits for the good of the Church or the faithful,"[31] no such claim is made for a presbyter's authority by virtue of his sacramental ordination even with the caution that it must be exercised in communion with his bishop. This is unfortunate since a presbyter's representation of the headship of Christ derives from his sacramental ordination, not by delegation of the bishop. A presbyter represents Christ sacramentally. His representation of the bishop is of another order.[32]

Although bishops, not presbyters, possess the highest degree of the priesthood, *Lumen gentium* does not specify how the priesthood of presbyters is restricted. This cannot simply be confined to the fact that priests depend on bishops for the "exercise" of their power, for it is the "state" of priesthood rather than its "exercise" that bishops possess in the highest degree.[33] It is difficult to define this as a restriction in sacramental "power," such as in the ability to ordain presbyters, since history bears witness to ordinations performed by presbyters.[34] The concept of a partial or incomplete priesthood is not suggested in any of the documents and is incongruent with a presbyter's ability to represent Christ and the community eucharistically.

A possible key to the distinction between the priesthood of the bishop and that of the presbyter lies in their respective relationships to church order. This implies that priesthood is related not only to the ability to offer eucharistic sacrifice in the name of Christ and the community, but also to represent the communion of eucharistic communities. In other words, priesthood is related not only to function or power, but also to a representative role with respect to church order. The bishop has fullness of the priesthood because he represents the communion of eucharistic communities under his jurisdiction in the communion of churches which comprises the universal Church. For bishops, their task of being the visible source and foundation of unity that is sacramentalized by their membership in the episcopal college is inseparable from their eucharistic presidency. A eucharistic community is never closed in on itself, but is in communion with other eucharistic communities. The liturgical role of the bishop is the sacramentalization of his governing role, the "liturgical dimension of a pastoral charge."[35] This governance has as its object the unity of the Church—not just the unity within the particular church in his charge, but the unity of that church with other particular churches. The presidency of the bishop in the Eucharist parallels his governance of the ecclesial body of Christ. That is, he presides over the Eucharist because he exercises pastoral oversight of the community. The task of ministry for unity and communion in the Church is inseparable from the Eucharist, the sacrament of unity. Finally, the bishop is related to universality and apostolicity in a way that a presbyter is not. This is not merely a difference of jurisdiction, but is a sacramental distinction grounded in ordination. The college of bishops is the successor to the college of the apostles in teaching authority and pastoral government, and in union and with the consent of their head, the Roman pontiff, exercises supreme and full power over the universal Church.[36]

Another key as to why the priesthood of the bishop is normative for our understanding of priesthood lies within a theology of the Eucharist as it relates to the Church. *Sacrosanctum concilium*, the Constitution on the Liturgy, clearly teaches that the Church is most manifest in the full, active participation of the people of God at one altar where the bishop is presiding surrounded by his presbyterate and his ministers.[37] In other words, the Church is most manifest in a eucharistic celebration of unity within a diversity of ministry. This is the definition of a particular church: an altar community around a bishop.[38] Fullness of priesthood exists where there is fullness of Church, recognizing that a particular church is wholly Church even though it is not the whole Church. The bishop possesses fullness of priesthood because he presides over, that is, has pastoral charge of the basic ecclesial unit, the particular church which is usually a diocese and brings that particular church into communion with the other churches through his membership in the episcopal college. Presbyters participate in this by exercising charge of portions of this unit, usually a parish. These portions are subordinated to the particular church as their priesthood is subordinate to the bishop. Historically, as we have seen, there was a link between the bishop's Eucharist and that of the presbyters signifying their unity.

As long as sacramentality is viewed as exclusively a power or as an authority, the subordination of presbyteral priesthood remains a problem. However, if the sacrament of order is seen as ordering the Church, as empowering an individual to stand as representative of the Church, the relationship of a presbyter to a bishop clarifies the presbyter's identity rather than diminishes it, for a presbyter exercises both *episcope* and priesthood in a limited, circumscribed fashion within a parish setting.[39] Even though presbyters are exercising an ever greater ministry of oversight due to the current shortage of priests, a significant difference between a presbyter and a bishop is that a presbyter exercises ministry within parish settings or in specialized ministries such as schools, hospitals, and retreat centers. That is, he exercises a form of episcopal ministry ordered to a smaller segment within a particular church. He does this under the oversight of the bishop.

The analysis of the rite of ordination of presbyters in the preceding chapter showed that even though the rite broadens the ministry of the presbyter beyond the Eucharist, his sanctifying role is still predominant. The Spirit invoked during the prayer of ordination is the "Spirit of holiness." This role is the liturgical expression of the presbyter's responsibility for the unity of the community in his role of pastoral leadership. In other words, the primary identity of a presbyter is representation and relationship with respect to the ecclesial community in a way analogous to the bishop's identity and role. His specific activities, whether related to pastoral leadership, teaching, or sanctifying, is related to that more fundamental identity best described as sacrament of the ecclesial community.[40] This means he stands in the place of the community, stands for the community, and becomes a type of corporate personality in which the community recognizes itself. Both bishop and presbyter share this relationship to the ecclesial community that is inseparable from their eucharistic presidency, although they do so differently according to how they represent church order. The bishop differs from the presbyter in that as a member of the episcopal college he sacramentally represents the particular church in the communion of churches.

The threefold office constitutes a unity wherein one office cannot be divorced from another without reducing that office to a function. The person who represents the community sacramentally and presides at its liturgy is not designated for that office apart from that person's leadership of the community. In other words, ministry arises out of a person's *ordo* or place within a community. If this were not the case, we would return to a solely cultic definition of priesthood and a functional view of ministry. This relationship between eucharistic presidency and pastoral governance is most evident in the person of the bishop, but, as we have seen, it sheds light on the theology and ministry of the presbyterate as well as through the relationship between bishop and presbyter articulated in the documents of Vatican II.

Relationship Among Presbyters

A person is ordained to the priesthood within the order of the presbyterate, a collegial office. In the ordination rite, the gesture of laying on of hands made by the bishop and his whole presbyterium signifies that the ordinand is received into the college of presbyters. This is further symbolized by the exchange of the kiss of peace among the presbyters within the rite of ordination after the presentation of the bread and wine.

The government of the particular church is fundamentally collegial rather than strictly monarchical and is a shared responsibility.[41] The college of presbyters is not distinct from the bishop, but a common college which includes the bishop: "As prudent cooperators of the episcopal order and its instrument and help, priests are called to the service of the people of God and constitute along with their bishop one presbyterium though destined to different duties."[42] The commonality in which bishop and presbyters share in the one presbyterium is the priesthood.

Here, clearly, the "order" of the sacrament of order is not to be equated with the priesthood. Order and priesthood are distinct. The episcopacy, presbyterate, and diaconate are three separate "orders" within the sacrament of order. Two of these, the episcopacy and the presbyterate, share the priesthood, but the third, the diaconate, does not. Consequently, the orders of bishop and presbyter are inadequately distinct, joined as they are in a common priesthood within one presbyterium. All participate in the laying on of hands in the rite of ordination. However, only the bishop lays hands on the deacon, who is not ordained to the priesthood. The deacons share a common ministry and thus exchange the kiss of peace during the rite of ordination, but they do not form a college of deacons and do not share a priestly fraternity with the bishops and presbyters.

Membership in the one presbyterium brings mutual responsibilities. The bishop is instructed to consider the priests his cooperators as brothers,[43] sons, and friends.[44] He takes an interest in their material and spiritual welfare and has a responsibility for their sanctification. He listens to them and seeks their advice concerning the pastoral needs and well-being of the diocese. To this end, a council or senate of priests is established to represent the priests and to advise the bishop in the management of the diocese.[45] The priests are to recognize the bishop as

their father and obey him with a spirit of cooperation.[46] Their brother-
hood with each other is manifested in spiritual and material mutual
help, whether spiritual or pastoral, in reunions, and in community life
work and fraternal charity.[47]

Both the rite of ordination and concrete pastoral structures at the
diocesan level emphasize the collegiality of the presbyterate. Nevertheless, tensions exist between this communal emphasis and the increasing
isolation experienced by many presbyters today as they minister alone
in their parishes. The theology of the council and the rite recall the ancient tradition, but the practical exigencies of pastoral life today often
militate against its realization.

Relationship to the Church, the Priestly People of God

The fundamental task of the priesthood is to "bring the people of
God into being and increase it."[48] Ordained priesthood must therefore
be understood in the context of the Church. The presbyter builds up
the Church by engaging in a threefold ministry of the preaching of the
word, the guidance of the faithful, and the celebration of divine worship that is rooted in his sacramental ordination. These tasks of ministry form a unity most evident in eucharistic worship where the presbyter
exercises "in a supreme degree" his sacred function, "when, acting in the
person of Christ and proclaiming his mystery, they unite the prayers of
the faithful to the sacrifice of their head, and in the sacrifice of the mass
make present and apply, until the coming of the Lord (see 1 Cor 11,
26), the one sacrifice of the New Testament, that is, the sacrifice of
Christ who once and for all offers himself as an unblemished victim to
the Father (see Heb 9, 11-28)."[49]

Given the fact that the most intense exercise of the priesthood occurs in the Liturgy of the Eucharist, the challenge today is to understand the relationship between priest, community and the Eucharist,
and at the same time to avoid reducing a theology of ordained priesthood to the power to recite the words of institution and confect the
Eucharist. The latter would result in a constricted theology of the priesthood and would separate the sanctifying office of the priesthood from
the offices of prophecy and pastoral leadership. Several points must be
kept in mind.

1. *The Relationship between Church and Eucharist*

First, as Thomas Rausch points out, the essential relationship is between the Church and Eucharist rather than between the priest and Eucharist.[50] The priest presides at the Eucharist while the liturgical assembly
is the subject of the eucharistic action. The eucharistic assembly is not
the people as distinct from the priest, but includes both priest/presider
and people. To say that the assembly is the subject of the eucharistic action does not in any way detract from the necessity of an ordained
priest for a eucharistic assembly or the priest's role in confecting the
Eucharist. It does, however, define his role in relation to the broader
priesthood of the entire Church. The emphasis is not on the priest's individual action in confecting the Eucharist. The Eucharist is confected
in order that we may be brought into communion with Christ and
formed together into the body of Christ. The emphasis is on the constitution of the Church by the sacramental unity of the Eucharist and
on the Eucharist as a sacrament of initiation which more deeply incorporates us into Christ and the Church. In other words, the sacramental
presence of Christ exists for union and communion.

A renewed liturgical consciousness today envisions the ordained priesthood in relationship to the priesthood of Christ and the priesthood of
the Christian People of God. However, as Mary Alice Piil notes, *Sacrosanctum concilium* did not develop the relationship between the participation of the faithful and that of the priest in the liturgical action.[51] To
do so entails envisioning the ordained priesthood within the nexus of
relations of the entire liturgical action of the Eucharist and not only in
the moment of consecration.

The distinction between the ordained and common priesthoods as
exercised in the Eucharist is first enumerated in number 12 of the Instruction, *Eucharisticum mysterium:*

> The priest alone, insofar as he acts in the person of Christ, conse-
> crates the bread and wine. Nevertheless the active part of the faithful
> in the Eucharist consists in: giving thanks to God as they are mind-
> ful of the Lord's passion, death, and resurrection; offering the spot-
> less victim not only through the hands of the priest but also together
> with him; and, through the reception of the body of the Lord, enter-
> ing into the communion with God and with each other that partici-
> pation is meant to lead to.[52]

This text clearly teaches that the priesthood of the faithful participates in also actively offering the sacrifice and by actively entering into

communion. However, even though *Eucharisticum mysterium* distinguishes between the ordained priesthood, which alone consecrates, and
the common priesthood, it does not sufficiently relate them to each other.

This relationship became clearer with the decree *Prece eucharaistica,*
23 May 1968, which promulgated three new Eucharistic Prayers and
the publication of guidelines, *Au cours des dernier mois,* 2 June 1968, to
assist catechesis on the anaphoras of the Mass. These made it clear that
the faithful are directly involved in four places in the prayer: the introductory dialogue, the Sanctus, the memorial acclamation, and the
Great Amen. In the revised Communion Rite, the Communion preparation of the priest and the people occur together in the one recitation
of the "Lord, I am not worthy." These elements of the Eucharistic
Prayer, along with the use of the vernacular and the series of acclama-
tions throughout the Eucharistic Prayer, facilitate the active participation
of the common priesthood. This is not only a desirable characteristic of
liturgical celebration but a right and duty which the Christian people
have by reason of their baptism.[53]

The priest, as presider/president of the assembly, greets the faithful,
carries on a dialogue between himself and the assembly, invites the
people to pray with him, and leads the people in the Eucharistic Prayer.[54]
However, the 1970 edition of the General Instruction also emphasizes
the priest's role as representative of Christ:

> Within the community of believers, the presbyter is another who pos-
> sesses the power of orders to offer sacrifice in the person of Christ. He
> therefore presides over the assembly and leads its prayer, proclaims the
> message of salvation, joins the people to himself in offering the sacri-
> fice to the Father through Christ in the Spirit, gives them the bread of
> eternal life, and shares in it with them. At the eucharist he should,
> then, serve God and the people with dignity and humility; by his
> bearing and by the way he recites the words of the liturgy he should
> communicate to the faithful a sense of the living presence of Christ.[55]

The priest, therefore, both engages the priesthood of the faithful and
represents the priesthood of Christ to that priesthood.

2. The Relationship between the Ordained Priesthood and the Priesthood of Christ

Both priesthoods, common and ordained, are rooted in the priesthood of Christ. The priestly act of Christ is twofold: the sanctification

of humankind in a descending act through the sacraments and the worship offered to God by the Church in an ascending act of worship.[56] Three liturgical principles ground the relationship of the common and ordained priesthood in the priesthood of Christ.

First, within the Liturgy of the Eucharist the emphasis is on the whole of the liturgical action, not just the isolated confection of the Real Presence of Christ. The liturgical movement is doxological and trinitarian. We give thanks and praise to the Father, we remember the Son, and we invoke the Holy Spirit to transform the gifts into the Body and Blood of Christ, but also to transform us into a community of unity as the body of Christ. The liturgy commemorates the great *exitus–reditus* wherein we recognize the Father as the creator and giver of gifts which are transformed in the power of the Holy Spirit into the Body of Christ and returned in thanksgiving and offering to the Father in the great doxology. This corresponds to the four basic actions that constitute the eucharistic sacrificial meal: taking, blessing, breaking, and giving.

The action is threefold. Christ is sent by the Father, anointed by the Spirit, and returns to the Father in sacrificial self-offering. Bread and wine, the gifts of creation, are given by the Father, transformed into the Body and Blood of Christ by the power of the Spirit, and offered to the Father as the sacramental representation of Christ's self-offering in his passion and death. The Christian, having received the gift of life, is transformed by the Spirit into the ecclesial body of Christ and is thus joined to Christ's self-offering to the Father. The Christian's self-offering is never individualistic, but becomes part of Christ's.

The Eucharistic Liturgy is not just oriented to the *res et sacramentum,* the real Body and Blood of Christ, but communion in the Body and Blood of Christ is oriented to the *res,* the unity of all of us in Christ. The Body of Christ does not exist sacramentally for its own sake, but is given to us that we may become what we eat, the Body of Christ. Again, this is not simply an individual communing, a "Jesus and I" relationship, but a communing with Christ in and through and with an ecclesial communion with other Christians. The sacrament is given for the glorification of God through Christ's self-gift to the Father and through our transformation into Christ and incorporation into that same self-gift.

The priestly community, brought into being through baptism, is thus formed in and through the Eucharist. It becomes the body of Christ, who is priest, and it joins itself to Christ the Priest in his return to his Father in his self-offering and thereby becomes a priestly community. It also becomes a priestly community in baptism for the same reason, but through another means—the incorporation into the priestly body of Christ by immersion into his dying and rising. The Eucharist continues on a daily or weekly basis what was accomplished in baptism. Even though a Christian becomes a member of the common priesthood through baptism, this priesthood is exercised principally in the Eucharist as the sacramental representation of Christ's self-offering.

Second, the Christian community as a whole is the subject of the liturgical action.[57] Initially, the Eucharist was understood as a rite celebrated corporately by the whole Church rather than a rite celebrated by a presider on behalf of the Church. Liturgical leadership was collegial. We can find evidence for this within three elements of the Eucharistic Prayer. (1) While it is true that the priest recites the words of institution in the first person and recites the anaphora by himself, we must note that aside from the words of institution, the anaphora is in the first person plural. Thus the priest is speaking it in the name of the rest of the assembly. Hervé Legrand's analysis of the liturgical vocabulary of the first millennium shows in the Roman Sacramentaries the subject of the verb "celebrate" is always the "we" of the assembly, never the "I" of the priest.[58] The liturgical "we" made Lombard say that a priest cut off from the Church could not validly celebrate Mass since he could not say *offerimus quasi ex persona Ecclesiae* in the anamnesis.[59] (2) The Fathers of the Church emphasized the dialogue between priest and people in the liturgy. For example, in the exchange, "The Lord be with you," and the response, "And also with you," there is a reciprocal recognition of the Lord's presence in both assembly and minister who is the primary celebrant of the sacred mysteries.[60] St. John Chrysostom commented that the Eucharistic Prayer is a common prayer because the priest does not give thanks (which is to say that he does not celebrate the Eucharist which means to give thanks) alone, but only with the people. He does not begin the Eucharistic Prayer without first gathering the faithful and assuring their agreement to enter into this action through the dialogue: "Lift up your hearts." "We lift them up to the Lord." "Let us give thanks to the Lord our God." "It is right to give him thanks and praise."[61] (3) The "Great Amen" represents an affirmation, endorsement, and commitment on the part of the assembly to what has just been accomplished.

In addition to these elements from the Eucharistic Prayer, the *General Instruction* introducing the *Roman Missal Revised by Decree of the Second Vatican Council* (1970) regards the entire assembly as the primary agent of the liturgical action: "For the celebration of the Eucharist is the action of the whole Church." (5) The new *Catechism of the*

Catholic Church also emphasizes that "it is the whole *community*, the Body of Christ united with its Head, that celebrates." (no. 1140) The Constitution on the Liturgy *(Sacrosanctum concilium)* teaches that the gathered people "should learn to offer themselves as they offer the immaculate victim—not just through the hands of the priest, but also they themselves making the offering together with him."[62]

Third, in addition to being grounded in the priesthood of Christ, the ordained priesthood is grounded in the priesthood of the People of God. The notion of the priesthood of the community is much older than the concept of ordained ministerial priesthood. In the New Testament, only Christ is called a priest in the letter to the Hebrews. An identification of the Church as a priestly community dates to such New Testament texts as 1 Peter 2:9 and Revelation 5:10, while the term "priest" was used to designate the bishop since at least the beginning of the third century.[63] It was applied to presbyters individually much later when they took over leadership and priesthood in smaller communities.[64] Its use with regard to church ministers is related to the idea of the Eucharist as a sacrifice and an analogy with the Old Testament levitical priesthood.

The ordained priest evokes and expresses the priesthood of the Church. The ordained priesthood is not only a ministry for the Church on behalf of Christ, but it is also a ministry done with the people.[65] There is a fear on the part of some that making the assembly the subject of the liturgical action makes the priest a delegate of the assembly, thus obliterating the distinction in essence between the priesthood of the baptized and the ordained priesthood.

Several distinctions may assuage these fears. First, there is a difference between delegation and authorization. Delegation would consist in arranging for a member of a congregation to preside at the congregation's assembly without empowering that person with a presbyteral relationship to the assembly. This constricts liturgical presidency to a liturgical function rather than relating it to a larger pastoral role. Authorization to ministry, however, always occurs in the context of prayer to the Holy Spirit accompanied by the laying on of hands. In the Roman Catholic Church authorization to ministry also links the present assembly to other assemblies in the recognition that no particular church can be Church apart from communion with the other particular churches or apart from the apostolic Church with which it is in continuity and communion. As Paul Gibson notes, "ministry is defined primarily by an act of worship."[66] He notes that anything less than this becomes an exercise of juridical legalism wherein a bishop's juridical act authorizing lay leadership becomes equivalent to a bishop's liturgical act, that is, ordination.

Second, a priest can also never be seen as a delegate of the assembly if we envision the priest and assembly with a head/body relationship. The Church is a sacerdotal community that precedes any division of ministries. The priest in speaking the Eucharistic Prayer in the name of the people *(in persona ecclesiae)* speaks as the head of that community that is the body of Christ. He also speaks *in persona Christi* as head of the community, for the community in union with Christ, its head, is the *totus Christus,* the whole Christ.[67] In this role there is a relationship of over/againstness of the priest to the community at the same time that the priest is within the community as a head is also a member of the body. This is not a relationship of democratic representation. Nor does it represent a horizontal relationship between priest and assembly.

The over/againstness of the priest acting *in persona Christi* as head of the community enables him to address challenging prophetic words to the community, to exercise a pastoral ministry of oversight and direction of the charisms of the community, and to preside sacramentally as the instrument of Christ's action in the sacraments. He is able to speak the "I" of "I absolve you" and the "my" of "This is my body" not because he is exclusively configured to Christ apart from all others who are also so configured in baptism, but because he represents Christ in headship.

There is a relationship of mutual interiority between the head and the body, the priest and the assembly. Cyprian expressed this relationship by saying that the bishop is in the Church and the Church is in the bishop.[68] John Chrysostom said the body is the fullness of the head and the head, the fullness of the body.[69] The ordained minister is in the Church, not above the Church, or apart from the Church. The Church is the primary subject of the liturgical action. It celebrates through the hands of the priests.

3. The Relationship between Liturgical Presidency and Governance

Presidency refers to the ecclesial life of the community before it refers to a liturgical function.[70] Ministry is first a pastoral charge before it is a liturgical function. As Hervé Legrand notes, the term "presider" is a term used since the time of Paul to designate "those who preside over the life of the community, expending themselves, without, however, any special reference to the liturgy (see especially Rom 12:6-8;

1 Thess 5:12-13; 1 Tim 5:17)."[71] The association of the priesthood of presbyters with that of the bishop dates to the *Apostolic Tradition* (ca. 215). This document does not mention presbyteral priesthood, but implies it since presbyters impose their hands over the gifts with the bishop. It also indirectly attributes the priesthood to presbyters where it contrasts deacons from the other two orders in their not being ordained to the priesthood, thus implying that bishops and presbyters are ordained to priesthood.[72] Presbyters share in the presidency of the Eucharist because they share in the governance of the community. Just as the bishop has the primary responsibility for governance, so he exercises the "high priesthood" within the liturgy where the various roles within the community are manifest.[73] The mutual sharing in these two roles by presbyters and bishop is most evident in their mutual concelebration. This signifies the one college or presbyterium comprised of both presbyters and bishops. David Power points to this common participation in governance with the college as evidence that the presbyterate is neither derived from the episcopate, nor solely a body of advisers to the bishop, but coworkers united in government and priesthood.[74] Government and priesthood are joined because the task of government is to promote the unity of the Church and the Eucharist is the sacrament of unity.

Third, the liturgy accomplishes sacramentally by means of signs what is fulfilled historically only eschatologically at the end time. In the Eucharist the Church is sacramentally formed into the body of Christ. Within sacramental theology that final unity between the Church and Christ is identified as the *res tantum,* the purpose and end of the *res et sacramentum.* Within the historical conditions of a fallen world, this Christification of the Church in the power of the Spirit is only in process. This is an example of realized eschatology and the tension between the "already" and the "not yet."

The "not yet" of realized eschatology furnishes the pastoral tasks to be accomplished. The identity of a priest, both bishop and presbyter, lies in the interrelationship between what is celebrated sacramentally and the slow work for the realization of sacramental unity in Christ by the power of the Spirit within the historical conditions of everyday life. The pastoral charge is to work for the building up and unity of the Church through pastoral presidency and sacramental presidency.[75] The one who presides over the ecclesial body of Christ also presides over the sacramental Body of Christ.

The first task of presbyters as coworkers of the bishop is to "announce the gospel of God to all."[76] The prophetic office of witnessing to the word of God is preliminary to the office of sanctification. This not only responds to mission in the fulfillment of Christ's command to "go into all the world and preach the gospel to the whole creation" (Mark 16:15), but corresponds to the dynamic of faith and conversion articulated in the letter to the Romans: "Faith comes from what is heard, and what is heard comes by the preaching of the gospel" (Rom 10:17). The task of preaching is not only liturgical, but includes the evangelization that precedes communal worship and the teaching that accompanies and follows it.

According to Louis-Marie Chauvet, there are four constitutive elements of the Liturgy of the Word—texts of past events accepted as authoritative, these texts proclaimed as living today, their reception by a community recognizing its own identity in them, and ministry, which guarantees both the apostolicity of what is read and assures that these texts function as an exemplar of the community's identity.[77] Ordination, because it is authorization in the power of the Spirit involving the election of the community, creates a living, personal link between a present faith community and the living word of God today and the community and faith of apostolic Christianity. The word as preached liturgically by an ordained person connects the faith experience of the community with apostolic faith of the gospel because of the connection between ordination and apostolicity.

Both the revisions of the rite of ordination and the theology of the priesthood articulated at Vatican II sought to expand the theology of the presbyterate beyond the Eucharist that had too narrowly circumscribed its theology. For example, in the Middle Ages the presbyterate was almost exclusively defined in terms of the sacral functions of celebrating Mass and forgiving sins. This, along with the practice of saying Masses for the living and the dead, led to the constriction of the presbyterate to its cultic dimension. This resulted in the medieval phenomenon of the Mass-priest who did not have a pastoral charge and whose only purpose and means of livelihood was to celebrate the Eucharist. However, in this instance, the Eucharist, often celebrated with a lone acolyte, was divorced from the active participation of the people.

Priestly identity can only be discerned within priestly relationships. Ordained priesthood must be seen in the perspective of the common priesthood of all the faithful. This relationship is best viewed within the eucharistic action wherein both priesthoods, the common priesthood and the ordained priesthood, are operative and in an interactive relationship. This is not to reduce priestly identity once again solely to its cultic dimension, but to examine both within the sacramental sign where both are most publicly visible.

Conclusion

The *exitus–reditus* of the eucharistic action and the formation of the ecclesial body into the unity of the body of Christ does not simply occur when the priest recites the words of consecration or the people receive Communion. Furthermore, what happens sacramentally by means of signs must also find its realization in the historical and concrete realities of daily existence. This is why the cultic exercise of the priesthood is insufficient for the priesthood's fullest realization. Teaching, sanctification, and pastoral leadership both prepare for their liturgical expression and flow from it in an analogous way as to how the liturgy is the "high point towards which the activity of the Church is directed, and, simultaneously, the source from which all its power flows out."[78] Pastoral leadership finds liturgical expression in liturgical presidency. What is achieved sacramentally—the upbuilding of the Church and formation of the Mystical Body of Christ—must then be concretized in the historical order through teaching, evangelization, the model of holiness of life, and orchestration of the various charisms within the Christian community.

Notes, Chapter Five

[1] Raymond E. Brown, *Priest and Bishop: Biblical Reflections* (New York: Paulist Press, 1970) 35. Elsewhere Brown comments: "It is generally admitted that in Acts, I Peter, and the Pastoral Epistles the titles are at least partially interchangeable . . . . In Acts 20:28 Paul addresses the presbyters of Ephesus as 'bishops.' I Peter 5:1 is directed to presbyters who in 5:2 are said 'to be exercising supervision' *(episkopein)*." The Pastorals speak of "the bishop" in the singular (1 Tim 3:12-17; Titus 1:7-11) and of "presbyters" in the plural (1 Tim 5:17-19; Titus 1:5). But since most commentators understand the singular usage to be generic, there is general agreement that we do not have here an instance of communities with only one bishop.

[2] Brown, 53.

[3] *Letter to the Magnesians* 6.1, in *Early Christian Fathers,* ed. Cyril C. Richardson (New York: MacMillan, 1970) 95.

[4] *Smyrnaeans* 8:1.

[5] Brown, 40.

[6] The earliest evidence for this comes from North Africa in the third century (Cyprian, *Ep.* 5.2.). The practice spread extensively in the fourth century. Cited by Paul Bradshaw, *Liturgical Presidency in the Early Church,* Grove Liturgical Study No. 36 (Bramcote: Grove Books, 1983) 24. For a discussion of the word *sacerdos* and its developing relationship to bishop and priest see P. M. Gy, "Notes on the Early Terminology of Christian Priesthood," *Sacrament of Holy Orders* (London: Aquin Press, 1962) 98–115.

[7] David N. Power, O.M.I., *Ministers of Christ and His Church: The Theology of the Priesthood* (London: Geoffrey Chapman, 1969) 110.

[8] Joseph Pascher, "Relation between Bishop and Priests according to the Liturgy Constitution," *Concilium* 2 (Glen Rock, New Jersey: Paulist Press, 1964).

[9] Mary M. Schaefer and J. Frank Henderson, *The Catholic Priesthood: A Liturgically Based Theology of the Presbyteral Office* Canadian Studies in Liturgy No. 4 (Ottawa: Canadian Conference of Catholic Bishops, 1990) 41.

[10] David Power observes that the terms *bishop* and *presbyter* are used of the same persons in Acts 20:17, 28 and 1 Pet 5:2. 1 Tim 3:1-10 and Titus 1:5-7 also suggest that they refer to the same person. One primary difference is that *bishop* is always used in the singular while *presbyters* are mentioned in the plural. *Ministers of Christ and His Church,* 24–25.

[11] M. Francis Mannion, "Catholic Worship and the Dynamics of Congregationalism," *Chicago Studies* 33 (1994) 60. This is also developed in his two-part article, "Sunday Without a Priest: What is at Stake?" *The Priest* 49 (1993) 31–36; 49 (1993) 29–34.

[12] Eugene LaVerdiere notes the same connection between a functional view of ministry and congregationalism in his address, "The Mission and Ministry of the Ordained," at the conference, *Ministry in the Year 2000,* sponsored by Saint John's University, Collegeville, Minnesota, 28 June–1 July 1994. This discussion of congregationalism appeared in Susan K. Wood, "Priestly Identity: Sacrament of the Ecclesial Community," *Worship* 69 (2) (1995) 111–12.

[13] Thomas P. Rausch, *Priesthood Today: An Appraisal* (New York: Paulist Press, 1992) 28, points out the same difficulty in his discussion of a leadership model of priesthood which focuses on ministry or service as the basic category of priesthood.

[14] *Lumen gentium* 28.

[15] *Presbyterorum ordinis* 2.

[16] David Power notes this relationship in *Ministers of Christ and His Church* (London: Geoffrey Chapman, 1969).

[17] See the suggested homily, fourth paragraph.

[18] Austin Flannery's translation of this passage reads: "its [the episcopal college's] support and mouthpiece." The Latin text is "Presbyteri, ordinis episcopalis providi cooperatores eiusque adiutorium et organum." The intent of the text is

clearly one of interdependence and cooperation. However, Flannery's translation diminishes the autonomy of the presbyterate more than the Latin text appears to do.

[19] *Presbyterorum ordinis* 7.

[20] *Presbyterorum ordinis* 2.

[21] *Presbyterorum ordinis* 7.

[22] Ibid.

[23] Ibid.

[24] *Apostolic Constitutions*, I, 57, 4.

[25] *Sacrosanctum concilium* 42.

[26] Pascher notes that in the history of the Latin Church there is not evidence of a concelebration with a bishop. The Constitution on the Sacred Liturgy, art. 47, permitted concelebration apart from the presence of the bishop or his official representative represents an innovation. Pascher, 29.

[27] Robert F. Taft, S.J., "One Bread, One Body: Ritual Symbols of Ecclesial Communion in the Patristic Period," in *Nova Doctrina Vetusque: Essays on Early Christianity in Honor of Fredric W. Schlatter, S.J.*, eds. Douglas Kries and Catherine Brown Tkacz (New York: Peter Lang, 1999) 32–35.

[28] Ninth century, *Ordo Romanus*, XXXVI, 23. Cited by Pascher, 28.

[29] *Decrees of the Ecumenical Councils*, ed. Norman P. Tanner, S.J., 2 vols. (London and Washington: Sheed and Ward; Georgetown University Press, 1990) 2:742.

[30] John W. O'Malley, S.J., "One Priesthood: Two Traditions," in *A Concert of Charisms: Ordained Ministry in Religious Life*, ed. Paul. K. Hennesy, C.F.C. (New York: Paulist Press, 1997) 12.

[31] *Lumen gentium* 27.

[32] See David Power, *Ministers of Christ and His Church*, 180–87.

[33] Aloys Grillmeier, "The Hierarchical Structure of the Church, with Special Reference to the Episcopate," in *Commentary on the Documents of Vatican II* Vol. I, ed. Herbert Vorgrimler (New York: Herder and Herder, 1966) 221.

[34] See chapter four, note 19.

[35] H. M. Legrand, "The Presidency of the Eucharist According to the Ancient Tradition," *Worship* 53 (1979) 407. So also J.-M.R. Tillard, *Eglise d'églises: L'Ecclésiologie de communion* (Paris: Cerf, 1987) 220ff., and Edward Schillebeeckx, *Ministry* (London: SCM, 1981) 70. This differs from the position taken by Gordon W. Lathrop, *Holy Things: A Liturgical Theology* (Minneapolis: Fortress Press, 1993) 185, who argues in chapter eight, "Leadership and Liturgical Community," that "symbolically formalized Christian leadership positions were liturgical positions" at their origin.

[36] *Lumen gentium* 22.

[37] *Sacrosanctum concilium* 41.

[38] *Lumen gentium* 26.

[39] John O'Malley rightfully points out four assumptions regarding ordained ministry underlying the documents of Vatican II: "1) Priestly ministry is a ministry by and large to the faithful; 2) It is a ministry that takes place in a stable community of faith, that is, in a parish; 3) It is a ministry done by clergy 'in hierarchical union with the order of bishops'; and 4) The warrant for ministry, including preaching, is

ordination to the diaconate or presbyterate." "One Priesthood: Two Traditions," 13. These pose difficulties for an understanding of presbyterate members of many religious communities. The present discussion presupposes the diocesan model of the presbyterate.

[40] Susan K. Wood, "Priestly Identity: Sacrament of the Ecclesial Community," *Worship* 69 (2) (1995) 109–27.

[41] Here the alternative to strictly monarchical governance is not democracy, but a collegiality where ultimate responsibility resides with the bishop while at the same time he has a responsibility to take counsel with the presbyterate. See canon 500.2.

[42] *Lumen gentium* 28.

[43] *Presbyterorum ordinis* 7.

[44] *Lumen gentium* 28.

[45] *Presbyterorum ordinis* 7. Canons 495–502.

[46] *Lumen gentium* 28. *Presbyterorum ordinis* 7.

[47] *Lumen gentium* 28.

[48] *Presbyterorum ordinis* 4.

[49] *Lumen gentium* 28.

[50] Thomas P. Rausch, S.J., "Priest, Community, and Eucharist," in *Finding God in All Things: Essays in Honor of Michael J. Buckly, S.J.*, eds. Michael J. Himes and Stephen J. Pope (New York: Crossroad, 1996) 263.

[51] Mary Alice Piil, "The Local Church as the Subject of the Action of the Eucharist," in *Shaping English Liturgy* eds. Peter C. Finn and James M. Schellman (Washington, D.C.: Pastoral Press, 1990) 178.

[52] Congregation of Rites, Instruction *Eucharisticum mysterium,* on worship of the Eucharist, 25 May 1967, no. 12; COL 179, no. 1241.

[53] General Instruction of the Roman Missal, no. 3; DOL 208, no. 1393.

[54] General Instruction of the Roman Missal, nos. 28, 14, 32; DOL 208, nos. 1418, 1404, 1422.

[55] General Instruction of the Roman Missal, no. 60, DOL 208, no. 1450.

[56] Josef Andreas Jungmann, "Constitution on the Sacred Liturgy," in *Commentary on the Documents of Vatican II* Vol. I, ed. Herbert Vorgrimler (New York: Herder and Herder, 1966) 14.

[57] Yves Congar, "L'Ecclesia ou communauté chrétienne, sujet intégral de l'action liturgique," in *La Liturgie après Vatican II,* Unam Sanctam 66, eds. J. P. Jossua and Y. Congar (Paris: Editions du Cerf, 1967) 241–82. See also Mary Alice Piil, "The Local Church as the Subject of the Action of the Eucharist," 173–95.

[58] Legrand, "Presidency," 432; Benedicta Droste, *"Celebrare" in der römischen Liturgiesprache* (Munich: Max Hueber, 1963) 73–80. Note the exception in the rubrics of the Gelasian Sacramentary, 80. Cited by Rausch, "Priest, Community, and Eucharist," 265–66.

[59] P. Lombard, *Sent.* IV, d. 13. See B. D. Marliangeas, *Clés pour une théologie du ministère. 'In persona Christi, in persona Ecclesiae'* (Paris: Beauchesne, 1978) 55–60. Cited by Louis-Marie Chauvet , "Ritualité et Théologie," *Recherches de Science Religieuse* 78 (4) (1990) 537.

[60] Ibid., 277.

[61] "The eucharistic prayer is common; the priest does not give thanks alone, but the people with him, for he begins it only after having received the accord of the faithful. . . . If I say that, it is so that we learn that we are all a single body. Therefore let us not rely on the priests for everything, but let us, too, care for the Church." *Com. In 1 Cor.* Hom. 18, 3 (PG, 61, 527) cited by Congar, 277–78. Also cited by Hervé-Marie Legrand, "The Presidency of Eucharist according to the Ancient Tradition," *Living Bread, Saving Cup,* ed. R. Kevin Seasoltz (Collegeville: The Liturgical Press, 1982) 218.

[62] *Sacrosanctum concilium* 48.

[63] Paul Bradshaw, *Liturgical Presidency in the Early Church,* 27.

[64] See Edward Schillebeeckx, *Ministry: Leadership in the Community of Jesus Christ* (New York: Crossroad, 1981) 44, 48–49.

[65] See Bob Hurd, "Liturgy and Empowerment: The Restoration of the Liturgical Assembly," in *That They Might Live: Power, Empowerment, and Leadership in the Church,* ed. Michael Downey (New York: Crossroad, 1991) 139.

[66] Paul Gibson, "The Presidency of the Liturgy," in *A Kingdom of Priests: Liturgical Formation Of the People of God* ed. Thomas J. Talley, Alcuin/GROW Liturgical Study 5 (Bramcote: Grove Books Limited, 1988) 35.

[67] The encyclical, *Mediator Dei,* defined the liturgy as "the public worship which our Redeemer gives to the Father as Head of the Church; it is also the worship given by the society of the faithful to its head, and through him, to the Eternal Father: it is, in a word, the integral worship of the mystical body of Jesus Christ, that is, of the head and its members." Cited by Congar, 269.

[68] *Epis.* 66, 8. Cited by Congar, 269.

[69] *In Ephes.,* c. 1, hom. 3,2 (PG, 52, 26). Cited by Congar, 281.

[70] See Paul Bradshaw, *Liturgical Presidency in the Early Church,* Grove Liturgical Study No. 36 (Bramcote: Grove Books, 1983) 7–8: "[In the New Testament] . . . no one was ordained or appointed to an office which consisted primarily of saying the eucharistic prayer, but whoever said it did so as the natural expression of what they already were within the community."

[71] Hervé-Marie Legrand, "The Presidency of the Eucharist According to the Ancient Tradition," *Worship* 53 (1979) 432.

[72] *Apostolic Tradition,* 8.

[73] See David Power, *Ministers of Christ and His Church,* 40.

[74] Ibid.

[75] Literature contrasting the diocesan priesthood with priesthood exercised by member of religious communities sometimes contrasts a "cultic priesthood," one that emphasizes sacramental ministry, with a "prophetic or kerygmatic priesthood," one that emphasizes a ministry of the word and priest as spokesperson and agent for a special kind of view. There may be a difference in emphasis and primary activity, but the present thesis here holds the two functions, pastoral charge and witness to the word in a necessary relationship to what a priest celebrates sacramentally, whether this be for a stable parish community or occasional special groups. For this literature see Thomas Rausch, "Priest Community, and Eucharist" (note 38); Michael Buckley, "Jesuit Priesthood: Its Meaning and Commitments,"

Studies in the Spirituality of Jesuits 8 (1976); John O'Malley, "Priesthood, Ministry, and Religious Life: Some Historical and Historiographical Considerations," *Theological Studies* 49 (1988) 223–57; and John W. O'Malley, S.J., "One Priesthood: Two Traditions," in *A Concert of Charisms: Ordained Ministry in Religious Life*, ed. Paul K. Hennesy, C.F.C. (New York: Paulist Press, 1997) 12.

[76] *Presbyterorum ordinis* 4.

[77] Louis-Marie Chauvet, *Symbol and Sacrament: A Sacramental Reinterpretation of Christian Existence*, trans. Patrick Madigan and Madeleine Beaumont (Collegeville: The Liturgical Press, 1995) 210.

[78] *Sacrosanctum concilium* 10.

Chapter Six

The Liturgical Rite
of the Ordination of Deacons

O f all the offices in the Church, the diaconate has changed most dramatically over time.[1] The ministries of the Church developed gradually to meet the ministerial needs and circumstances of a developing Church. Ordained to assist bishops and presbyters in the ministry of word, the liturgy, and charity, the service of deacons has varied in terms of its relative permanence, emphasis, and specific tasks. Since deacons currently both preach and preside at the liturgies of baptism, matrimony, and at times of Christian burial, their ordained ministry is more closely connected with the ordained priesthood than in previous history.

Acts 6:1-6, the account of the appointment of seven Hellenists by prayer and the laying on of hands to serve at the tables of Jerusalem widows, is frequently identified as recounting the origin of the diaconate. However, scholars point out that it is anachronistic to think of this text as the institution of the permanent diaconate.[2] Stephen is never called a deacon in this text. Stephen and Philip preach, and Philip baptizes (Acts 8:12), functions performed at the time by the apostles and presbyters (Acts 6:8; 8:5). One cannot speak of an "ordination" to an ecclesiastical office at this stage of ecclesiastical development, although in some situations, persons chosen for a special task such as missionary work received a laying on of hands within a context of assembly, prayer, and prophecy.[3] The office of deacon did not exist in the first century church in the form it assumed in the second century. The clearest indication of office of deacon occurs in the pastoral epistles in 1 Timothy. Even here neither bishop nor deacon was yet defined as they were later, and the letter does not describe their functions. The meaning of the laying on of hands is ambiguous and depends on its context for meaning since it does not always indicate an office or installation in a ministry.[4] For example, in Acts 13:1-3 Paul and Barnabus are selected for a missionary work, but not "ordained" to be apostles. In Acts 6:5-6 it is not even clear who lays hands on the seven, whether it is only the apostles or the gathered community. From the New Testament texts and the witness of the Apostolic Fathers, we can say that the diaconal ministry of material aid did not become institutionalized in the Church until the end of the first century or at the very beginning of the second century.[5] This text from Acts does, however, show the church structuring its ministry to meet the needs of the community. The Church later returned to this text for a description of the diaconal tasks once the office had developed. Originally, however, *diakonia* broadly refers to "service," and is descriptive of the ministry of the whole Church prior to its later more technical use to describe a specific office within the Church.

A variety of offices including bishop-presbyters, deacons, traveling prophets, and teachers existed well into the late first century. The earliest writings witnessing to a clearly delineated threefold office of bishop, presbyter, and deacon are the letters of Ignatius of Antioch and Polycarp of Smyrna at the turn of the first century. In the second century ministerial structures tended to be very fluid. However, in the tradition that comes down to us in the early third century from the *Apostolic Tradition* (ca. 215) a deacon is ordained to serve the bishop, is not ordained to the priesthood, and does not share in the counsel of the presbyterate.[6] Nathan Mitchell points out, however, that this was not universal, for Optatus of Miletus (ca. 370) considered deacons the third rank of priesthood.[7] Fourth-century conciliar prohibitions against deacons exercising priestly functions like celebrating the Eucharist are another indication that this position was held by others.[8]

Diaconal ministry included charitable works, liturgical ministry, and evangelical tasks such as proclaiming the gospel and teaching the catechumens. In the early Roman church, deacons, as assistants of the bishop, exercised authority over the other ministers, presided at the distribution of alms and the care of the hungry and homeless, were responsible for financial matters, educating the young clergy and presenting them, attesting to their worthiness, at their ordination.

Evidence regarding the sacramental ministry of deacons is varied. Paul Bradshaw reports that with respect to baptism Tertullian distinguished between presbyters and deacons, who could baptize with the bishop's authorization, and lay men, who could do so in cases of necessity. He notes, however, that only bishops and presbyters were the normal ministers of baptism in later practice.[9] The *Apostolic Constitutions* (late fourth century) prohibits deacons from administering baptism.[10] Although there were no later instances of this practice, Cyprian was willing for a deacon to reconcile penitents if no presbyter were available.[11] The issue here, however, is not so much the regular ministry of deacons as it is the extent of the delegation of episcopal functions. Bradshaw concludes that in the fourth century, when presbyters were deputized for this by bishops on a more regular basis, "they came to be thought of as possessing certain inherent liturgical functions, which were consequently to be denied to the diaconate and the laity, in other words that such powers were treated as theirs by right and not merely by concession."[12]

The deacon's role in the liturgical assembly was a natural extension of his role in the church and his close association with the gifts of the people. Although he did not preside at the eucharistic celebration, he walked in liturgical procession, was seated next to the bishop, carried the gifts to the altar, read the gospel, distributed the Eucharist, and carried viaticum to the sick. Scholars dispute whether deacons preached in the early Church.[13] Certainly the bishop preached at liturgical assemblies when he was present.[14] Deacons assisted with the preparation of candidates for the baptismal rites, performed some of the more private services such as the anointing of the body during the initiation rites, and often continued a mentoring relationship with the newly baptized.

Deacons became a very powerful group in the church during the first three centuries. According to the *Didascalia Apostolorum,* a third-century Syrian or Palestinian work, the deacon is the bishop's "hearing . . . and his mouth and his heart and his soul." The archdeacon was the closest collaborator of the Bishop of Rome.[15] Rome maintained the practice of appointing seven deacons. Pope Fabian, in the middle of the third century, further increased the diaconal power by placing each of these deacons in charge of the administration of two of the fourteen regions of Rome. In the second and third centuries it was not unusual for the senior deacon, who functioned as the executive assistant to the bishop, to be elected to succeed the bishop.[16]

The development of the diaconate was particularly dependent upon the shifting relationship between presbyters and bishops. Deacons had a more defined function when presbyters constituted a council for the bishop. Deacons had been powerful assistants of the bishops. When the presbyter developed as an individual apart from the corporate presbyterate, becoming more "sacerdotalized," assuming episcopal functions, such as presiding at the Eucharist, there was a shift in power. Then presbyters thought that deacons should assist them as they had assisted the bishops and be subject to them. Service at table came to be considered inferior to the power to make the Body and Blood of Christ present, and a person's role in the Eucharist determined one's role in the Church.[17] The decision of the Council of Nicaea (325) to limit the powers of deacons because of their attempts to usurp the position of the presbyters contributed to the decline of the diaconate in the West.[18] Beginning in the sixth century, Benedictine monasteries contributed to the decline by assuming diaconal service through their charitable work and hospitality. A negative aspect of this was the loss of connection between this monastic charity and the local bishop and the association with the Eucharist it had had since the house churches in the New Testament.[19]

In the pre-Nicene Church the diaconate was generally considered to be a permanent vocation. Although it was possible for deacons to become presbyters, this was not common practice.[20] By the tenth century, however, the diaconate was a preliminary step to the priesthood almost everywhere in the West. The United States Catholic Conference eloquently sums up the change which occurred in the diaconate from the fourth to the twelfth century:

> Once a minister of charity, now a mere "waiter at tables"; once a minister of worship, now a ceremonial appendage. While the deacon still retained some function within the ministry of the word, this too would disappear. And all because the deacon was not a presider of the Eucharist. The deacon was no more than a "secretary at the altar," as Peter Cantor declared.[21]

The vision of the diaconate as a separate order witnessing to the centrality of charity, the ministries of word and worship flowing from that service of charity, disappeared in the Middle Ages only to reappear in *Lumen gentium* and *Sacrum diaconatus ordinem.*

Vatican II taught that although a deacon is not ordained into the priesthood, the diaconate is one of the degrees of the sacrament of order.[22] After the lapse of a millennium, it restored the diaconate as a permanent ministry in the Church, but left to local episcopal conferences the decision whether and where to appoint permanent deacons.[23] Paul

VI established canonical norms for the permanent diaconate in his apostolic letter *Sacrum diaconatus ordinem* (June 18, 1967). He promulgated a revision of the rite of ordination in 1968,[24] and then in 1972 established norms for the diaconate, addressing the admission and training of deacons, and the requirement of celibacy for unmarried deacons.[25]

In the United States, the National Conference of Catholic Bishops requested the permission to restore the permanent diaconate on May 2, 1968. By August 30, 1968, permission for this had been granted and a Bishops' Committee on the Permanent Diaconate was established.[26] Implementation of the permanent diaconate is at the discretion of the local diocese. In the United States, as elsewhere, some dioceses have them and others do not.

In the United States, the National Conference of Catholic Bishops gave the following reasons for their request for permission to restore the permanent diaconate:

- To enrich and strengthen the many and various diaconal ministries at work in this country with the sacramental grace of the diaconate;

- To enlist a new group of devout and competent men in the active ministry of the Church;

- To aid in extending needed liturgical and charitable services to the faithful in both large urban and small rural communities;

- To provide an impetus and source for creative adaptation of diaconal ministries to the rapidly changing needs of our society.[27]

Vatican II also opened the possibility to confer the diaconal order upon married men, provided they be of more mature age. Married men may be ordained to the permanent diaconate at age 35, and they must obtain the consent of their wife. Unmarried men may be ordained at age 25, but they must remain celibate. This means that the diaconate is not to be considered as only a step toward the priesthood, but has its own sacramental character and grace so that those who are called to it can permanently serve the Church in this way.[28]

When the permanent diaconate was first restored, a deacon could not remarry upon the death of his wife. However the Congregation for Divine Worship and Discipline of the Sacraments issued a circular letter June 6, 1997, to diocesan bishops and heads of men's religious orders informing them that John Paul II had stipulated that any one of the three following conditions taken singly are sufficient for a favorable consideration of the dispensation from the impediment for remarriage: (1) the great and proven usefulness of the ministry of the deacon to the diocese to which he belongs; (2) that he has children of such tender age as to be in the need of motherly care; and (3) that he has parents or parents-in-law who are elderly and in need of care.[29]

According to the statistics dated January 1998, there are approximately 24,063 deacons serving in 129 countries.[30] The diaconate exists in about 1,100 of 2,800 dioceses worldwide. A comparison of geographical regions reveals a highly unequal distribution: Africa, 331 deacons in 25 countries; the Americas, 16,022 deacons in 35 countries, 11,837 of these in the U.S.A.; Asia, 142 deacons in 22 countries; Australia and Oceania, 160 deacons in 14 countries; Europe, 7,408 deacons in 34 countries with 1,250 in France, 2,100 in Germany, and 1,900 in Italy, but only 32 in Poland.

In the United States approximately 80 percent of deacons are Caucasian, 14 percent are Hispanic, 3 percent are African American, and 2 percent are Asian or of other ethnicity. Fifty percent of deacons have a graduate or postgraduate degree, but a third have only a high-school or some other education other than college.[31] More than one-third of all deacons are spending 50 percent or more of their time in community and peace and justice ministries. Twenty-eight percent of deacons spend 50 percent or more of their time in sacramental and liturgical ministry. Deacons serve as administrators in 122 of the 2,161 parishes in the U.S.A. without a resident pastor. A very small percentage of deacons receive compensation for their ministry: 3.4 percent are salaried as deacons in full-time ministry; 1.6 percent are salaried in part-time ministry; and 5.6 percent are unpaid in parishes or institutions where they work 30 or more hours per week. In 1996 there were 2,248 candidates for the diaconate enrolled in 108 dioceses in the United States, representing an 11 percent increase over the previous year.

The Revised Rites

The revision of the rite of ordination to the diaconate was unique in that the revision preceded the actual experience of the permanent diaconate in the Church. Therefore, it does not reflect a tradition of lived experience of the diaconate as a permanent order within the Church, but rather anticipates it.

The present rite of ordination for deacons is parallel in structure to that of bishops and presbyters in order to emphasize the unity of the three degrees of ordination. The 1990 rite reflects the experience of the permanent diaconate by indicating options within the suggested homily for ordinations of either married or unmarried candidates. The promise of celibacy is integrated into the other promises of the elect rather than standing alone at the end of the homily as in the 1968 rite. The 1990 rite, unlike previous rites, includes a promise of obedience and respect to both the diocesan bishop and the legitimate religious superior by those elect belonging to a religious community.

The outline of the 1990 rite is as follows:

Outline of the Rite

Introductory Rites
Liturgy of the Word
Liturgy of Ordination
    Election
        Calling of the Candidates
        Presentation of the Candidates
        Election by the Bishop and Assent of the People
    Homily
    Promises
        Promises of the Elect
        Promise of Obedience
    Litany of Supplication
        Invitation to Prayer
        Litany
        Concluding Prayer
    Laying on of Hands and Prayer of Ordination
    Explanatory Rites
        Investiture with Stole and Dalmatic
        Presentation of the Book of the Gospels
        Kiss of Peace

Liturgy of the Eucharist

Concluding Rite

Solemn Blessing

Introduction to the Rite for the Ordination of Deacons

Parallel in structure with the introductions to the other two rites, the introduction is divided into four sections: the importance of the ordination, the duties and ministries of the participants in the ordination, instructions for the celebration of the ordination, and the requisites for the celebration.

The first section traces the diaconate to primitive apostolic times and lists the duties of the deacons: "administer baptism solemnly; care for the Eucharist and give holy Communion; assist at and bless marriages in the name of the Church; bring viaticum to the dying; read the Sacred Scriptures to the faithful and instruct and exhort the people; preside over worship and the prayer of the faithful; administer sacramentals; and officiate at funeral and burial rites."[32] Even though deacons engage in a threefold service: the liturgy, the gospel, and works of charity, the diaconal duties listed in the introduction focus more on liturgical functions than on the other two services. Service of the word is broader than proclaiming the gospel at liturgical services, but can include catechetical instruction and other teaching. *Lumen gentium* 29 also mentions administrative service as a diaconal function.

Liturgy of Ordination

Election

A deacon calls the names of those to be ordained and asks them to come forward. Each answers "present" and makes a sign of reverence before the bishop. A presbyter designated by the bishop, usually someone who has been associated in some way with the formation of the candidates, presents them to the bishop on behalf of the local church. The bishop asks whether they are judged to be worthy. The presbyter testifies to their worthiness and to the inquiry made among the Christian people and the recommendation of those concerned with their formation. The bishop then chooses the candidates and all present say "Thanks be to God" or give their assent in some other way.[33] Applause is a common response in the United States. Many dioceses in the United States observe the custom of seeking some visible form of consent or assent from the wives of married candidates at this point.[34]

Homily

The bishop first instructs the assembly on the ministerial duties of the deacons as ministers of the word, of the altar, and of charity. His homily emphasizes the service of deacons and connects the charity they perform to their service at the altar.

The bishop then addresses the elect, exhorting them to imitate the Christ whom they serve, to serve in love and joy and avoid all unchastity and avarice. If unmarried elect are to be ordained, an instruction on celibacy follows, reminding the elect that celibacy is a sign and a motive of pastoral charity and a source of spiritual fruitfulness in the world. It will enable the elect to devote themselves joyfully to the unhindered service of God and neighbor in the ministry of Christian conversion and rebirth. All the elect are exhorted to be people of faith and hope and above every suspicion of blame so that their actions will express what they proclaim by word of mouth.

Promises of the Elect

The elect makes the following promises to undertake the diaconal ministry in the service of the liturgy, of the gospel, and of works of charity:

1. He states his intention to be ordained to this office.

2. He states his resolve to discharge the office of the diaconate with humility and love in order to assist the priestly Order and to benefit the Christian people.[35]

3. He states his resolve to hold the mystery of faith with a clear conscience and to proclaim this faith in word and action according to the gospel and the Church's tradition.

4. If the elect is unmarried, he promises to remain celibate as a sign of dedication to Christ in serving God and humankind for the sake of the kingdom.

5. The candidate promises to maintain and deepen a spirit of prayer appropriate to his way of life and to celebrate the Liturgy of the Hours for the People of God and the whole world according to what is required of him.

   This promise makes provisions for differing requirements for celibate and married deacons. Celibate deacons are bound to the Liturgy of the Hours and married deacons are subject to whatever requirements are determined by the episcopal conference.[36]

6. He promises to shape his way of life always according to the example of Christ, of whose Body and Blood he is a minister.

Notably missing from this list is a promise regarding the works of charity, identified as a distinguishing mark of the diaconal order in *Lumen gentium* 29.[37]

Paul VI, in his *motu proprio, Ad pascendum* (August 15, 1972), decreed that the public commitment to celibacy before God and the Church is to be celebrated, even by religious, in a special rite which is to precede ordination to the diaconate. Furthermore, he decreed that a married deacon who has lost his wife cannot enter a new marriage, although John Paul II relaxed this in 1997.[38] The decree of promulgation for the 1990 rite explains that this rite of commitment to celibacy conforms both to this prescription and to John Paul II's express mandate. It also fulfills the prescriptions of canon 1037 which requires unmarried candidates for the permanent diaconate to assume publicly before God and the Church the obligation of celibacy.

The editor of the February 1990 issue of *Notitiae,* the journal of the Congregation for Divine Worship and the Discipline of the Sacraments, apparently presuming that those candidates for the diaconate who promise celibacy are destined for the presbyterate, explains that the requirement of making the promise of celibacy also by those who have already taken religious vows or who have a similar juridical responsibility makes the bond between celibacy and presbyteral ordination more evident to the gathered assembly: "The revised rite shows that ecclesiastical celibacy is not only a personal question of a spiritual relationship between the Christian and God, but that, in the case of sacred ministers, besides being an eschatological sign it is also an ecclesiological sign. The presbyter is impelled to a love of a total dedication of his whole person to the Church, of which he is minister and pastor, in communion with and in imitation of the spousal love of Christ."[39] In other words, there is a symbolic difference between the celibacy professed by a religious and that professed by an ordained minister, the first being a sign of the eschaton, the second being a sign of single-minded dedication to the Church. The two, however, are really not that distinct since *Perfectae caritatis,* the Decree on the Up-To-Date Renewal of Religious Life, describes chastity "for the sake of the kingdom of heaven" as a demonstration of "that astonishing alliance, initiated by God himself, to be completed in the world to come, when the church has Christ alone for consort."[40] Both entail nuptial imagery between Christ and the Church.

Michael Joncas points out that in comparison to the 1968 rite the promise of celibacy heightens the distinction between married and celibate deacons.[41] He asks whether married candidates should profess publicly their commitment to Christ, his kingdom, and the service of God in the modality of the sacrament of marriage if celibate candidates are asked to do so in the modality of celibate living.

The requirement that vowed religious repeat a promise of celibacy in response to John Paul II's mandate represents a change from the exemption in canon 1037 of the 1983 Code of Canon Law. Kevin Seasoltz suggests that "the bishop's questioning of the religious candidate for the diaconate regarding his commitment to celibacy is both embarrassing and awkward because it gives the clear impression that the previous profession of chastity has not been taken seriously."[42] In his opinion, when bishops try to contextualize this promise in terms of a prior profession of chastity, the new commitment appears to be redundant.

Promise of Obedience

The elect promises respect and obedience to the diocesan bishop and, in the case of a member of a religious community, to both the diocesan bishop and his legitimate superiors. The promise of obedience directly relates to the purpose of diaconal ordination, which is "to serve the bishop."[43] Ordination to the diaconate effects both entrance into the clerical state and incardination into a diocese which brings with it an obligation to the local bishop.[44] The promise of obedience on the part of those deacons who belong to a religious community implements the principle enunciated in *Christus Dominus* 35, 1, the Decree on the Pastoral Office of Bishops in the Church: "Religious should at all times treat the bishops, as the successors of the apostles, with loyal respect and reverence. Moreover, whenever legitimately called upon to do apostolic work, they must carry out these duties in such a way as to be the auxiliaries of the bishop and subject to him." This same section of the document balances this obligation with the requirement to take into consideration the special character of each religious institute and the obligation of individual religious to obey their religious superiors.

The liturgical issue concerning the appropriateness of the feudal gesture of placing joined hands in the hands of the bishop, pending a change initiated by the national episcopal conference, is essentially the same as in the rite for the ordination of presbyters.

Litany of Supplication

The litany of supplication is very similar to the one used for the ordination of presbyters, with the addition of an example of fourth-century permanent deacon, Saint Ephrem the Syrian (d. 373). Theologian, exegete, and Doctor of the Church, Ephrem was ordained a deacon but apparently never became a priest. He managed to escape episcopal consecration by feigning madness.[45]

The character of the concluding prayer of the litany differs from those used for the ordination of bishops and presbyters. Instead of summing up the prayer of the people, as is customary in collects, it reflects the preoccupations of the ordaining bishop, asking for help in this act of the bishop's ministry.[46]

Laying on of Hands

Only the ordaining bishop lays hands on the candidates for the diaconate since a deacon is not ordained into the priesthood. After the laying on of hands, the ordaining bishop sings or prays the prayer of ordination.

Prayer of Ordination

1 Be with us, we pray, almighty God;
2 you bestow every grace,
3 you apportion every order and assign every office.

4 You remain unchanged but make all things new;
5 in your eternal providence you watch over all creation
6 and make due provision for every age
7 through the one who is your word, your power, and wisdom,
8 Jesus Christ, your Son, our Lord.

9 You enable your Church, Christ's body,
10 to grow to full stature as a new temple,
11 adorned with every kind of heavenly grace,
12 united in the diversity of its members,
13 and formed into a wonderful pattern of unity by the Holy Spirit.

14 As once you chose the sons of Levi
15 to minister in the former tabernacle,
16 so by gifts of grace
17 you established the threefold rank of ministers
18 to serve your name.

19 And so, in the first days of your Church,
20 through the inspiration of the Holy Spirit
21 your Son's Apostles appointed seven men of good repute
22 to assist them in the daily ministry,
23 that they might devote themselves more fully
24 to prayer and preaching of the word.
25 By prayer and the laying on of hands
26 they entrusted to these chosen men the ministry of serving at table.

27 We ask you, Lord:
28 look with favor on these servants of yours
29 who will minister at your holy altar
30 and whom we now humbly dedicate to the office of deacon.

[Paul VI decreed that the following words constitute the form of the sacrament and are required for validity:]

31 Lord, we beg you:
32 send forth upon them the Holy Spirit,
33 that they may be strengthened
34 by the gift of your sevenfold grace
35 to carry out faithfully the work of the ministry.

36 May they excel in every virtue of the Gospel:
37 in love that is sincere,
38 in concern for the sick and poor,
39 in unassuming authority,
40 in the observance of spiritual discipline,
41 and in purity of heart.

42 May your commandments shine forth in their conduct
43 so that by the example of their way of life
44 they may become a model for your holy people.
45 May they remain strong and steadfast in Christ,
46 offering the witness of a clear conscience.
47 Your Son came not to be served but to serve:
48 may they imitate him in this life
49 and so be found worthy to reign with him in heaven.

50 We ask this through our Lord Jesus Christ, your Son,
51 who lives and reigns with you in the unity of the Holy Spirit,
52 God for ever and ever.

     All answer:
53 Amen.

The prayer is essentially the ancient consecratory prayer of the Sacramentary of Verona (fifth or sixth century). The reference to the seven men of good repute was added to the 1968 text in order to balance the reference to the sons of Levi so that the service of charity is in tandem with service at the altar.[47] It is structured according to an invocation (ll. 1–13),[48] anamnesis (ll. 14–26), epiclesis (ll. 27–35), prayer of invocation for the newly ordained (ll. 36–49), and concluding doxology (ll. 50–53).

The invocation is trinitarian in structure. It first calls on God as the source of every gift who assigns everyone their rank and ministry. The reference is to God the creator who provides what is needed for every age. This is accomplished through the word, power, and wisdom who is Jesus Christ, God's Son, our Lord. Christ's body is the Church. The Church, characterized by a diversity of members, is formed into a unity by the Holy Spirit.

The anamnesis situates the diaconate within a threefold ministry and presents a typology of diaconal service in recalling the sons of Levi, an allusion to the sacral service of the diaconate, who ministered in the former tabernacle in the Old Testament. The seven men of good repute who assisted the apostles in the New Testament constitute a second typology for the diaconate and represent the charitable service of the diaconate. The diaconal ministry is identified as "daily," suggesting a regular rather than occasional ministry. This may be a significant criterion as the Church discerns who it should ordain to the diaconate as the office continues to develop in the life of the Church. It is also a ministry identified as "serving at table," underscoring the service character of this ministry.

Service at table, however, is transposed to ministry "at your holy altar" in the epicletic section which immediately follows. The service of charity and service at the altar are intrinsically connected because "what the church does at the altar and in the celebration of its rites and sacraments summarizes, and at the same time initiates its mission in the world."[49] A deacon's service in the world finds expression in his liturgical ministry, and, conversely, his liturgical ministry sends him back into the world to enact in charity that service he has sacramentally ritualized at the altar. The link between charity and liturgical service appears here by the simple juxtaposition of "table" and "altar" rather than by more direct explanation.

The Spirit invoked is the Spirit who strengthens by the gift of sevenfold grace. The expression "sevenfold grace" signifies a multiple and abundant grace and is a reference to the list of the gifts of the Spirit in Isaiah 11:1-2 which were given to Christ for the accomplishment of his messianic work: wisdom, understanding, counsel, fortitude, knowledge, piety, and fear of the Lord.[50] In each of the ordination rites, the Spirit invoked in this section of the ordination prayer specifies the grace and primary work of that particular office.

The intercessory prayers which follow the epiclesis list yet another set of virtues which should characterize the deacons: sincere love, concern for the sick and the poor, unassuming authority, self-discipline, and holiness of life. They are to model the commandments, be steadfast and of pure conscience. Finally, Christ the Servant is the model for diaconal ministry in the ordination prayer. Deacons imitate Christ the Servant and by their example are to lead people to imitate their lives.

The prayer of ordination for deacons spells out the holiness of life expected of them in much more detail than do the ordination prayers for presbyters or bishops, both of which focus more on the specific tasks of ministry. This indicates that people minister more by who they are than by what they do, also indicating that diaconal ministry is more about presence than task, about who a deacon is than what he does. This is reflected in the 1984 revised guidelines of the NCCB for the formation and ministry of deacons which emphasize that the essence of diaconal ministry is not *what* a deacon does in terms of sacral functions, but *who* he is as an embodiment of what all believers are called to pursue in a life dedicated to serving others in the manner of Jesus Christ.[51] However, the absence of mention of specific tasks of ministry may also be a sign that the rite developed prior to significant experience of the diaconate in the life of the Church or an indication that diaconal ministry is not as easily specified as presbyteral or episcopal ministry.

The major changes in the 1990 prayer of ordination are indicated in the following table:[52]

1968 Prayer of Consecration	*1990 Prayer of Ordination*
"Almighty God, giver of honors, distributor of orders, and apportioner of offices"	"you bestow every grace, you apportion every order and assign every office." This eliminates reference to honor with its corresponding interpretation of office as status elevation.[53]

1968 Prayer of Consecration (cont.)	*1990 Prayer of Ordination* (cont.)
"You enrich it with every kind of grace and perfect it with a diversity of members to serve the whole body in a wonderful pattern of unity." This translation, however, fails to translate the fact that this unity is ascribed to "the law": "Cuius corpus, Ecclesiam tuam, caelestium gratiarum varietate distinctam suorumque conexam distictione membrorum, *per legem totius mirabilem compagis unitam. . . .*" (emphasis added)	"You enable your Church, Christ's body, to grow to full stature as a new temple, adorned with every kind of heavenly grace, united in the diversity of its members and formed into a wonderful pattern of unity by the Holy Spirit." Here the unity of the Church is ascribed to the Holy Spirit.
"You established a threefold ministry of worship and service for the glory of your name. As ministers of your tabernacle you chose the sons of Levi and gave them your blessing as their everlasting inheritance." This translation eliminates the military language in the Latin original: "nomini tuo militare constituens": "performing as a soldier."	"As once you chose the sons of Levi to minister in the former tabernacle, so by gifts of grace you established the threefold rank of ministers to serve your name." (nomini tuo servire constituens) This form eliminates the military references as well as mention of the reward promised to the sons of Levi. The emphasis is clearly on service.
"May his conduct exemplify your commands and lead your people to imitate his purity of life." ("In moribus eorum praecepta tua fulgeant, ut suae castitatis exemplo imitationem sanctae plebis acquirant. . . .") The literal Latin text prayed that deacons might lead God's people to holiness through the example of their "chastity."	"May your commandments shine forth in their conduct so that by the example of their way of life they may become a model for your holy people." ("In moribus eius praecepta tua fulgeant, ut suae conversationis exemplo imitationem sanctae plebis acquirant. . . .") The literal Latin text prays that deacons might lead God's people to holiness through the example of their conversion of life. The change from "by the example of his chastity" to "by the example of his conversion of life" adapts the prayer of ordination to the ordination of married deacons at the same time that it broadens the concept of virtue that must characterize a deacon's life.

The changes emphasize diaconal service and de-emphasize ordination as a bestowal of an honor.

Explanatory Rites

Investiture with Stole and Dalmatic

Some of the assisting deacons or other ministers put a deacon's stole and dalmatic on each deacon. The stole is the major indispensable sign of ordination and is worn for all liturgical services. Deacons wear it across their chest from left shoulder to right hip, a custom dating from the seventh century as directed by the Council of Toledo (ca. 633). The council gives this explanation: "The right side of the body he must have free, in order that he may without hindrance, do his service."[54]

The dalmatic is a tunic in the color of the liturgical season worn as the liturgical outer garment of deacons for all Sunday and feast day liturgical celebrations. Its history bears witness to the prestige of deacons in the early Church and to the close relationship between the papal deacons and the Bishop of Rome. Constantine granted the honor of wearing the dalmatic, a sign of authority of the fourth-century magistrates, to major Christian bishops. The dalmatic was a privilege usually reserved to the pope who wore it under the chasuble. Pope Sylvester (314–35) conferred the dalmatic on papal deacons. Three centuries later Pope Gregory the Great usually reserved it to himself and his deacons, although he sometimes bestowed it on other archbishops. It was required for all bishops and deacons in the eleventh century. Today only deacons wear it as an outer garment.[55]

No prayer formula accompanies the vesting, but Psalm 84 or another appropriate song of the same kind may be sung.

Presentation of the Book of the Gospels

Service to the gospel represents one of the three services to which a deacon is ordained, the other two being service in the liturgy and service in charity. In the tenth century the presentation of the Book of the Gospels signified that the deacon was a minister of the liturgical proclamation of the gospel.[56] Writing at a time when the diaconate was transitional and almost exclusively liturgical, St. Thomas Aquinas refers to the proclamation of the gospel as the highest task of the deacon.[57] According to the present rite, the presentation of the Book of the Gospels "symbolizes the duty of the deacon to proclaim the gospel reading in liturgical celebrations and to preach the faith of the Church in word and in deed."[58] He is instructed:

> Receive the Gospel of Christ, whose herald you have become.
> Believe what you read,
> teach what you believe,
> and practice what you teach.[59]

In addition to the proclamation of the gospel, the deacon's ministry of the word includes a ministry of exhortation, instruction, catechesis, and sometimes preaching.[60] Since a deacon also preaches the gospel in deeds, his works of charity are another form of proclaiming and embodying the gospel message.

The Roman Catholic Church in the United States currently authorizes deacons to preach when presiding at the baptism of infants and some of the adult rites of Christian initiation, matrimony, benediction of the Blessed Sacrament, a wake or Christian burial service apart from the Eucharist or in a cemetery, morning or evening prayer or other rites of the Liturgy of the Hours, and the visitation of the sick.[61] However, the function of preaching here corresponds with the function of presiding. In a Eucharistic Liturgy, the homilist should ordinarily be the presiding bishop or presbyter. James Monroe Barnett argues rather convincingly that preaching was not a diaconal function in the early Church and that it should not be today.[62] He sees this as a presbyteral function requiring a specialized theological education not appropriate for all deacons. Although he suggests providing deacons with homilies prepared by people properly trained in theology and homiletics, this does not really solve the issue. Those who preside at the occasions listed above should be theologically astute enough to interpret the texts and rituals for the faith community.

Kiss of Peace

The bishop gives each of the newly ordained the kiss of peace, sealing the deacons' admittance into their ministry. Then all or some of the deacons present give them the kiss of peace, indicating their reception of the new deacons into their shared ministry. This parallels the rites for bishops and presbyters even though *Lumen gentium* says nothing concerning a diaconal college analogous to the presbyteral college *(presbyterium)*[63] or the episcopal college.[64]

Conclusion

The rite of ordination to the diaconate certainly highlights the service which is characteristic of this order and which brings to visibility the service which is characteristic of the nature of the Church. This is evident in the suggested homily, in the prayer of ordination, and the symbolism within the diaconal manner of wearing the stole. As noted, however, it does not precisely specify the forms this service may assume within the Church other than naming a threefold ministry to the liturgy, the gospel, and works of charity, thus allowing a flexibility to the exercise and development of this order in the life of the Church.

Prior to the revision of this rite, the experience of the Church was that of transitional and celibate deacons. The present rite still continues to reflect this experience with its emphasis on celibacy for those who are making that promise and its failure to contextualize the rite according to the experience and responsibilities of married candidates. It is possible that future revisions of the rite may become necessary as the Church gains experience with the permanent diaconate.

Notes, Chapter Six

[1] For a history of the diaconate see Jean Colson, *La Fonction diaconale aux origines de l'Eglise* (Brugge: Desclée de Brouwer, 1960); Jean Colson, "Diakon und Bischof in den ersten drei Jahrhunderten der Kirche," 23–31; and Walter Croce, "Aus der Geschichte des Diakonates," 92–128, in *Diaconia in Christo*, eds. Karl Rahner and Herbert Vorgrimler (Freiberg: Herder, 1962). Some of these essays with others are in P. Winninger and Y. Congar, eds., *Le Diacre dans l'Eglise et le monde d'aujourd'hui*, Unam Sanctam 59 (Paris: Cerf, 1966). Histories in English include Edward P. Echlin, *The Deacon in the Church* (New York: Alba House, 1971); James Monroe Barnett, *The Diaconate: A Full and Equal Order*, rev. ed. (Valley Forge, Pa.: Trinity Press International, 1995); Joseph W. Pokusa, "The Diaconate: A History of Law Following Practice," *The Jurist* 45 (1985) 95–135.

[2] See Edward P. Echlin, *The Deacon in the Church* (New York: Alba House, 1971) 3–25. Joseph Lécuyer, however, thinks the text represents the institution of the first Hellenistic deacons in "Les diacres dans le Nouveau Testament," in *Le Diacre dans l'Eglise et le monde d'aujourd'hui*, eds. P. Winninger and Y. Congar (Paris: Cerf, 1966) 15–26. James Monroe Barnett gives a complete discussion concluding that the Seven were not deacons in *The Diaconate: A Full and Equal Order* (Valley Forge, Pa.: Trinity Press International, 1995 revised) 28–42. Gottfried Hammann considers the use of the term "deacon" to describe the seven Hellenists anachronistic in *L'amour retrouvé: Le ministère de diacre, du christianisme primitif aux Réformateurs protestants du XVIe siècle* (Paris: Cerf, 1994) 23.

[3] See Nathan Mitchell, *Mission and Ministry: History and Theology in the Sacrament of Order* (Collegeville: The Liturgical Press, 1982) 158–67, and Kenan B.

Osborne, O.F.M., *Priesthood: A History of The Ordained Ministry in the Roman Catholic Church* (New York: Paulist, 1988) 70–81.

⁴ Kenan B. Osborne, O.F.M., *Priesthood: A History of The Ordained Ministry in the Roman Catholic Church*, 72; also Nathan Mitchell, *Mission and Ministry: History and Theology in the Sacrament of Order* (Collegeville: The Liturgical Press, 1982) 158–67.

⁵ Hammann, 24.

⁶ *Apostolic Tradition*, 3.

⁷ Nathan Mitchell, *Mission and Ministry: History and Theology in the Sacrament of Order*, Message of the Sacraments 6 (Collegeville: The Liturgical Press, 1982) 206.

⁸ See Council of Arles, canon 15; Council of Nicaea, canon 18. Texts in Hermann T. Bruns, ed., *Canones Apostolorum et Conciliorum Seaculorum IV–VII* (2 vols; Bibliotheca Ecclesiastica; Berlin: G. Reimeri, 1839; repr., Turin: Bottega d'Erasmo, 1959), II, p. 109 (Arles); I, p. 19 (Nicaea). Cited by Mitchell, 206.

⁹ Paul Bradshaw, *Liturgical Presidency in the Early Church*, Grove Liturgical Study No. 36 (Bramcote: Grove Books, 1983) 26–27.

¹⁰ *Apostolic Constitutions*, 3.11, 20; 8.28, 46.

¹¹ Cyprian, *Ep.* 18.1. Cited by Bradshaw, 27.

¹² Bradshaw, 27.

¹³ See the discussion in James Monroe Barnett, *The Diaconate: A Full and Equal Order*, rev. ed. (Valley Forge, Pa.: Trinity Press International, 1995) 80–83.

¹⁴ Paul Bradshaw comments that "Justin Martyr's description of the Sunday Eucharist, where it is the president who 'in a discourse admonishes and exhorts,' has usually been interpreted as implying that by the middle of the second century only a bishop might deliver the homily at a liturgical assembly, and the Jewish (and early Christian) practice of inviting others to give an exposition of the Scriptures had already disappeared. This development, however, does not seem to have been quite as rapid and as straightforward as that in every place, and may not even have been so at Rome." Preaching eventually became restricted to bishops in the West, but Bradshaw cites evidence for presbyteral preaching in the East. Bradshaw's discussion concerns the presence or absence of lay preaching. Deacons are not mentioned. *Liturgical Presidency in the Early Church*, 16–20.

¹⁵ James F. Puglisi, *The Process of Admission to Ordained Ministry: A Comparative Study*, Vol. 1: Epistemological Principles and Roman Catholic Rites, trans. Michael S. Driscoll and Mary Misrahi (Collegeville: The Liturgical Press, 1996) 153.

¹⁶ James Monroe Barnett, *The Diaconate: A Full and Equal Order*, rev. ed. (Valley Forge, Pa.: Trinity Press International, 1995) 66–67.

¹⁷ See St. Jerome, "To Evangelus," in *The Principal Words of St. Jerome* (New York, 1893) 288–89, cited in United States Catholic Conference, *Study Text VI: The Deacon, Minister of Word and Sacrament* (Washington, D.C.: United States Catholic Conference, 1979) 19–20.

¹⁸ Council of Nicaea, canon 18.

¹⁹ Claude Bridel, *Aux seuils de l'espérance: Le diaconat en notre temps* (Paris: Delachaux et Niestlé, 1971) 29, 30–31.

²⁰ James Monroe Barnett, *The Diaconate: A Full and Equal Order*, 83.

²¹ United States Catholic Conference, *Study Text VI: The Deacon, Minister of Word and Sacrament* (Washington, D.C.: United States Catholic Conference, 1979) 20.

²² *Lumen gentium* 29.

²³ *Lumen gentium* 29; *Ad gentes* 16.

²⁴ Paul VI, apostolic constitution, *Pontificalis romani recognitio,* June 17, 1968.

²⁵ Paul VI, *motu proprio, Ad pascendum,* August 15, 1972.

²⁶ For a history of the restoration of the permanent diaconate in the United States see Richard L. Rashke, *The Deacon in Search of Identity* (New York: Paulist Press, 1975).

²⁷ NCCB Bishops' Committee on the Permanent Diaconate, *Permanent Deacons in the United States: Guidelines on Their Formation and Ministry,* rev. ed. (Washington, D.C.: United States Catholic Conference, 1984) 1–2.

²⁸ Paul VI, apostolic letter issued *motu proprio,* "General Norms for Restoring the Permanent Diaconate in the Latin Church" (Sacrum Diaconatus Ordinem) June 18, 1967.

²⁹ *Origins* 27 (11) (August 28, 1997) 171.

³⁰ The statistics in this section are from the Secretariat for the Diaconate, National Conference of Catholic Bishops/United States Catholic Conference, http://www.nccbuscc.org/deacon, 1/25/99.

³¹ At the time of writing this book, the most recent statistics for the United States were as of December 21, 1996. Secretariat for the Diaconate, National Conference of Catholic Bishops/United States Catholic Conference, http://www.nccbuscc.org/deacon, 1/25/99.

³² *De Ordinatione Episcopi, Presbyterorum et Diaconorum,* 174, citing *Lumen gentium* 29.

³³ General Introduction, 11. Note, however, that appointment to diaconal ministry by the laying on of hands was present in apostolic times. The "order" of deacon was a later development.

³⁴ United States Catholic Conference, *Study Text VI: The Deacon, Minister of Word and Sacrament* (Washington, D.C.: United States Catholic Conference, 1979) 31.

³⁵ In the *Apostolic Tradition* deacons were ordained for the service of the bishop. The Latin text of this promise is "Ordinis sacerdotalis." Here "priestly order" should be interpreted as including bishops and presbyters since both belong to a priestly order.

³⁶ Paul VI, "General Norms for Restoring the Permanent Diaconate in the Latin Church," stipulates that "It is a supremely fitting thing that permanent deacons recite every day at least part of the Divine Office, to be determined by the episcopal conferences" (no. 27); reiterated in *Ad pascendum,* Laying Down Norms Regarding the Order of Diaconate, August 15, 1972, DOL 2588.

³⁷ Noted by Jan Michael Joncas, "The Public Language of Ministry Revisited: *De Ordinatione Episcopi, Presbyterorum et Diaconorum* 1990," 395.

³⁸ Paul VI, *Ad pascendum,* August 15, 1972, DOL 2586. For a report of the circular letter from the Congregation for Divine Worship and the Sacraments communicating the new legislation concerning the remarriage of permanent deacons see *Origins* 27 (11) (August 28, 1997) 171.

[39] As reported in "Rites of Ordination and the Synod of Bishops," *Bishops' Committee on the Liturgy Newletter* 26 (June 1990) 23.

[40] *Perfectae caritatis* 12. *Decrees of the Ecumenical Councils. Volume Two: Trent to Vatican II,* ed. Norman P. Tanner, S.J. (Washington, D.C.: Georgetown University Press, 1990).

[41] Jan Michael Joncas, "The Public Language of Ministry Revisited: *De Ordinatione Episcopi, Presbyterorum et Diaconorum* 1990," *Worship* 68 (10) (1994) 395.

[42] Kevin Seasoltz, "Institutes of Consecrated Life and Ordained Ministry: Some Canonical Issues," in *A Concert of Charisms: Ordained Ministry in Religious Life,* ed. Paul K. Hennessy, C.F.C. (New York: Paulist Press, 1997) 154.

[43] Introduction, 179, citing Hippolytus, *Traditio Apostolica,* 8.

[44] Paul VI, *Ad pascendum,* August 15, 1972, DOL 2589, Introduction, 176.

[45] E. des Places, "St. Ephrem the Syrian," *New Catholic Encyclopedia,* vol. 5 (Washington, D.C.: The Catholic University of America, 1967) 463.

[46] Pierre Reinhard, O.F.M., "L'Ordination des diacres," *La Maison-Dieu* 98 (1969) 88.

[47] Antonio Santanoni, "Ordination and Ministry in the West," trans. David Cotter, notes that the Veronese prayer locates the diaconate in the area of liturgy and worship, underplaying the ministry of charity completely.

[48] The division here differs from how the text is divided with spaces on the page. However, the anamnesis begins with the Old Testament reference and continues with the reference to the seven men of good repute. The definite trinitarian structure of the opening stands as a unit.

[49] United States Catholic Conference, *Study Text VI: The Deacon, Minister of Word and Sacrament* (Washington, D.C.: United States Catholic Conference, 1979) 11.

[50] Bruno Kleinheyer, "Le diaconat à la lumière du rituel d'ordination selon le Pontifical Romain," in *Le diacre dans l'Eglise et le monde d'aujourd'hui,* eds. P. Winninger and Y. Congar, Unam Sanctum 59 (Paris: Cerf, 1966) 110. The Isaiah text, however, does not mention "piety," traditionally listed as one of the seven gifts even though the *Catechism of the Catholic Church,* 1831, also cites Isaiah 11:1-2 as the source. Joseph Jenson, *Isaiah 1–39* (Collegeville: The Liturgical Press, 1984) 133, gives this explanation: "The repetition of *fear of the Lord* at the beginning of v. 3 is an insertion by a later editor, but the Greek translation of the Old Testament (the Septuagint) avoided the repetition by translating the first *fear of the Lord* as "reverence" *(eusebeia);* thus it provided seven terms instead of the six (in three pairs) of the Hebrew, and from this derives the list of the traditional seven gifts of the Holy Spirit."

[51] NCCB Committee on the Permanent Diaconate, *Permanent Deacons in the United States: Guidelines on Their Formation and Ministry* (Washington D.C.: USCC Office of Publishing and Promotion Services, 1984) nos. 35–38.

[52] Jan Michael Joncas enumerates these changes in "The Public Language of Ministry Revisited: *De Ordinatione Episcopi, Presbyterorum et Diaconorum* 1990," *Worship* 68 (1) (1994) 397–98.

[53] For a critique of the language of ordination rites with respect to status elevation see Mary Collins, "The Public Language of Ministry," in *Official Ministry in a New Age,* ed. James H. Provost, Permanent Seminary Studies No. 3 (Washing-

ton D.C.: Canon Law Society of America, 1981) 7–40; Jan Michael Joncas, "The Public Language of Ministry Revisited: *De Ordinatione Episcopi, Presbyterorum et Diaconorum* 1990," *Worship* 68 (1) (1994) 386–403. Joncas argues that the elevation language has been much mitigated in the 1990 rite.

⁵⁴ Council of Toledo, canons 28 and 40, in Hefele, *History of the Councils* 4:453, 454. Cited by James Monroe Barnett, *The Diaconate: A Full and Equal Order,* 169.

⁵⁵ John Laurance, s.j., "Liturgical Vestments," *The New Dictionary of Sacramental Worship* (Collegeville: The Liturgical Press, 1990) 1306–07.

⁵⁶ Matthieu Cnudde, "L'Ordination des diacres," La *Maison-Dieu* 98 (1969) 90.

⁵⁷ *Summa contra gentiles* 4:75.

⁵⁸ *De Ordinatione Episcopi, Presbyterorum et diaconorum* 188.

⁵⁹ Ibid., 210.

⁶⁰ Bishops' Committee on the Liturgy, *The Deacon, Minister of Word and Sacrament,* 36.

⁶¹ Ibid., 46.

⁶² James Monroe Barnett, *The Diaconate: A Full and Equal Order,* 80–83, 211–212.

⁶³ *Lumen gentium* 28.

⁶⁴ *Lumen gentium* 19.

Chapter Seven

Questions Concerning the Diaconate

D espite the disappearance of the permanent diaconate until its restoration after Vatican II, the Church has retained an intuition of the necessity of the diaconal office. As we have seen, the rite for the ordination to the diaconate was revised before the Church had significant experience of the permanent diaconate. In many ways it has proceeded experimentally, and many questions remain to be answered. Does the theology of the orders require that a person must be ordained to a "lower" order before ordination to a "higher" order? How is the diaconate distinct from the other orders? What is the distinction between a deacon and a layperson since both may service the Church in similar ways?

1. Need the Church necessarily continue to ordain to the "lower" orders before ordaining to the "higher" orders?

There is but one rite of ordination to the diaconate, but it may be conferred on either transitional deacons or permanent deacons. Transitional deacons are those men who are ordained deacon in the course of their preparation for ordination to the presbyterate. These men must make a promise of celibacy at the time of ordination and can be ordained at a younger age. Canon 1032 stipulates that "men destined for the presbyterate are to be admitted to the order of diaconate only after they have completed the age of twenty-three." An interval of six months is to be observed between the diaconate and the presbyterate.

Permanent deacons are men who will not be ordained to the presbyterate. They may be married, but if married, they must be at least 35 years of age. Unmarried men may be ordained at age 25, but must make a promise of celibacy.

It may be time to rethink the necessity of being ordained to the lower orders before being admitted to the higher orders as well as the imagery of "lower" and "higher." More specifically, it is time to rethink the necessity of the transitional diaconate. Conditioned by our most recent past, we are accustomed to thinking of deacons as a "lesser" rank, the first of three sacramental orders. From a historical perspective, before the diaconate became a stepping stone to the presbyterate, deacons, especially those in Rome, were often more prestigious than presbyters. Orders were distinct offices in the Church, fulfilling distinct roles of service. Although deacons were sometimes ordained to another order, it was quite normal for a deacon to be consecrated bishop without passing though the presbyterate.[1] In our own time, from the perspective of the Second Vatican Council as well as the rites of ordination, the bishop is described as having the "fullness of order" rather than being the "highest order," a significant nuancing of terminology which carries important theological implications.

Historically, at the time of Hippolytus, in the early third century, the presupposition was that the various orders were permanent. A person did not move from one to the other or need to be ordained to a lower office before being ordained to a higher office. The episcopate followed years of service as an ordinary Christian, deacon, or presbyter.

Through the scholarship of Gregory Dix it had been commonly thought that the idea of an ordination to a succession of offices dates from the later fourth century.[2] However, more recent scholarship suggests that the idea of a fixed pattern of sequential ordinations was a development of the high Middle Ages. Louis Weil and Balthasar Fischer challenge the assumption of such scholars as Gregory Dix,[3] F. H. Dudden,[4] and Henry Chadwick[5] that Ambrose of Milan received a series of transitional ordinations during the week between his baptism and his ordination as bishop in 373.[6] According to Ormonde Plate, when Photius was the first man elected as the Patriarch of Constantinople in 858 he was the first bishop who was required to receive a rapid sequence of ordinations.[7] The sequential pattern became normative from the time of the election of Pope Gregory VII in 1073 and was eventually established in canon law. Gradually the diaconate became only a step on the way to priestly ordination, to the point that it was reduced to an almost entirely liturgical function by the ninth century.

The advantage of such a succession was that time spent in the minor offices tested the faith, reputable life, steadfastness of character, and general fitness for office of a candidate. That this was not the universal practice is evident in Gregory's oration on Basil the Great, bishop of Caesarea (d. 379). He says that Basil received the honor according to the law and order of spiritual advancement, unlike the majority of those who aspire to the episcopate who are cleansed (baptized) and instructed in wisdom at the same time.[8]

Must one be ordained a deacon before being ordained presbyter, or be ordained a presbyter before being ordained bishop? This is currently the discipline of the Church according to canon law, but the history of ministry in the Church as well as two changes in the rites of ordination raise this question.

First, the present ordering within the Roman Pontifical moves away from the practice of presenting lower orders as stepping stones to higher order. As of 1990 it begins with the rite for a bishop and presents the three orders in a descending rather than an ascending pattern. This emphasizes the bishop as constituting the fullness of orders in which the other two orders participate. The orders of deacon and presbyter no longer appear as ascending steps to the episcopacy.

Second, Vatican II clearly teaches that episcopal consecration is sacramental. A bishop is ordained to the threefold office including the governing office of pastoral leadership, the sanctifying office of priesthood, and the prophetic office of preaching and teaching. Thus when a person is ordained bishop, he is by that action ordained a priest and receives the fullness of the priesthood and orders. This means that he possesses in full what is only partial in the other two orders. Prior to Vatican II, when the sacramentality of episcopal consecration was still a disputed theological question, episcopal consecration was seen as a jurisdictional canonical mission. Ordination to the presbyterate and diaconate then necessarily preceded episcopal consecration.

Even before the restoration of the permanent diaconate, Karl Rahner argued that "the very short interval of time between ordination to the diaconate and ordination to the priesthood does not give the impression that the diaconate is a means for testing the suitability of a candidate for the priesthood."[9] He also suggested that the official duties of a deacon are so different from those of a priest that the diaconate is not a true test of someone's suitability for the priesthood. He concludes that the diaconate does not have of its very nature the character of a step to the priesthood, and that the Church can ordain to the various offices without prior ordination to other offices.

With respect to the presbyteral office, we must inquire into the necessity and meaning of prior diaconal ordination. In actual practice the brief period of the transitional diaconate, frequently spent in the final year of seminary studies, provides a limited internship for the presbyterate rather than a distinctive service to the Church. According to the theory articulated by Paul VI, "The exercise of the office of deacon enabled those who were to become priests to give proof of themselves, to display the merit of their work, and to acquire preparation—all of which were requirements for receiving the dignity of the priesthood and the office of pastor."[10] The diaconate was intended to "furnish that proof of life, of maturity and of aptitude for the priestly ministry which ancient discipline demanded from candidates for the priesthood."[11] "By gradual exercise of the ministry of the Word and of the Altar," meaning both service in the ministries of lector and acolyte as well as diaconal service, "candidates for sacred orders should through intimate contact understand and reflect upon the double aspect of the priestly office."[12] While there is certainly great value in testing a candidate's suitability for orders, and while the Church may recruit candidates for the presbyterate among those who have proved themselves in the diaconate, this interpretation raises several problems. First, is diaconal service during the final year of seminary study an adequate test of a candidate's suitability for advancement to the presbyterate? More importantly, according to this theory the ministry of Word and of the Altar is seen as oriented to the priestly office of ordained ministry, is seen as a partial exercise of that office, and is ultimately subsumed within that office. The diaconate is ordered to priesthood rather than being an integral office in and of itself.

The first explicit conciliar legislation requiring progression through a succession of orders, canon 2 of Nicaea I (325) and the Council of Sardica (343 or 344), were directed against the abuse of advancing recent converts to the episcopate or the presbyterate as soon as they had been baptized.[13] The intent of the canons was that a candidate "should continue for some years in every order, to give some proof of their behavior to the Church."[14] This argument from experience is very different from a more legalistic concept of passing through various grades of office as was the experience of early medieval popes such as Otto I or Leo VIII.

We must ask whether we really need to ordain someone for an internship. According to current discipline, one must be ordained in order to
preach in many liturgical settings, preside at weddings and funerals, and
solemnly baptize. However, ordination to an office charged with these
functions in order to give a presbyteral candidate ministerial experience
and practice for a more complete ministry he will receive later is an insufficient reason for diaconal ordination. It is a functional rather than relational understanding of ordained ministry. A deacon is not someone who
is almost a priest but not quite; he is, rather, someone who is authorized to
exercise a distinctive public ministry in the Church. Significantly, *Lumen
gentium* 29 clearly states that a deacon is ordained "not unto the priesthood, but unto the ministry." Therefore, even though deacons and priests
may share some duties in common, in no way do deacons fulfill a "lesser"
priestly role. They fulfill no ordained priestly role at all.

The restoration of the permanent diaconate corrects a number of
problems created by the transitional diaconate. First, since a permanent
deacon does not proceed to presbyteral ordination, the diaconate is not
a training or proving ground for something else, but an office with its
own integrity within the Church. Unlike transitional deacons, those
ordained as permanent deacons approach the office with a sense of vocation to the diaconate rather than to the presbyterate.

Second, since the period of time spent in the transitional diaconate
is usually brief, the duties of deacons, inclusive of the diaconal functions in the liturgy, cannot be performed on a regular basis in the
Church if there is no stability within the office. In 1969 the General
Instruction of the Roman Missal prohibited one minister serving in
another ministry in the liturgy. The absence of the diversity of ministries in the liturgy diminishes the diversity which reflects the nature of
the Church. Other duties, especially those pertaining to charity, also
need the stability of a stable office.

Arguments sometimes advanced for the retention of the transitional
diaconate is that bishops and presbyters should also be outstanding in
their identification with and service of the poor in the community.
Their leadership of the Eucharist is authentic only as an expression of
their leadership in showing charity to and respecting the dignity of the
poor. Does not the *cursus honorum* give a more holistic understanding
of both the episcopate and the presbyterate by indicating that personal,
lived leadership in full Christian life, includes diaconal service of others, especially the poor? Does this not indicate the need for both bishops and presbyters to receive diaconal ordination?

In response to such arguments, the bishop has the ultimate responsibility for charity as a bishop, not because he has passed through the transitional diaconate. He promises to "show compassion and kindness for the sake of the Lord's name to the poor, to strangers, and to all who are in need." Bishops and presbyters do not "pick up" the responsibility for service along the way which they then bring with them to another office. One office is not added to another as an accretion or another piece of the puzzle that makes the picture more complete. The bishop has fullness of orders by virtue of episcopal ordination itself, not by virtue of having passed through the other orders on his way to the episcopacy.

The very nature of priesthood is a participation in the priesthood of Christ who lays his life down for others. Certainly, the Eucharist is fundamentally diaconal at its very core, and to preside at the Eucharist as bishop or presbyter is to imitate Christ, who, in washing the feet of his disciples, taught us the nature of priesthood. A priest does not derive this diaconal responsibility from his ordination to the diaconate, but from his ordination to the priesthood as bishop or presbyter. One can also argue that every Christian is called to diaconal service of the neighbor because of the common priesthood assumed in baptism.

The diaconal order in the Church is witness to the fact that there is public, ordained, official diaconal service in the name of the Church apart from the ordained priesthood. In fact, it exists in service of the priestly order.[15] Although *diakonia* must characterize all the Church's activity and particularly that of all its ordained ministers, ordained deacons perform charity in the name of the bishop or the pastor, thus in the name of the Church.[16] Thus the diaconal service of deacon derives from the bishop and pastor rather than the diaconal service of the bishop and presbyter being derived from their ordination to the diaconate. "Lesser" orders are related to the fuller orders rather than fuller orders being an addition to the lesser orders.

2. How are the three orders distinct?

When the three orders are seen as partial or complete expressions of ordained priesthood, there seems to be little reason to be content with a partial expression when a more complete participation in the priesthood is possible. As we have seen, the diaconate is not a participation in the ordained priesthood despite the fact that the transitional diaconate may sometimes give that impression since it occurs as a step within presbyteral training. When the orders are distinguished with respect to liturgical functions in isolation from how those liturgical roles reflect relationships within the ecclesial community, this contributes to this impression. The episcopacy, the presbyterate, and the diaconate are participations in the one sacrament of order, not the priesthood. We cannot adequately sort out the distinctiveness of the three orders on the basis of liturgical ministry or other pastoral functions, since many of these may overlap, but must do so on the basis of ecclesial relationships.

Each order in the Church sacramentalizes the nature of the Church in some way. This does not negate the fact that each ordained person, as also each of the People of God, has responsibilities related to word, worship, and furthering the reign of God corresponding to the prophetic, priestly, and kingly threefold office. The service of one order in the Church does not exhaust that particular service. The three orders contribute in distinctive ways, although there is a closer relationship between the episcopacy and presbyterate than between these two orders and the diaconate.

As we have seen, the episcopacy relates the local church to the universal Church and sacramentalizes the communion of churches through the college of bishops. The eucharistic presidency of the bishop corresponds directly to his responsibility for the unity of communion of the local church and its communion with other local churches.

In the contemporary life of the Church, now that the presbyterate does not function as a council of elders advising the bishop, it is in many ways the least distinctive order in the Church because of its close association with the episcopacy. Presbyters extend the bishop's presence to the parishes of the diocese. Like the bishop, they make visible the universal Church in their own locality.[17] They exercise governance, but in a more restricted locale and in a subordinate relationship to the bishop.[18] *Lumen gentium* 28 is careful to note the limits of their authority: "According to their share of authority they exercise the office of Christ the shepherd and head, they gather together the family of God as a fellowship inspired by the spirit of unity and lead them through Christ in the Spirit to God the Father."

Priests are consecrated in the image of Christ the high and eternal priest "to preach the Gospel and nourish the faithful and celebrate divine worship." In doing this, the presbyterate sacramentalizes the holiness and prayer of the Church. Preaching and sanctification, that is, leading the Christian community in worship and exhorting them to Christian lives, are arguably the primary responsibilities of the pres- byterate. The episcopacy exercises a high priesthood, but by and large it is the presbyters who are in daily contact with the spiritual lives of the vast majority of the people within a diocese. We have seen this empha- sis in the rite of ordination to the presbyterate, but this is also sup- ported by *Lumen gentium* 28 which states that priests exercise their sacred functions in a supreme degree in the eucharistic worship.

A deacon is ordained for service with respect to the liturgy, the gospel, and the works of charity. The deacon identifies himself with the Servant Jesus who washed the feet of the apostles. This same Servant Jesus interpreted his public mission through the words of Isaiah: "The Spirit of the Lord is upon me, because he has anointed me to bring good news to the poor. He has sent me to proclaim release to the cap- tives and recovery of sight to the blind, to let the oppressed go free, to proclaim the year of the Lord's favor."[19]

Both the episcopacy and the presbyterate have responsibilities toward the word and the liturgy, but the diaconate is unique in singling out the work of charity. The bishop, because he has the fullness of orders, has the ultimate responsibility towards the poor, the weak, and the perse- cuted, but historically this responsibility was exercised with diaconal assistance.[20] In many respects, the work of charity is central to the dia- conate because it both specifies diaconal liturgical service, which sacra- mentalizes the charitable extraliturgical service of a deacon,[21] and constitutes a living interpretation of the core gospel message.

The permanent diaconate recognizes the service of charity as a spe- cific ministry as an essential part of Church order.[22] Gottfried Ham- mann argues that the normative and professional function to which the diaconate is ordered lies in "the service of tables," that is, the work of charity.[23] In his opinion, this takes precedence over the ministry of the word in the apostolic sense of the term. He argues that if this were not the case, the solution of Acts 6 would be in vain, and charitable work would again be abandoned. The diaconate was especially tied to chari- table and liturgical functions in the second century when the churches were developing on the margin of official society. During this period, aid for needy people, symbolically indicated by the biblical phrase "or- phans and widows," was the measure of the Church's diaconal con- science.[24] Hammann argues that contrary to the prevailing society, to live in the Christian community, especially as a needy and socially dis- enfranchised person, meant finding a salvific communion assuring the necessities of life thanks to a new awareness of human poverty and the vocation to share arising from that awareness. In his opinion the diaconal ministry exists as a vocation to charity to respond to this need, to remind all the church members of it, and to envision ways of fulfilling this vocation and of assuring the just distribution of goods.[25]

Hammann maintains, however, that charity must be lived as a spiritual gift. The task of giving charity its transcendent dimension belongs to the diaconal minister. This dimension lies at the heart of the eucharistic worship of the Christian community. There, in the awareness of universal poverty before God, praise is offered to God and service given to all. In the Church of the first two centuries, the Eucharist took place in the context of a communal meal contributed by all the members. Deacons collected the gifts, inventoried them, selecting some for the eucharistic meal and then supervising the distribution of the rest to those who had the greatest need. Thus the sharing of material goods is tied to this table ministry from its origins. The deacon finds his responsibility and his place in Christian worship in this material service of charity. The liturgical service of the deacon gives a spiritual meaning to his charitable work in the community, and the charitable work in the community is represented liturgically in his service at the altar.

The service of charity is not a transitional function, but essential to the permanent ordering of the Church itself. The diaconate is a sacrament of the Church; that is, it represents and makes visible the service aspect of the Church. Since ordained ministry orders the Church, the Church being the referent of the sacramental symbol of ordination, we can look at ordained ministry and discover something about the nature of the Church itself. In this case, we see that charity, in addition to proclamation of the word and the sacraments of the altar, is an essential component of what it means to be the Church of Christ.

Once the centrality of the service of charity is recognized, it is well for the contemporary diaconate to take a lesson from history. The demise of the diaconate between the fourth and seventh centuries was due to a number of factors. Gottfried Hammann thinks that in the fourth century the diaconate became more a service of the bishop, inclusive of pastoral work and teaching, than a service of the poor.[26] In his opinion, the work of charity constituted the foundation of the diaconate. The diaconate receded with the demise of the service of charity, a loss of relative autonomy with respect to this proper work, and the development of a more hierarchical clergy which subordinated the diaconate to the priesthood.[27] Walter Croce attributes it in no small part, however, to the desire of deacons to take on more of a priestly and liturgical role and distance themselves from more menial service tasks, leaving them to be carried out by lesser clerics.[28] Claude Bridel reads the decline of the diaconal order in the West as the history of the rupture between life and worship as the liturgical service of the deacon became separated from its roots in the practical tasks of service to the people.[29]

Historical documents witness to the growing liturgical role of deacons. For example, letters from Caesareus of Arles indicate that a deacon could read a patristic homily if the priest was prevented from preaching.[30] He accompanied the priest for the prayer for the sick.[31] The Council of Orleans in 511 authorized deacons to baptize in the case of necessity.[32] In 516 the Synod of Tarragone decreed that the deacon alternate with the priest in saying the divine office in the country churches.[33] The Council of Vaison prescribed that deacons preach if the priest cannot in 529.[34] In 534 the Council of Orleans prohibited the ordination of deacons if they could not read or did not know the order of baptism.[35]

The tendency was for the deacon to become an authorized supplement to the priest, while an effort was made for them not to supplant him.[36] A correspondence between the growing liturgical role of the deacon and the demise of the work of charity is evident at the Synod of Rome (595) which gives evidence that deacons preferred the singing of psalms to caring for the poor. It ordered them to no longer chant in order to consecrate themselves again to preaching and charitable work. However, the writing of Gregory the Great indicates that Roman deacons of this period were often very important personages serving as messengers for bishops and invested with an authority superior to that of priests.[37]

This led to confusion in the roles of the two offices and to conflicts between priests and deacons as is evident in a number of councils and synods. The Council of Nicaea (325) decreed that deacons should not give the Eucharist to presbyters or be seated above them.[38] An unknown author of a tract, now included in the works of Ambrosiaster, entitled *Concerning the Boasting of Roman Levites*, criticizes the then current opinion that deacons can claim for themselves the same rank as priests. The Council of Angers decreed in 453 that deacons should have a humble respect for priests.[39] St. Jerome likewise levied similar criticisms of the situation.

That deacons have an important liturgical role is indisputable. This role is directly related to their service of charity. However, if this becomes divorced from their extraliturgical service, history teaches us that the office is doomed. One factor in our own time contributing to this danger is the priest shortage, which occasions deacons assuming many functions normally associated with the priesthood. The discrepancy between a celibate priesthood and a married diaconate may in some instances encourage a person to choose the diaconate rather than the priesthood when they really desire presbyteral rather than diaconal ministry. The requirements for the permanent diaconate give evidence that the bishops fear that vocations to the diaconate would detract from vocations to the presbyterate. Thus a married person must be 35 in order to be ordained to the permanent diaconate, and an unmarried person must remain unmarried.[40] The shortage of presbyters and restrictions on who can be ordained are insufficient reasons for conflating the two offices. These problems are not solved by ordaining more deacons but by addressing the declining presbyterate on its own terms.

3. What is the distinction between a deacon and a layperson since both may serve the Church in similar ways?

Today the word "ministry" is generally used to refer to almost any service in the Church despite the Vatican's efforts to restrict its meaning.[41] Thus when the work of laypersons and deacons sometimes overlap, it may be difficult to distinguish functionally between them even though certain functions like administering solemn baptism are restricted to deacons. Some people oppose the restoration of the permanent diaconate on the grounds that it will inhibit the growth of lay ministry. Yves Congar helps to sort out some of the differences by distinguishing between services, ministries, instituted ministries, and sacramental consecration.[42]

"Services" include everything that the faithful do for others. "Ministries" are services which exceed occasional services and which have a certain stability. They engage a person at a vocational level, are recognized or validated in a community, integrated into its life, and associated with a charism received from the Holy Spirit. "Instituted ministries" are ministries bestowed by installation, both a juridical act and a liturgical act, by the bishop or his representative. Acolyte and lector are presently installed ministries in the Church replacing the former minor orders. Finally, sacramental ordination gives a sacramental character, permanently conforming the ordinand to a certain aspect of imitation of Christ and creating a particular relationship with the Church. For example a bishop imitates Christ the Shepherd, a presbyter, Christ the Priest, and a deacon, the Servant Christ. The distinction between these categories lies not in what each does, but in the stability and ecclesial validation which accompanies the ministry, the vocation from which each arises, and how radically the ministry orients a person's core self.

Diaconal ordination confers entrance into the clerical state and incardination in a diocese or personal prelature.[43] The permanent diaconate requires us to ask, in a vivid way that the transitional diaconate does not, what it means to be a cleric and not to participate in the priesthood. Here we have both to distinguish between deacon and priest, and between deacon and lay person. The term "lay deacon" is an interesting oxymoron that is becoming common usage to designate a permanent deacon. A deacon, by definition, is not a layperson, but a cleric.

The confusion grows when permanent diaconate is often seen as an intermediary state between the laity and the clergy even though a deacon is a cleric. According to this view, the "world" is somehow present in the hierarchy in the person of the deacon. Very often the deacon engages in a secular profession, lives in a neighborhood among the laity, and may be married. In a sense he has a foot in two worlds: the sacred sphere of the hierarchy and the world of business and family. For example, Paul VI describes the permanent diaconate as "an intermediate order between the high ranks of the Church's hierarchy and the rest of the people of God."[44]

Such a view reinforces a dualism between the sacred and the secular and distances bishops and presbyters from the laity. All Christians are called to be "in but not of the world," according to their proper vocation.[45] Presence in the world does not specify what is distinctive about the diaconate. Furthermore, there is no need for an intermediary since the laity do have direct access to bishops and presbyters. However, the service of the diaconate among the people gives them an awareness of pastoral needs. Originally the "eyes and ears of the bishop," deacons make the needs of the laity known to them. Liturgically, this intermediate function is expressed by the deacon's receiving the gifts of the faithful and presenting them to the presider, by reciting the intercessory prayers of the faithful, and by inviting and exhorting the people to pray and make ritual gestures. Permanent deacons, however, are not "super-Christians," but are constituted in a different kind of relationship to the communion and mission of the Church.[46]

Even though many of the works assigned to deacons can be and already are being performed by the laity, three reasons for diaconal ordination suggest themselves. First, some ministry is actually diaconal ministry and needs to be officially designated as service in the name of the Church by ordaining those persons who are performing this ministry. This does not simply publicly recognize someone who is already a deacon, but places them in a specific ordained relationship with the Church. Second, diaconal ministry is not only identified by what it is, but by the motivation and vocation of those who perform it. Those who evince this motivation and vocation are candidates for ordination. Finally, the Vatican II documents indicate that ordination to the diaconate confers sacramental grace to strengthen those performing diaconal ministry and that those actually carrying out the functions of the deacon's office should be strengthened by this grace.

1. Diaconal ministry needs to be recognized as such by ordaining those who perform it to the diaconate.

Some ministry in the Church is clerical because it officially represents the ministry of the Church as institutional Church rather than the ministry performed by individual Christians out of their baptismal identity. It is probably impossible clearly to delimit diaconal tasks properly speaking from many activities of lay people. The general rule of thumb is that diaconal ministry is an extension of the hierarchic Church which represents the Church in an official and public way. Through this ministry the Church becomes itself and is actualized at a certain point in space and time in the most intensive way.[47] The nature of the Church becomes visible in an official way through ordained ministry. Because ordination in the Roman Catholic Church constitutes a permanent state of life, there is also a permanent quality to the choice for ministry. Three examples from diaconal service to sacrament, word, and charity may help to illustrate the nature of diaconal ministry.

Within the liturgical activity of a deacon, the witnessing of Christian marriage serves as an example of properly diaconal ministry. The ministers of the sacrament are actually the woman and man who exchange their marriage vows. The function of the minister of the Church is to witness this exchange of vows in the name of the Church. Even though a layperson could receive jurisdictional empowerment to do this, it is properly the function of a minister ordained to represent publicly the Church.

An example of diaconal ministry of the word could include permanent catechists who devote their lives to catechetical work. Here catechists are distinct from teachers of theology. Catechists are extensions of the teaching office of the bishop who teach the faith in order to elicit faith. They have an obligation to transmit the tradition and teachings of the Church so that the Church may continually perpetuate itself in its members.

An example of diaconal ministry of charity could possibly include people who work for Catholic Charities or other church organizations on a permanent basis and out of a sense of vocation. They do not do this because it may be one counseling job or organizational job that happens to be available to them, for which they are qualified, and which they may choose to do for a time, but rather they do it from a vocational decision. This would be reflected in the permanent state of life of the diaconate.

2. Diaconal ministry is identified by the vocation of those who perform it.

Diaconal ministry may be full or part time, but it necessarily arises from a life-orienting vocation to do ministry for the Church. Karl Rahner has perhaps best expressed the nature of this vocation by using the example of St. Paul who was a tentmaker by trade and who was forced to devote a great deal of time to this in order to support himself.[48] Rahner describes the vocation of Paul:

> By his inner attitude . . . he was an apostle and nothing else, i.e. his apostolic vocation and task was the only real, personal motive force of his whole life; it formed his life, it was the only guiding line of his actions, everything else was subordinated to it, and even his economic vocation, by which he earned his bread, served this other vocation and nothing else, no matter how time-consuming it may have been. His apostolate, if we may put it this way, was not a spare-time job, it was not merely a hobby or just an additional though extremely ideal occupation transforming his life, but the real existential, formative principle of his life, even though it may of necessity have taken up less of his time than his trade of tentmaking.[49]

Rahner concludes that the Church should ordain only persons for whom the diaconate is a vocation in the theological and existential sense. This means that it must constitute the inner structural principle of that person's life. It is insufficient for ministry to be an idealistic spare-time occupation which is not somehow defining of who the person is. Finally, ordination to the diaconate should never be a reward or decoration for a zealous apostolate.

If we understand ordination to be the official designation and mandate of a person to exercise his or her role of service to the community, and if we further understand that the ministry entrusted to a person "does not result from a simple recognition by the community, but that it is part of the movement of the sending of the Son by the Father and of the sending of the apostles by Christ,"[50] then public, official ministry in the name of the Church must be an ordained ministry. Charles Wackenheim argues that "all ministers must be ordained, failing which their 'ministry' is only a private initiative (however precious it may be)."[51]

If this is the case, many people ministering in the name of the Church fulfill the requirements for the diaconate. Their service needs to be designated as official service of the Church through ordination. Perhaps we need to multiply ordinations to the diaconate rather than to restrict them too narrowly. Nathan Mitchell argues that this would correct an overemphasis on the presbyterate which does not reflect "the classical theological norm."[52] Joseph Komonchak has asked what it would mean for the practical life of the Church if there were seven deacons in each parish.[53] This is certainly not unimaginable; in many parishes there are easily this many who would fulfill the vocational and ministerial criteria. The potential of the diaconate is that it may open the Church to a greater variety of ministries within, for, and in the name of the Church.

If the Church chooses to ordain those persons who show evidence of a diaconal vocation and who are already doing diaconal ministry, the requirements for diaconal ordination with respect to age, marital status, and gender may have to be changed. While it is true that married men can be ordained deacons, they have to be older than men ordained to be deacons who are studying for presbyteral ordination. Certainly, some women are already doing this kind of ministry. The historical evidence for women deaconesses is somewhat controverted, although clearly deaconesses existed to assist women in the baptismal rites of the early Church. Arguments disallowing the ordination of women because this need for this particular service no longer exists will also have to account for the changing roles of male deacons in the Church. Their role has undergone historical development from the supervision of the collection of goods contributed to the *agape* meals of house churches, to an assistant to the bishop, to a variety of liturgical functions. An overview of the historical, theological, and canonical issues of ordaining women to the diaconate are clearly presented in the report of the Canon Law Society of America, *The Canonical Implications of Ordaining Women to the Permanent Diaconate.*[54]

Some may argue against expansion of the diaconate, seeing this as a clericalization of the Church to the detriment of lay ministry. Wackenheim counters that the primary sense of ordination has nothing to do with clerical status. Even though a deacon is a cleric in the Church, the permanent diaconate has not assumed the symbols and life style associated with clericalism. Deacons are generally forbidden clerical attire aside from liturgical vestments. Most are married and live regular family lives in their neighborhood communities. Frequently they hold secular jobs in additional to their diaconal duties. This lifestyle has contributed to the term "lay deacon," which, while theologically incorrect, is symbolic of the perception that the deacon is not set apart from the laity as priests and bishops frequently have been. For too long we have associated all instances of "clerical" with "priestly" and have identified clerical with a rather elitist caste system within the Church.

3. Ordination to the diaconate confers sacramental grace.

Finally, ordination to the diaconate gives that person performing the office of the diaconate the sacramental grace of the office. Paul VI says that ordination would "strengthen that person by sacramental grace" for those works.[55] This is also the reason given in *Ad gentes* 16:

> There are men who are actually carrying out the functions of the deacon's office, either by preaching the word of God as catechists, or by presiding over scattered Christian communities in the name of the pastor and the bishop, or by practicing charity in social or relief work. It will be helpful to strengthen them by that imposition of hands which has come down from the apostles, and to bind them more closely to the altar.

It is important to identify what this sacramental grace is. This quotation seems to presume that ordination to the diaconate does not authorize the ministries mentioned. That is, it is not a prerequisite for performing these services. However, it is a gift of sacramental grace, which strengthens the deacons and binds them more closely to the altar.

Two observations are in order. First, sacramental grace is not simply an infusion of something akin to a supernatural vitamin, which strengthens what a person can do naturally. That which is supernatural is always of an entirely different order from the natural order. Second, sacramental grace is not something privatized that exists simply for the benefit of the person who receives it. Sacraments are acts of the Church and also actualize the Church. The sacramental grace of office is not primarily for the individual who receives it, but for the Church. In Karl Rahner's words, the "grace of office" "sanctifies" the holder of the office "precisely inasmuch as it equips him not to seek his own sanctification in an 'egotistical' manner, but rather, by directing his gaze away from himself and forgetting himself, to serve his neighbor in the Church."[56]

Finally, sacramental grace is not invisible. Sacramental grace, by the very fact of being sacramental has a *visible* dimension because sacraments are signs and involve materiality. In other words, ordination to the diaconate creates a visible bond between diaconal service and the Church. It identifies that service as a service of the Church and not merely the service of an individual Christian.

Conclusion

These theological considerations lead to several conclusions.

1. The permanent diaconate is normative for our understanding of the theology of the diaconate.

Just as the adult baptism within the context of the Rite of Christian Initiation for Adults (RCIA) is normative for our understanding of baptism today, even though most Catholics continue to be baptized as infants, so too should the permanent diaconate be considered as normative for our understanding of the theology of the diaconate regardless of the relative number of permanent or transitional deacons. Normativity does not depend on the relative number of permanent deacons vis-à-vis transitional deacons, but on which experience gives us our most complete understanding of the meaning of the sacrament.

Sacramentally, there is no distinction between those who are ordained deacon as part of their formation for ordination to the presbyterate ("transitional deacons") and those who exercise this office in a stable manner ("permanent deacons"). However, the manner of exercis-

ing this office within the permanent diaconate may more clearly indicate the true nature of the office. A more permanent service to the
Church extending beyond liturgical service, but which is ritualized by
and integrated with liturgical service, is a better indicator of the office
than the temporary service possible to transitional deacons.

2. *The diaconate strengthens the relationship between the liturgy and the world.*

In creating a visible bond between the person performing charitable
services and the altar, the sacrament of the diaconate strengthens the
relationship between the liturgy and the world. What is enacted symbolically in eucharistic worship has a referent outside of the liturgy.
John's Gospel recounts the episode of Jesus washing the feet of the disciples at the point where the Synoptic Gospels place the institution
narrative. The footwashing represents the diaconal service that they are
to render to one another at all times, not just when they are at table together. Similarly, diaconal liturgical service at the altar is a reminder
and sacramentalization of service given in the name of the Church outside of the liturgy. The institution of the diaconate does not exist for
liturgical service at the altar, but its service at the altar is an important
link between sacramental worship and service to Church and world in
the name of the Church.

3. *The permanent diaconate does not represent a solution for the problem of the shortage of presbyters.*

When the diaconate is seen primarily in terms of liturgical function,
there is the temptation to see it as a partial realization of the priesthood. Unfortunately, the current shortage of priests in the Roman
Catholic Church is reinforcing this perception. If no priest is available,
deacons can fill in, short of pronouncing words of absolution and consecration. Thus their function is seen more and more to be priestly
rather than diaconal, resulting in a confusion of orders. The argument
that we need the diaconate because "the lack of priests forces us to
transfer many of the functions previously exercised by priests to those
who should nevertheless belong to the clergy" is simply not a good argument.[57] That is an argument for more priests rather than an argument for the distinctive office of the diaconate. In terms of liturgical
service we need to see how each and every liturgical functional of deacons

is diaconal rather than presbyteral. With the decline of the permanent diaconate beginning in the fourth century, the presbyterate tended to absorb all ministries to itself. Now is the time to sort out what is distinctive to each order.

Notes, Chapter Seven

[1] David N. Power, *Ministers of Christ and His Church: The Theology of the Priesthood* (London: Geoffrey Chapman, 1969) 72.

[2] Gregory Dix, "The Ministry in the Early Church," in *The Apostolic Ministry,* ed. K. E. Kirk (London: Hodder & Stoughton, 1947) 284.

[3] Ibid.

[4] F. H. Dudden, *The Life and Times of St. Ambrose* (Oxford: Clarendon, 1935) 72–74.

[5] Henry Chadwick, *The Early Church* (Grand Rapids, Mich.: Eerdmans, 1967) 167.

[6] Louis Weil, "Aspects of the Issue of *Per Saltem* Ordination: An Anglican Perspective," in *Rule of Prayer, Rule of Faith: Essays in Honor of Aidan Kavanagh, O.S.B.,* eds. Nathan Mitchell and John F. Baldovin (Collegeville: The Liturgical Press, 1996) 200–17; Balthasar Fischer, "Hat Ambrosius von Mailand in der Woche zwischen seiner Taufe und seiner Bischofskonsekration andere Weihe empfangen?" in *Kyriakon,* vol. 2, eds. P. Granfield and J. A. Jungmann (Münster/Westfalem Aschnendorff, 1970) 527–31.

[7] Ormonde Plater, "Direct Ordination: The Historical Evidence," *Open* 37 (4) (1992) 1–3.

[8] Gregory Nazianzen, *Oration on St. Basil the Great,* 25, 26, in *Funeral Orations by St. Gregory Nazianzen and St. Ambrose,* trans. Leo P. McCauley, vol. 22 of *Fathers of the Church* (New York: Fathers of the Church, 1953) 50. Cited by Barnett, *The Diaconate: A Full and Equal Order,* 107.

[9] Karl Rahner, "The Theology of the Restoration of the Diaconate," *Theological Investigations,* vol. V, trans. Karl-H. Kruger (Baltimore: Helicon Press, 1966) 272.

[10] Paul VI, *motu proprio,* "Laying Down Certain Norms Regarding the Sacred Order of the Diaconate," August 15, 1972.

[11] Ibid.

[12] Ibid.

[13] *Council of Nicaea,* in *Nicene and Post-Nicene Fathers,* 2d ser., 14:10; *Council of Sardica,* in *Nicene and Post-Nicene Fathers,* 2d ser. 14:424–25. See also Canon 80 of the *Apostolic Canons* (ca. 550).

[14] Bingham, *The Antiquities of the Christian Church,* 1:131; Nicetas David of Paphlago, *Vita s. Ignatii,* in *Patrologiae sive Latinorum, sive Graecorum,* ed. J. P. Migne

(Turnholt, Belgium: Brepols, n.d.) 105:511–12. Cited in Barnett, *The Diaconate: A Full and Equal Order,* 111.

[15] Note the deacon's promise "to discharge the office of the diaconate with humility and love in order to assist the priestly order and to benefit the Christian people" (200).

[16] The suggested homily says, "Since they are consecrated by the laying on of hands that comes to us from the Apostles and once they are bound more closely to the service of the altar, they will perform works of charity in the name of the Bishop or the pastor" (199).

[17] *Lumen gentium* 28.

[18] *Lumen gentium* 28.

[19] Luke 4:18-19.

[20] For the bishop's responsibility see Karl Rahner, "The Second Vatican Council on the Diaconate," in *Foundations for the Renewal of the Diaconate,* 190.

[21] For some specific connections between a deacon's liturgical service and his diaconal identity see Patrick McCaslin and Michael G. Lawler, *Sacrament of Service: A Vision of the Permanent Diaconate Today* (New York: Paulist Press, 1986) 103–14. Timothy J. Shugrue comments that "in the estimation of many observers, the truly distinctive identity of the deacon and his most effective contribution to the life of the Church are more integrally tied to that charitable service which the U.S. Bishops in 1984 characterized as 'the ministry of love and justice.'" *Service Ministry of the Deacon* (Washington, D.C.: National Conference of Catholic Bishops, Bishops' Committee on the Permanent Diaconate, 1988) 9.

[22] USCC, *Study Text VI: The Deacon, Minister of Word and Sacrament,* 12.

[23] Hammann, 25–26.

[24] Ibid., 37.

[25] Ibid.

[26] Ibid., 68.

[27] Ibid., 80.

[28] Walter Croce, S.J., "From the History of the Diaconate," in *Foundations for the Renewal of the Diaconate,* trans. David Bourke, Karl H. Kruger, and William F. Schmitz (Washington, D.C.: National Conference of Catholic Bishops, Bishops' Committee on the Permanent Diaconate, 1993) 61–89.

[29] Bridel, 35.

[30] *Ep.* 13.21. Cited by Claude Bridel, *Aux seuils de l'espérance: Le diaconat en notre temps* (Paris: Delachaux et Niestlé, 1971) 28.

[31] *Ep.* 87.3. Cited by Bridel, 28.

[32] Can. 212.

[33] Can. 7.

[34] Can. 2.

[35] Can. 12.

[36] Bridel, 29.

[37] Bridel, 29.

[38] Can. 18.

[39] Can. 2.

[40] See Richard L. Rashke, *The Deacon in Search of Identity* (New York: Paulist Press, 1975) 85.

[41] See "Some Questions Regarding Collaboration of Nonordained Faithful in Priests' Sacred Ministry," *Origins* 27 (24) (November 27, 1997) 397–410. Kenan Osborne observes that Vatican II reserved the word "ministry" to the three offices of the ordained ministry: "In the case of the lay minister, the documents of Vatican II consistently employ the term 'apostolate.' This distinction of terms—'ministry' = ordained; 'apostolate' = nonordained—was deliberately done to indicate the 'essential difference' between the ordained and unordained ministries in the Church. However, after the council closed, this distinction in naming has not been followed, even by documents which have come from the Roman curia itself." *Priesthood: A History of the Ordained Ministry in the Roman Catholic Church* (New York: Paulist, 1988) 324.

[42] Yves M.-J. Congar, "Le diaconat dans la théologie des ministères," in *Le diacre dans l'Eglise et le monde d'aujourd'hui,* 124. I follow Congar's schema, here but update the application and interpretation.

[43] *De Ordinatione Episcopi, Presbyterorum et diaconorum,* 176.

[44] Paul VI, *moto proprio,* "Laying Down Certain Norms Regarding the Sacred Order of the Diaconate," August 15, 1972.

[45] Émile Marcus, "La spécificité du diaconat," in *Le diacre dans l'Eglise et le monde aujourd'hui,* 150–51.

[46] Canon Law Society of America, *The Canonical Implications of Ordaining Women to the Permanent Diaconate* (Washington, D.C.: Canon Law Society of America, 1995) 33.

[47] Karl Rahner, "The Theology of the Restoration of the Diaconate," 298.

[48] Ibid., 305–07.

[49] Ibid., 305.

[50] Charles Wackenheim, "Esquisse d'une théologie des ministères," *Revue des Sciences Religieuses* 47 (1973) 2–26, at 17–18. Translated and cited by Joseph A. Komonchak, "The Permanent Diaconate and the Variety of Ministries," *Diaconal Quarterly* 4 (1) (1978) 21.

[51] Ibid.

[52] Nathan Mitchell, "Ministry Today: Problems and Prospects," *Worship* 48 (1974) 336–46, at 345.

[53] Joseph A. Komonchak, "The Permanent Diaconate and the Variety of Ministries," *Diaconal Quarterly* 4 (1) (1978) 15.

[54] Canon Law Society of America, *The Canonical Implications of Ordaining Women to the Permanent Diaconate* (Washington, D.C.: Canon Law Society of America, 1995).

[55] Paul VI, *moto proprio, Sacrum diaconatus ordinem,* June 18, 1967.

[56] Karl Rahner, "On the Diaconate," in *Foundations for the Renewal of the Diaconate,* 208.

[57] This is Karl Rahner's argument in, "The Theology of the Restoration of the Diaconate," 285.

Index of Documents

Index of Scripture References

Index of Proper Names

Seasoltz, Kevin, 111, 153
Severian of Gabala, 44, 45
Sylvester, 159
Synod of Rome, 175
Synod of Tarragone, 175

Tertullian, 145
Thomas Aquinas, 66, 159
Trent, Council of, *see* Council
Tromp, Sebastian, 17

Union of Superiors General of
  Men, 107
United States Bishops' Committee
  on the Liturgy, 37, 91

United States Catholic Conference
  (USCC), 146

Vatican Council I, 1–3, 17
Vatican Council II, xi, xv, 1–2,
  5–7, 11, 13, 18, 23, 29, 31,
  64–65, 70, 93, 118–19,
  121–23, 126, 136, 146–47,
  166–68, 178
Veni Creator Spiritus, 36, 106

Wackenheim, Charles, 180, 181
Weil, Louis, 167

Zizioulas, John, 41, 71–75, 78

Index of Subjects